AGHORA II: KUNDALINI

AGHORA II: KUNDALINI

Robert E. Svoboda

Foreword by Robert Masters, Ph.D.
Illustrations, Captions and Appendix
by Robert Beer

Brotherhood of Life Publishing
Albuquerque, New Mexico, USA

©1993 Robert E. Svoboda
Illustrations, Motifs and Captions: With Thanks to and ©1993 Robert Beer
First Printed 1993, Reprinted 1995
by Brotherhood of Life Publishing
110 Dartmouth, SE
Albuquerque, NM 87106-2218

ISBN 0-914732-31-5

Typeset in ITC Berkeley Oldstyle and ITC Mona Lisa Recut

PRINTED IN THE UNITED STATES OF AMERICA

DEDICATION

She, the Eternal One, is the Supreme Knowledge, the cause of freedom from
delusion and the cause of the bondage of manifestation.
She indeed is sovereign over all sovereigns.
(Devi Mahatmya, I.57-58)

Dedicated to the Great Goddess, the Divine Mother of the Universe:
the Kundalini Shakti.

CONTENTS

ILLUSTRATIONS

ACKNOWLEDGEMENTS

With Thanks To...

Robert Beer, Tibetan Iconographer and Friend of the Dharma for providing his exquisite artwork and indefatigable support for the Aghora volumes.

Dr. Frederic M. Smith for providing the terms and definitions in the Glossary.

Inner Traditions International for permission to re-draw several of the Siddha illustrations from *Masters of Enchantment* by K. Dowman & R. Beer.

Allied Publishers Limited, New Delhi, India for permission to reproduce the Sadashiva painting which graces the cover of this volume.

About the cover:

Vimalananda explains the concept thusly (from Chapter Two): "The purpose of Kundalini Yoga is to reunite Shiva and Shakti, to create the eternal form of Shiva, *Sadashiva*. Sadashiva's left side is female and right side is male; the two principles have united but have not merged. If they were to merge that would be the end of the play, and that would be no fun at all. Sadashiva exists on the cosmic scale; in an individual this deity is called *Ardhanarishvara* ('the Lord Who is Half Female'). In order to manifest Sadashiva the Kundalini must be made to rise fully, because the highest manifestation of Shiva in the human being is in the head, the highest part of the body.

"In an ordinary person Kundalini is asleep at the base of the spine, and so Shiva is bereft of Shakti. Such a person is not Shiva but merely *shava* (corpse). I look at everyone I meet as a skeleton because that is what they are; until a person's Kundalini Shakti awakens and begins to dance on Her Shiva, that person is as good as dead."

Shri Yantra

The sacred Shri Yantra is the most well known and fascinating of all yantras because of its intriciate geometric harmony. It consists of nine interlocking triangles, the union of five downward pointing yoni triangles (shakti) with four upward pointing fire triangles (Shiva), and is also known as the Navayoni (nine yoni) chakra. The configuration produces a pattern of forty-three triangles which represent the goddess Tripurasundari at the center surrounded by her retinue of forty-two deities. These triangles are arranged in a series of five chakras that house one, eight, ten, ten and fourteen triangles progressively from the center outwards. This structure is enclosed by two concentric lotus circles of eight and sixteen petals enclosed within a square Bhupura or ground plan. (continues on page 316)

— For a more thorough understanding of Yantras please refer to
the Appendix beginning on page 285 —

FOREWORD

Aghora, described in this volume as "super-tantra," is a Path of Devotion to the Great Mother Goddess Kundalini, here manifesting with the Name and Image of the Goddess Tara. This Way is one of extraordinary extremes and intensities, even for tantra, and its aim is nothing less than to destroy the human limitations of the practitioner, so that he or she becomes a super-human—in fact, a kind of deity.

Aghora II is the second volume of a trilogy describing and explicating this Way as practiced by the Aghori Vimalananda, and as recounted by his student, the ayurvedic physician Robert Svoboda. The result is certainly one of the most unusual works to be encountered in the whole wonder-filled literature of world religions. It is also a work very much of this time, shredding and trampling on universal and almost-universal prohibitions. The Aghori sets out to overcome human limitations by shattering internally every restraint, no matter how ancient or powerful the taboo, and also by creating a body/mind that is able to contain emotional, sensory and other experiences which would consume anyone not properly prepared.

The Aghori, as presented by Vimalananda, must literally and systematically create a body (and subtle bodies) with a nervous system and other systems able to explore levels of consciousness and to tolerate kinds and intensities of energies which would otherwise result in madness, terrible suffering, destruction of gross and subtle body/mind organs, and death. Crucial to avoiding those outcomes are access to the necessary esoteric

[13]

teachings and trainings and, above all, to the Goddess.

As Vimalananda says again and again, in this present time the external forms of the spiritual disciplines are of much lesser importance than the inner work and, above all, the immediate and personal relationship to deity. It is possible to relate to the Great Mother Goddess in such a way that most of the requirements, temporal and material, of a spiritual discipline may be cast aside. However, what is dispensed with in the way of formalities must be compensated for by duration and intensity of both Practice and Devotion. Much present-day ritual and ceremony can be understood as aids or even crutches of a kind for those who lack the courage, dedication and devotion to proceed in unmediated interaction with Deity.

In speaking of intensities involved in such practice, here reference is to something going well beyond, for example, the "dionysiac element" in religions *as experienced in practice*. Those intensities are almost always reserved for special occasions, limited in time, and experienced within the context of different kinds of protections. But the Aghori, or similar figure, must always be willing to do without human supports of any kind and to venture into the awe-ful worlds of the nonhuman supported only by activated latent potentials and by confident belief that the Mother Goddess will guide and protect. Such a practitioner must be willing to venture into *anything or nothing*, knowing that in either case a successful experience will bring further isolation from the human and immersion in realities from which there can be no turning back. We are indeed speaking here of a "cosmic thrill-seeker" at home in realms of either terror or rapture—an ultimate psychenaut who is also our most authentic contemporary *saint*.

Despite the uniqueness and emphasis on inner work there is in this book an enormous wealth of information of value to the student of Eastern spiritual disciplines. Often even a sentence or two will shed more significant light on profound states of consciousness or very complex stages of meditation than the reader is likely to find in whole volumes intended to illumine the same subjects. The book is of value to advanced practitioners of yoga and other paths of self-actualization while, at the same time, it should be fascinating reading for anyone interested in the farther reaches of human experiences and human potentials.

Let it be added that there is much in this volume, and more in its predecessor, that will be startling and shocking to almost all. How much is to be taken as "objective truth," and how much is to be taken as "subjective truth," often is unclear. Vimalananda makes it plain that this distinction is for him not one of great importance—and, if he is going to make a judgment in the matter, then "subjective truth" is doubtless of greater value. Vimalananda also belongs in the tradition of spiritual teachers who deliberately speak and behave in such a manner as to shock, and often dismay, the observer. Such Teachers are to be found in many Traditions—for our own time, the very saintly Fourth Way Master G. I. Gurdjieff is a wonderful example.

There are other Paths or Ways which have strong similarities to Aghora—most notably, ones associated with Kundalini and the Great Mother Goddess in some other religions and esoteric Traditions. I would particularly mention as examples the ancient and still-enduring esoteric Schools of the Goddess Sekhmet in Egypt, the Goddess Hera in Greece, the Goddess Kapo in Hawaii, the Goddess Kali in India—there are also others. Each of these powerful and authentic mystery Traditions offers Paths of equal intensity, equally demanding of dedication and devotion to the Great Mother. Each uncompromisingly requires that the subtle and gross body/mind systems of the person become transmuted into vehicles or instruments having experiential capacities which by any ordinary standards are "superhuman." Only when this has been accomplished can there be that level of interaction with deity and other nonhuman beings which the higher Work requires.

Finally, I feel obliged to say that I do not know whether Vimalananda was an actual person. His name, and other names in the book, are said to be pseudonyms intended to prevent readers from being "distracted" by "externals." We are told that Vimalananda died about ten years ago, so that there is no question of searching him out—as many tried to do with another such mysterious character, the shaman Don Juan in the books of Carlos Castenada.

In personal conversation with the author, he states that Vimalananda was indeed an actual person and that the mystery surrounding his identity is mainly at the insistence of Vimalananda's own family. Considering the shock content of various of the Teachings, that is quite understandable. Some may wish to pursue this matter further. Most will find it sufficient to benefit from the extraordinary contents of *Aghora II* and its predecessor.

As for myself, I take pleasure in writing this Foreword even in the absence of any verifiable certainties about the Aghori Vimalananda, and despite strong personal reservations concerning some of the practices described. What I do know from many years of first-hand experience is the immense power of the Way of Devotion to the Great Mother Goddess and how, as this book sets forth, such a Way differs from those which are more dependent on human teachings and such objectifications in the world as ceremonies and

rituals. From my own experiential knowledge of the Fifth Way of the Goddess Sekhmet, I recognize in what is here called "Aghora" another Path that
has been provided as a *real* and powerful means of unveiling truth and
effecting transformation.

Robert Masters, Ph.D.
Co-Founder and Director of Research, The Foundation for Mind Research,
Pomona, NY; author of *The Varieties of Psychedelic Experience, Forbidden Sex-
ual Behavior and Morality, The Goddess Sekhmet* and many other books.

INTRODUCTION

"The study of philosophy without a longing for liberation is like dressing up a corpse."— Tripura Rahasya

In earlier times, when esoteric knowledge was under jealous guard, a spiritual aspirant usually had to endure years of patient waiting before being taught. Now that information has become an article of commerce, all manner of secrets would seem to have become available to anyone who has the price of a book or tape; however, simply because secret doctrines can now be purchased and thus easily possessed does not mean they can be easily comprehended. Though words can be bought and sold, that living wisdom which cannot be confined within words must still be earned.

Among the long-hidden arcana now being packaged for sale is the lore of Kundalini, the root from which all spiritual experiences sprout, and most of the writers who have tried to present to the world this living knowledge, which is the source of all knowledge, produce only dead words. As Heinrich Zimmer observed, "The best things can't be told; the second best are misunderstood."

Carl Jung, who many decades ago delivered a series of lectures on Kundalini, explains why:

> Therefore the Yoga way or the Yoga philosophy has always been a secret, but not because people have kept it secret. For as soon as you keep a secret it is already an open secret: you know about it and other people

know about it, and then it is no longer a secret. The real secrets are secrets because no one understands them. One cannot even talk about them, and of such a kind are the experiences of Kundalini Yoga. That tendency to keep things secret is merely a natural consequence when the experience is of such a peculiar kind that you had better not talk about it, for you would expose yourself to the greatest misunderstanding and misinterpretation. (Jung, p.20)

The experiences of Kundalini Yoga are peculiar because Kundalini is the source of all your experiences. Kundalini is that in-dwelling energy which by self-identifying with your opinions and character traits accretes and preserves your identity. In Jung's words,

... according to the Tantric teaching, there is an urge to produce a personality, something that is centered, and divided from other beings.... It is what one would describe in Western philosophical terms as an urge or instinct toward individuation. The instinct of individuation is found everywhere in life, for there is no life on earth that is not individual. Individuation takes place only when you are conscious of it, but individuality is always there from the beginning of your existence. (Jung, p. 2)

So long as the urge toward individuation is mainly directed toward benefiting your own limited temporary individual self it is called *ahamkara*, or egoism, the force which makes it possible for you to unquestioningly accept the world as it is on the surface. This same force is called Kundalini when it turns away from the mundane and toward the spiritual, the permanent and eternal. After Kundalini awakes it becomes impossible to continue believing that external reality is the sole reality. Ahamkara makes you who you are now; Kundalini makes you into what you will become.

Kundalini has remained secret for so long because, as Jung notes, it cannot be understood; it can only be experienced. The process of spiritual evolution cannot be objectified and separated from the subject who evolves, for Kundalini functions simultaneously as descriptive consciousness, as the thing described, and as its description. Since human language is made up of subjects and objects, descriptions of Kundalini tend to be skewed, either toward objective comment on the experience, which devitalizes it, or toward description of the raw subjective experience itself, which is usually distorted by the experiencer's mental imbalances, stresses and fantasies.

Among the writers who have made valuable contributions to the literature on Kundalini are Sir John Woodroffe (Arthur Avalon), an Englishman who was initiated into Tantra while serving as a judge in India; and Gopi Krishna, a Kashmiri Pandit who suffered terrifying consequences when his own Kundalini was awakened before he knew how to deal with it. While neither perfectly conveys Kundalini's incomprehensible secrets, since their words get in their way, here and there in inspired passages Kundalini's radiance flashes momentarily through, like lightning through a somber sky.

These accounts succeed, albeit partially, because their information has not been lifted out of context. Kundalini can be understood solely within the context of Indian culture. But ever since the time of the early Theosophists most Western interpreters of Kundalini, unfortunately, in order to import into their own systems of psychology concepts which they believe to be Tantric, have not hesitated to assign to Tantric words denotations which often vary significantly from their original meanings.

Jung himself borrowed concepts from Kundalini Yoga, including the very concept of Kundalini, which he called the anima, and so he bears some of the blame for this situation. At least he was more forthright than are most distorters of Kundalini:

> One needs a great deal of psychology in order to make these matters palatable to the Western mind, and unless we try hard and dare to commit many errors in assimilating it to our Western mentality, we simply get poisoned. For these symbols have a terribly clinging tendency. They catch the unconscious somehow and cling to us. But they are a foreign body in our system—*corpus alienum*—and they inihibit the natural growth and development of our own psychology. It is like a secondary growth or poison. Therefore one has to make really heroic attempts to master these things, to stand up against these symbols, in order to deprive them of their influence. Perhaps you cannot fully realize what I say, but take it as a hypothesis—though it is more than a hypothesis. It is a truth. I have seen too often how dangerous their influence may be. (Jung, p. 9)

Rejecting those concepts that "we do not need" for a systematic psychological description of Western experiences with the unconscious, Jung rationalized:

> We can only understand their picture of the world in as much as we try to understand it in our own terms. Therefore I make the attempt to approach it from the psychological point of view. I am sorry to have bewildered you, but you will be more bewildered if you take these things literally (you had better not). If you think in these terms, you will build up an apparent Hindu system with the psychology of the Western mind, and you cannot do that. You simply poison yourself! (Jung, p. 13)

Possibly those who try hard and dare to commit many errors in order to assimilate concepts from Kundalini Yoga into popular psychology do avoid the fate of the many Westerners who have poisoned themselves by dressing their minds in Indian vestments. But while replicas of Kundalini Yoga may function well enough in the external world of consensus reality to be useful psychological tools, they cannot substitute for the real thing when it comes to spiritual development. This is particularly true for those people who, by design or by accident, have broken through some of the barriers which separate objective from subjective reality and live lives in which waking reality and symbolic reality compete with one another for attention. Such individuals risk being trapped on an unknown ocean in a leaky conceptual boat if they try to rely on psychology alone to carry them safely to shore.

An awakening into the reality of the nonphysical in a person who lacks adequate prior preparation usually precipitates a personal crisis; such people may seem crazy, are often thought to be crazy, and sometimes believe themselves to be going crazy, all because they can no longer unquestioningly accept our "standard" reality. Most of those who lose touch with everyday reality are actually insane, of course, but in a sizable number of cases the cause is a spiritual crisis.

The prophet Ezekiel once heard a divine voice command him to sleep on his right side for 390 nights and then to switch to his left side for 40 more. (Ezekiel 4:4–6) Unless you know, as yogis do, that the position in which you sleep exerts a profound effect on your physiology, and so your consciousness, you will agree with *Time* magazine that Ezekiel and St. Teresa of Avila who like Ezekiel heard voices, were schizophrenic. When in fact they were most likely inspired by a reality of which the unawakened know nothing.

A spiritual awakening alters forever the way in which an individual experiences the world, for after the initial crisis abates one discovers that there is no way to return to one's previously comfortable mindset. Once aroused and unboxed Kundalini is not "derousable"; the genie will not fit back into the bottle. "After the awakening, the devotee lives always at the mercy of Kundalini," says Pandit Gopi Krishna, who experienced several crises during which the speed, insouciance and authority of the power he had unleashed terrified him. That power which caused his terror, which he had to face without the help of any guide, can terrify or incapacitate anyone who awakens Kundalini without proper guidance.

So long as Kundalini remains within the realm of psychology, our relative objectivity can shield us from the influence of symbolic existence. Once we enter subjective reality, however, that realm in which symbols "cling," we are at their mercy unless we have been taught how to deal with them. Those who ride Kundalini without knowing their destination risk losing their way.

The result may be "ego inflation," which occurs when one's limited personality survives the crisis intact and the individual then "claims the lustre of the archetypal world for his or her own person," or "ego deflation," if the awakening thoroughly disrupts one's self-integration and garbles one's self-image.

The savants of India have for thousands of years worked to perfect user-friendly methods of spiritual advancement that when properly implemented prepare individuals for and guide them through the process of individuation without terrorizing them. Each of these methods arouses the evolutionary power inherent in every individual, but this power appears as Kundalini in one system alone: the Tantric tradition. Anyone who wants to understand Kundalini as Kundalini must first come to grips with Tantra.

Though it has for centuries been maligned by the orthodox and puritanical among Indians, Tantra is not a religion of sensory indulgence which teaches the instant gratification of one's cravings. A good Tantric believes in truth and reality, and in the facing of facts, the first of which is the fact that all of us are part of the manifested universe, subject to its laws until we develop the power to redefine ourselves in other terms. A Tantric aims to become *sva-tantra* ("self-functioning"), to be free of all limitations, including especially the limitations of his or her own personality.

Tantra is not a subject one can learn in school, nor are Tantric texts "how-to" books, because Tantra is not bookish knowledge; it is living wisdom which must be obtained directly from an experienced practitioner. A good guide, a guru who has already followed the path and knows all its pitfalls, is absolutely essential if one hopes to follow the Tantric path and arouse Kundalini without calamity; a powerless or ignorant guru is far worse than none at all.

One such expert, the Aghori Vimalananda, taught me what I know of Kundalini. His uniquely original way of perceiving the world developed thanks to the awakening of his own Kundalini through a midnight ritual on a corpse. When Kundalini awakened for him, she took the form of the Tantric goddess Smashan Tara, the goddess of the burning grounds who enables one to cross over from the reality of life to the reality of death. Smashan Tara, the "Savioress of the Cemetery," enabled Vimalananda to cross over from his ordinary consciousness into states in which he could perceive reality from a different vantage. His experiences at the time of this awakening and thereafter are recounted in my book *Aghora: At the Left Hand of God*.

Aghora summarized the paths an Aghori follows in his or her odyssey from the darkness of unexamined mundane existence into the light of the celestial realms, all the while maintaining consciousness of both. Aghora is a sort of super-Tantra, a Tantra in which all sense of limitation is removed. Aghora is the Path of the Shadow, the "shadow" being all those aspects of our lives that permit us to exist as individuals at the expense of other beings. We can know the light of altruism only because we have known the darkness of self-ishness; only after passing through the Valley of the Shadow of Death do we learn how to live. Aghoris are psyche explorers who go down into the black-ness of their individual conceits to find their way to true freedom. Their spiritual path is no anemic "sweetness and light" experience; an Aghori must be "as hard as diamond and as soft as wax" as the situation demands. Only after the grapes of your ego-attachments have been thoroughly trod-den into juice can you vint the sweet wine of spiritual wisdom.

Aghoris play the game of life with the utmost sobriety, fully aware of the wagers staked. No means to awakening is too disgusting or frightening for them, for they worship death, the Great Transformer. *Aghora* literally means "non-terrifying"; an Aghori takes the most terrifying experiences possible and transmutes them into devotion to Reality. Tradition sends Aghoris to seek God in the cremation grounds, where death is ever-present, but a good Aghori sees the entire world as one vast ongoing cremation. Aghoris person-ify and deify death, selecting one face of this Universal Reality as their Beloved and worshipping this deity with an intense and all-consuming love. Every day for Vimalananda was a day of play with the cosmos, his Lover, and he never tired of playing the games that lovers play, for those games brought him ever closer to his sweetheart.

Because when the goddess Kundalini awoke in him, She had a form and a personality that he could interact with, Kundalini spared Vimalananda the sort of anguish that She awarded Pandit Gopi Krishna. Had Panditji perhaps concentrated on a god or goddess instead of a lotus he too might have found a haven in which to rest when the tempest tossed him. To Vimalananda Kundalini was not a wild unapproachable force that batted him about according to Her whim; She was instead his Beloved Mother, in whose lap he sat, allowing Her to protect him from all dangers with Her irre-sistible clout.

Vimalananda always preferred the path of worship of God-with-form to that of worship of the Impersonal Absolute. To him, the highest expression of divinity is the Motherhood of God, the God who protects and loves Her children no matter what errors they may make. This attitude was to him the best of all possible attitudes when dealing with Kundalini, because once you enter into such a mother-child relationship all fear of damage by the energy disappears. Also, as he liked to say, "Bhakti is Shakti": the energy (*shakti*) that you put into devotion (*bhakti*) to your chosen form of God is returned to you manyfold, benevolently amplified by the universe. As your devotion grows, so does your own personal power, which you are less likely to misuse since all you can think about is the One you love.

An Aghori's ache for a vision of the Beloved is so fierce that no means to achieve it is too extreme. This divine fury, a sort of cosmic thrill-seeking, is Aghora's hallmark. "Aghoris always overdo a thing," as Vimalananda liked to say, and *Aghora* documents how he frequently overdid things in his life. Overcome by his craving for his Beloved he worshipped with every element and substance and hobnobbed with every sort of ethereal being, all his rituals becoming, by Tantric transmutation, offerings to the divine.

Aghora's field of activity is not limited to enthralling or repugnant practices. The path of Aghora is the path of spontaneity; every action must be performed at the moment most appropriate for its performance, and it must be appropriate to the context in which it is performed. Worship is worship to an Aghori, be it in a temple or in a cemetery; with the surrender of all self-interest except that single-minded quest to achieve the Beloved, an Aghori can accept with love and thankfulness everything that God offers, bliss and misery alike, and transmute every experience, even a trip to the toilet, into an act of worship of the Absolute. Everything an Aghori touches, desired and despised, clean and unclean, he drags from the periphery of his experience into the purity of his center to help develop the "critical mass" needed to ignite and sustain a "spiritual chain reaction."

Vimalananda was a man of action, both "right-handed" and "left-handed," and cared little for scholarly views on what might or might not be classifiable as Aghora. He embraced accepted doctrine when it suited his purposes, while always retaining the right to innovate at any moment when necessity demanded. Philosophical systems have come and gone in India over the ages, but the spiritual springs from which they have sprung have continued to overflow. Indian spiritual tradition, Tantra particularly, has always ebbed and flowed between the twin shores of theory and practice. Theory perpetually regulates practice, and practice inexorably modifies theory. As fast as theologians erect and legitimize mountains of dogma, iconoclasts weather them down with their own individual interpretations; the heresies of yesterday are the orthodoxies of today.

Contemporary India is filled with individuals and sects working to legitimize their own unique aggregate of philosophy, cosmology and technique by assimilating their systems to the mainstream of "Vedic tradition" or

"Kashmir Shaivism" or whatever, while other individuals and sects—often paradoxically the same ones—move away from such standardized definitions of religion, calling them convenient fictions that limit and mislead. Maintaining that modern circumstances (time, place, people) are too different to permit precise recovery or revival of the ancient ways, they assert that what must be revived within a system is the flame which gives it life, not its external form.

For his part Vimalananda cheerfully combined many seemingly contradictory theories and practices into "his" Aghora, quoting in his support the ancient text which taught that only bewildered people dispute about truth, for "what proposition is there that the learned cannot defend?" Though highly educated Vimalananda's knowledge of Sanskrit texts was modest, and he neither knew nor cared to know much of the Tantric literature in Gujarati, Hindi or English translation, languages in which he was fluent. His textbook was life itself, and he could read from it meanings which are accessible only to those who know the secret language of spirituality.

While he called himself an Aghori, Vimalananda's disdain for organized religion distanced him from all recognized Aghori lineages, nor did he refer to his own mentors as Aghoris (and it is doubtful that they would describe themselves thus). He preferred to follow his own path:

"I have never believed in religion. Religions are all limited because they concentrate only on one aspect of truth. That is why they are always fighting amongst one another, because they all think they are in sole possession of the truth. But I say there is no end to knowledge, so there is no use in trying to confine it to one scripture or one holy book or one experience. This is why I say, when people ask what religion I follow, 'I don't believe in *Sampradaya* (sect), I believe in *Sampradaha* (incineration).' Burn down everything which is getting in the way of your perception of truth." (*Aghora*, p. 167)

In this at least he agreed with Jung, who once observed that "the function of religion is to protect us from an experience of God." The Aghori Vimalananda was too much the iconoclast and too determined to perceive reality to be imprisoned within dogma; his Aghora is a religion of consciousness, its precepts engraved not on tablets of stone but on the heart of the individual practitioner who must use them to create an individual system, thereby carving out his or her own spiritual niche.

There are not now and there never have been large numbers of Aghoris abroad in the world, nor did Vimalananda create many. He was quick to tell most people, "Do as I say, not as I do," and never permitted anyone to slavishly imitate him, because only those fit to dine on human brain will derive spiritual advantage from such a diet. He never devised any system of spiritual practices for the world to admire and follow. After carefully evaluating each individual who came to him he would teach certain lessons, directly or obliquely, or he would teach nothing at all, depending on his perception of his karmic connection with that person and his or her fitness and aptitude for spiritual disciplines. He never hesitated to challenge anyone's assumptions on spirituality and yogic discipline, and was not afraid to step on toes if he thought that he might arouse someone from their slumber by doing so.

Vimalananda wanted his views to be spread to anyone willing to listen because he felt acutely the anguish of the emptiness of the modern world, whose god is Mammon and whose predominant religion is an arrogantly emotionless science which seems bent on suppressing what humanity remains within us. As society disintegrates and meaning dissolves from life, people tend either to descend into despair or to return to their roots. We in the West have for years been cutting ourselves off from our roots, and now, nearly rootless, we are slowly dying from lack of cultural nourishment.

Some Westerners seek to live without roots, hydroponically, through futurism, while others try to reinvent the past via the "men's movement," Goddess Worship, Afrocentrism and the like. Yet others search for roots in such still-living cultures as the Indian, Native American, Tibetan or Chinese, as if perhaps by donning their visages they can somehow assimilate their ways. We have, however, become so superficial that few of us know how to dive deep enough into the cultures we seek to emulate to tap into their roots, and so we usually, as Jung feared, poison ourselves.

Vimalananda had no more faith that mass spiritual movements can save us than he trusted in social programs, political activism or enforced morality to rescue us, since all such solutions are superficial; they change our clothing, not our inner beings. He believed that real change can come only through those individuals who are brave enough to examine all of their reality assumptions and change those which must be changed. The numerous misconceptions about spirituality which permeate our modern world make his teachings on Kundalini valuable for everyone trying to follow a spiritual path. Before his death Vimalananda charged me with the responsibility of presenting his musings to those willing to listen, as much for the purpose of organizing my own knowledge, refining my understanding and manifesting my own creativity as for the purpose of instructing others. He also wanted me to have something solid to remember him by, so that whenever I want to be with him again I need only open the book.

Like other great teachers Vimalananda had a knack for being right, as well as an outstanding ability to impart his knowledge to those around him, usually when they least expected it, via an uncommon perspective, mixing theory with anecdote or letting anecdote reveal theory. His urbanity and ready humor betrayed a virtuosity in his play with the world which often masked an extraordinary shrewdness. He was never shy to speak out, and at times he seems as arrogant, harsh, critical, opinionated, pretentious and ready with stereotypes as much as at others his words are filled with sweetness, compassion, love, devotion, farsightedness and attention to detail. In his opinions and often peculiar views he was unequivocal and unshakeable, which earned him both fear and respect, and a reputation variously as a genius, crank and man of wisdom and God. Whatever else he may have been, Vimalananda was always real, always true to himself and his vision of reality, and he encouraged anyone who couldn't stand his heat to leave his kitchen.

Those who are convinced that the real is limited to that which our senses can perceive will ask, "Did all the events described by Vimalananda actually 'occur' in the outward sense of our consensus reality, or did they occur solely within his individual consciousness?" Better they should ask this question of themselves, for few people realize just how much of their reality is manipulated. Today's mass media daily synthesize miraculous phenomena for our amazement, that they may manipulate our emotions. Are these images "real" or not? With the rise of computer-generated "virtual reality" soon we will literally be unable to believe our eyes and ears; dare we rely on the "objective" truth of our sensory perceptions any longer?

One of the chief arguments against "subjective" reality is that since it has no physical substance it is ephemeral. This is certainly true, at least on the surface (which is where objective reality operates, after all). But below the surface it is objective reality which is found to be impermanent, while the reality of ideas, memories and reflections goes on and on. This truth is brought home to me regularly in India, where people when giving directions often refer to landmarks which were demolished years before. Clearly, a structure's ethereal reality may persist long after its physical form has disappeared.

Though all living beings eventually lose their physical existence, they continue to live on in the hearts of those who remember them. Some live on in memory for generations; a few, like Jesus, will live and continue to transform human lives forever. Others, like the gods and goddesses of India, are remembered even though they may never have lived in physical bodies. Are they real? We in India believe that they are far more real than humans are, even though their existence may not be provable by methods acceptable to materialistic science.

Whether these acts that Vimalananda recounts actually "happened" in the physical world or not is impossible to say, for India is truly a mysterious country and strange things do happen there. Many people who knew Vimalananda experienced many unusual things when in his vicinity, and most of them attributed such occurrences to him, while he attributed them to the Great Goddess: "I am talking as if I do these things, but in fact it is beyond me to do anything. Only Ma can do it; She does it all. This is the foundation of all my confidence in my abilities. Do I have any capabilities? Ha! Everything is from Ma." Vimalananda was an artist of consciousness, and it is enough to know that his experiences were intensely real and true to him, and that they can be real and true for anyone who is open to the possibility of their being so. Every time I reread an incident from his life it suddenly becomes real for me again, no matter how long ago it transpired, and Vimalananda thus continues to live for me.

Vimalananda was convinced by his experiments, as some modern physicists have become convinced by their experiments, that it is really impossible to speak of objective reality without taking the assistance of a subjective observer, a "knower" whose observation irrevocably alters the reality thus observed. That shift in perception which allows Aghoris to know that knower, known and the process of knowing are one and the same Reality allows them to perceive miraculous phenomena, whether obvious to others or not. Aghoris control their thoughts and emotions themselves that they may better enjoy the reality they so crave: the company of the Beloved.

Since human consciousness requires objects, this book speaks of Kundalini as if She can be considered in isolation from the individual in whom She exists. Kundalini cannot be objectified, but until She is awakened in an individual She exists for him or her only as a concept, and so She can be relatively objectified. As She awakens, this relative objectification is progressively converted into relative subjectification, until when Kundalini has been completely aroused one moves wholly into subjective consciousness, and descriptions lose their utility.

This was one of the reasons that Vimalananda preferred to deal with people individually, and never discoursed in public. When he met someone he would use words to express the objective portion of what he had to communicate, and would express the subjective part by other means. Since each individual's consciousness is made up of a particular ratio of subjective to objective awareness, the targeted individual would often get the message while other people in the room might miss it entirely. I have tried to select from the many objective messages directed at me over the years those which are sufficiently general to be of use to readers who knew neither of us, and I have tried to compile them in such a way as to permit some of his subjective messages to come through as well.

Vimalananda insisted on anonymity in these books because the less people know of the external details of his life the less they will be distracted from looking at what he wants them to see: the internal details. Anonymity protects his message—the subjective story of his life—from any scholarly nitpicking over its objective details. A consummate actor, he compiled his teachings in the book of his life, in actions rather than in words, his every action a well-thought-out statement in the chapters of his saga. Though he insisted on anonymity both for himself and for his mentors, the name Vimalananda is not wholly pseudonymous; he used it occasionally in his younger days. It means both "son of Vimala" (his mother's name was Vimala) and "he whose bliss is stainless." Through all the ups and downs of his life, in days of anguish or exaltation, Vimalananda's bliss was ever stainless, because he was a true Aghori, perpetually intoxicated with love for God.

As I struggled over *Aghora* I realized that no single angle provides a truly accurate view of Vimalananda, and so I decided to use three angles. In *Aghora* Vimalananda told his own story subjectively, presenting his life and work in his own words much as they were spoken to me, his scribe. In this book he appears much as I saw and objectified him, and in the third volume will appear the artist that was Vimalananda, constantly at work in the atelier of the world around him.

This book deals predominantly with Vimalananda's approach to the details of Tantra, as outlined in the preface to *Aghora*, and has three protagonists: the teacher (Vimalananda), the taught (me), and the teaching. A majority of it is dialogue, or rather trialogue, since the teaching has its own voice. Living wisdom cannot be confined within words, but it can be hinted at through situations, much as a specific feature of an otherwise undistinguished landscape can often be discerned by following the path projected by a pointing finger. "Them that have ears, let them hear," said Jesus; whoever "hears" the inner import of Vimalananda's words will be able to "see" their inward meaning.

AGNI

When I met Vimalananda I had already been living in the city of Poona for more than a year, studying Ayurveda, India's ancient medical system, and yoga. I had spiritual ambitions but despite guidance from saintly personages I had no real idea of my ultimate spiritual aim. Still, I dutifully invested many hours each day in postures and breathing exercises, holy books, incense and meditation while I waited impatiently for something to happen.

To help pay for my schooling I had competed for and won a grant to report on how Ayurveda was being practiced in Poona. I interviewed physicians of all sorts in the area for this purpose, and one day my Sanskrit professor, who had been helping me locate interviewees, announced that he had located a most unusual doctor who was also a Tantric as well as a racehorse owner, someone who deserved to be met.

I greeted this news warily, as I had been cautioned of the great dangers inherent in Tantra. But since my mission was to obtain a cross section of healers and therapists, certainly I needed at least one Tantric, since many of the Ayurvedic remedies in common use today have been derived directly from Tantric alchemy; and Tantra like Ayurveda has its roots in the Atharva Veda.

Vimalananada was at that time staying with a family in an Irani colony just a few blocks from my own residence. The first time I went to meet him he had gone to the racecourse, where an elderly mare he had recently purchased was running. When I retraced my steps to meet him later in the day

I found the flush of victory suffusing his broad and handsome face.

I remember very little of that meeting, other than that when I mentioned a questionnaire that I wanted to use on him he suggested we talk about it on the following day. When I discovered on reflection that he had answered all my questions without my even asking them, I was impressed enough to return eagerly the next day, and the next. During these first days he predicted (correctly, as it turned out) that none of his immediate family would attend his funeral, and that I would cremate him. Such a prospect seemed almost as strange as his prediction of it, but he had taken me as his foster son almost from the moment we met, and it was soon natural enough to see him as friend instead of informant, and then to accept the proffered role of offspring.

Soon I was a frequent visitor to the Irani colony. These Iranis are a sect of Zoroastrian fire worshippers who exited Iran more recently than did their brethren the Parsis, who have lived in India for more than thirteen centuries. Soon I, like Vimalananda, became an auxiliary family member, tutoring at his behest the family's younger daughter and spending many pleasant, quiet hours chatting with him when he made the trip up from Bombay to attend the races.

I had known him for only a week or two when he invited me to accompany him outside Poona on the occasion of a lunar eclipse for me to see, as he said, "how I do my rituals." A month earlier I would have attended as a skeptical observer; now I accepted with alacrity, unsure of what I would find but certain that this was the right course of action for me.

We left Poona one morning by autorickshaw, a motorized three-wheeled taxi, and a jolting three-quarters of an hour later we reached Alandi, our first stop. Alandi is the home of Jnaneshwar Maharaj, who lived there seven hundred years ago with his brothers and sister. (A guru is often called *maharaj*, "great king," because he has become master of himself, and because he is the disciple's absolute master.)

Jnaneshwar translated the Bhagavad Gita from Sanskrit into Marathi, the local language, and composed a commentary for it to make its teachings accessible to the common people. His book the *Jnaneshwari* is the most beloved book in the state of Maharashtra, and his story is known to every Maharashtrian.

Jnaneshwar, who is reknowned for making a buffalo speak the Vedas and causing a wall to fly in the air, tired of the world around the age of twenty-one and took *jeevan samadhi* ("living trance"): he entered a cave and had its entrance sealed behind him so he could continue to meditate without interruption. His resting place was forgotten until a few hundred years later when another famous saint of Maharashtra, Eknath Maharaj, had a dream in which Jnaneshwar begged him to come to Alandi and save him from the tree above his head whose roots had begun to grow around his neck. Eknath Maharaj located Alandi, discovered the cave, found Jnaneshwar Maharaj, and removed the roots. Before resealing the cave he took with him the manuscript of the Jnaneshwari, which was resting on Jnaneshwar's lap. So it is thanks to Eknath Maharaj that the Jnaneshwari, which had been lost until that time, again saw the light of day.

A shrine now stands atop Jnaneshwar, and throngs of people come there regularly to worship God and to request Jnaneshwar's assistance in solving their problems. Hundreds of pilgrims crowd the shrine each morning, making the rounds of each tree and image and offering their respects to the black stone beneath which he is said still to be sitting. In 1974 a group of "rationalists" demanded that the government excavate the area beneath the shrine to determine if indeed Jnaneshwar continues to be resident there in the flesh. The ensuing public outcry prevented this from occurring, and Jnaneshwar sits there yet, enjoying the mingling of the devotional singing of the pilgrims who concentrate in his front courtyard with the murmuring of other penitents who recite the Jnaneshwari under the slim branches of the tree whose roots were the cause of its reappearance.

We sat at Jnaneshwar's stone that morning with other members of our party for over an hour, ritually requesting his assistance for our own more individualized worship scheduled for later that night. After similarly saluting Siddheshwar Mahadev, the *Shiva Linga* (phallic symbol of Shiva, the god of death and transformation) in the temple adjoining Jnaneshwar's, we all repaired to our officiating priest's nearby home. After a frugal meal and a short rest Vimalananda took me aside to explain some things.

"You are a student of Ayurveda," he began. "Have you studied Sankhya?"

The *Sankhya* philosophy is the theoretical basis of Ayurveda, and I considered myself to be well-acquainted with its principles, so I replied, "Yes."

"So you know that the entire world is made up of the Five Great Elements; you do know the Five Elements?" Yes, I did: Earth, Water, Fire, Air, and Ether. These Great Elements are not elements in the chemical sense that hydrogen and helium are elements; they are rather states of matter. The Earth Element predominates in everything that is solid in the universe, the Water Element in that which is liquid, and the Air Element in gases. The Ether Element is the space in which things occur, and the Fire Element is the force which changes solid to liquid to gas and vice versa. Everything in the manifested universe, including the human being, is made up of these Five Elements.

"As long as you are alive, your consciousness is limited by the vessel in which it is kept: the body. And since the body is made of the Five Elements your consciousness is limited by those very Elements. Knowing that your consciousness is limited is all well and good, but what are you going to do about it? You don't want to remain limited, do you?"

"Not in the least."

"Theoretical knowledge is necessary, but it is not enough; practical knowledge, experience is also needed. We have a proverb in Hindi: 'Where even *ravi* (the sun) cannot reach, there will go a *kavi* (poet).' But that does not go far enough. I say, 'Where even a kavi cannot reach, there will go an *anubhavi* (experiencer).' I believe that you should go out and experience what you have learned, so that it will have some practical value in your life. This is why I have brought you with me today.

"The essence of Tantra is purification of the Five Elements, to awaken the Kundalini Shakti, which is your own personal shakti (power, energy). Any spiritual practice, in any religion, is basically some process or other of awakening Kundalini, and Kundalini can only be awakened once the Elements in your body have become purified. Do you understand?"

I kept quiet in a way designed to reply, "Somewhat."

"I will explain all of this to you—eventually. For now, just think about the Five Elements. You can make spiritual progress by worshipping any of these Elements, but I think it is best to worship the Fire Element. Worshipping Earth may take you eons, because the chief characteristic of Earth is its stability. Worship of Water is unwise nowadays because Water is the main substance which makes up the body, and most of us identify too strongly with our bodies anyway. Worshipping Air is likely to make you seriously unstable, and there are difficulties in worshipping the Ether Element also. I think Fire is best.

"The first word in the Rg Veda, the most ancient of the Vedas, is *agni*, fire. The Vedic religion is basically a religion of fire worship. The *Rishis*, the Seers who wrote the Vedas, worship the fire because it is the representative of the sun on Earth. Life could not exist on Earth were it not for the sun, and most people think the Rishis are trying to propitiate the sun by their fire worship. In fact they are feeding the sun. If they were ever to stop their continuous offerings of nourishment to the sun, all creation would go to hell. As a by-product of this service that they perform for the benefit of all embodied beings, they obtain the might of the sun."

As amazing as I found all this talk of the Rishis and their pastimes I kept quiet, since I wanted to hear everything he had to say, and Indian teachers are notoriously intolerant of interruption.

He went on: "The Rishis used fire in their worship because fire both purifies and amplifies whatever is put into it. Even NASA [the U.S. National Aeronautics and Space Administration] has realized that the flames of its rockets amplify whatever sound is fed into them. For those of us who are not Rishis, worship of the fire is meant to purify the Fire Element in the body and to purify the consciousness by amplifying the mantras we repeat."

(A scientist has now developed a combustion chamber which resonates with sound power, so that a furnace's own roar fans its flames. *Mantras*, which are words of power that may or may not have meaning in known human languages, fan different flames in a different way.)

"A good sadhu lives for his fire; an Aghori is always near a fire. Every sadhu maintains his own fire, which is called a *dhuni*, and no one but that sadhu can sit there. You enter into such an intense relationship with the fire that only you two can share the experience. Do you invite a third party into your bedroom to watch you and your spouse make love?"

I shook my head and quickly asked for a clarification: "A *sadhu* is a wandering religious mendicant, I believe; do all sadhus keep dhunis?"

"Not all; actually, nowadays, only a few are left who do. But Nagas do. A Naga, a naked sadhu who gives up everything, gives up everything except his fire. Because of the hours he spends with his fire his consciousness eventually becomes the consciousness of his fire, and his fire becomes a part of him. A sadhu's dhuni is like a king's throne; whoever sits there becomes imbued with its accumulated power. When I lived as a sadhu at Mount Girnar I always kept a dhuni, and whoever tried to sit at it had to run away, because it was mine.

"Why maintain a fire?" My question though unspoken was heard nonetheless. "First, because fire causes life to exist; it is the very form of the lord of creation, the god that sadhus worship. Second, because it serves as his television, as his viamedia to get information from all corners of the Earth. During the times I have roamed as a sadhu I kept up with all the people who loved me with the help of my dhuni.

"Zoroastrians worship fire, but they don't understand this principle. I have seen their priests sitting and fanning themselves while they make offerings, as if they were being put to great trouble by the flames. What I say is, if you can't stand the heat, get out of the kitchen. If you don't love flames, don't worship fire.

"My way is quite different. I have always treated the fire as my beloved friend. When I sit and worship the fire, I play with it. Tonight you will see what I mean. I call it to me and let it come and kiss me. Don't you kiss the ones you love? And because I don't fear it, it doesn't burn me. It will never burn me; it loves me, because I have changed its fundamental characteristic. You can also use mantras to control the fire, and you can use mercury or many other things, but the highest way is to so overpower the fire with love that it loves you in return. Any other method involves changing its nature against its will. You should cause the fire to voluntarily drop its characteristic of burning. That is a *real* achievement.

"When you worship anything, even a rock, you will always get a better result if you personify it. Fire is no different. Give it a personality and then you can love it, play with it. How can you love fire as fire, which is so hot and destructive and burns anything with which it comes in contact? You have to bring it to a level where you can relate to it and love it. All *sadhana* (the collective name for any method of spiritual development; a sadhu is a renunciate who practices sadhana) is just the preliminaries for falling in love with your deity.

"Now that I live in Bombay again I can't very well keep a dhuni going all the time, so I make up for it by going out and performing *homa* on a regular basis. Vedic worship of the fire, *yajna*, is extremely detailed and complicated. Each ritual requires a fire pit of a unique shape, unique substances for offering, unique mantras, and so on. Nowadays no individual can perform an external yajna; it is simply too elaborate for the common person. You may be unable to do yajna, but you can still worship fire and derive benefits from doing so by performing homa. What we will be doing tonight is homa, which is a lot like yajna but much simpler."

I wondered diffidently why he thought I might be qualified to participate in this ritual and again, as usual, he answered my question before I could speak it.

"By doing homa you make progress in the spiritual field in spite of so many defects in your body and mind. In fact the fire will gradually burn away all your defects. After doing homa you always feel light and energetic because of all the bad karmas the fire has burned away. This will not happen if you worship Air, which you do when you control *prana*, the life force, in the practice of *pranayama*."

I had just spent a year and a half practicing pranayama, stopping after I had weakened my system significantly by overdoing it, so I knew he was referring particularly to me.

"I know that you have been practicing asanas and pranayama under the guidance of someone who tells you he is teaching you yoga. I am sorry to inform you that such a system of physical jerks is not the yoga that is fit for today.

"Were you not taught that all your defects must be removed before you practice pranayama? If you make a mistake in pranayama you run the risk of becoming physically or mentally ill; you may turn completely to the mundane world, or you may lose contact with the mundane entirely. Neither state is healthy. I know that Patanjali in his Yoga Sutras says to practice pranayama, but Patanjali was not a Rishi. He forgot that he was not living in the Golden Age, and that people get worse as *Kali Yuga* (the dark age in which we live) progresses. In Kali Yuga it is actually dangerous to practice too much pranayama. Our water and air are polluted, our nervous systems are bombarded by noise and radiation. Very few places today have the peace and purity essential for successful pranayama. Worshipping Fire is much better.

"My spiritual 'children' are not sadhus, so they cannot keep dhunis, so I encourage them to perform homa. Each of my 'children' repeats a certain mantra. Maybe they picked it up from a book, or maybe some guru gave it to them, or whatever; that doesn't matter. What matters is that they are reciting those mantras with sincerity, and everyone who repeats a mantra regularly should do regular homa to purify that mantra and amplify its effects.

"Several times a year I and my 'children' get together to perform homa. There are a number of reasons for this. First, many of them are poor and could not afford to purchase on their own all the *ghee* (clarified butter) and other expensive ingredients which go into the homa. So, the more affluent among them pay for everyone else, and in this way even the poorest can fulfill their yearly percentage of homa.

"Second, their being together encourages them to concentrate harder. You always try to show off when someone else is watching you; it's human nature. At first this had a negative effect: a few were treating the whole thing as a picnic and spending all their time worrying about filling their stomachs. You can't worship on a full stomach. One day I got wild and told them, 'We have come here to do penance, not to eat. If you can't do without food even for a day, please don't come.' Now these elements have been weeded out of our group, and everyone else is doing much better than before.

"Third, these 'children' of mine think they are performing the homa on their own—human beings typically self-identify with what their bodies do—but they are just puppets. Some ethereal being comes and sits inside each one without their knowing it and performs the homa with far more concentration than they could do it themselves, and my 'children' get the benefit of this worship."

"There must be other restrictions to homa other than avoiding a full stomach," I remarked.

"There are plenty of restrictions. Just as a woman during her menses must never enter a temple, she must not sit and do homa; she should not even handle the offerings, because of the odor she will transmit to them. The beings we are trying to please eat by smell, and they are not at all fond of the smell of menstrual blood. This is also the reason why you must never sniff or smell the offerings before you offer them. Would you take a big bite out of a piece of cake you were serving to someone? Only if you wanted to offend them.

"If you are an Aghori none of these restrictions apply—but until you become an Aghori all of them apply. Unless you are a veteran Aghori you must never eat meat, fish or even eggs on the day on which you plan to worship the fire. You must if at all possible bathe immediately before your homa, and better yet you should bathe your insides by performing purifications like an enema beforehand. You should never even try to do homa on your own without someone to show you how to do it properly first; otherwise you may make some mistakes which will play havoc with you. I have brought you out here today because I want to show you how to do homa properly, so that eventually you can do it on your own and make progress on your own."

And so that night under his watchful eye Vimalananda and I performed homa together, under the rays of the eclipsed moon. Thereafter I accompanied him on his homa expeditions whenever possible.

Alandi is a small town on the Indrayani River, which like most of the rivers of the Deccan Plateau flows freely only during and immediately after the monsoon. The land near the river is fertile and intensively farmed, but surrounding this zone of prosperity is a much larger region of rocky, treeless hills where even goats graze with difficulty. Our group investigated other shrines and unusual spots in the vicinity. And when one day our priest told the strange story of a nearby Shiva temple Vimalananda immediately decided to visit there, with a view to performing homa in such a unique location.

According to the story this village is one of the places where Kubera, the god of wealth, is supposed to reside, and a fantastic treasure is said to be buried nearby. An inscription carved in stone, which is now submerged in the river, states that if a human sacrifice is performed in a certain way there, unimaginable wealth can be obtained.

Once there was a king who heard of this inscription and decided to perform a human sacrifice and get the money for himself. He could find only one suitable victim in his entire kingdom: a young Brahmana boy, the son of the temple's priest; the child's mother and father sold the boy to the king out of greed.

When the time for the sacrifice arrived the poor innocent boy threw his arms around the Shiva Linga and sobbed, "Lord, these people want to take my life just to gain wealth. What have I done that I deserve to be sacrificed in this way?"

Shiva's favorite being in the whole universe is Lallu, the Baby Krishna, because of His innocence. He sees Lallu in every child. When this child invoked Shiva with such sincerity how could Shiva refuse to help? Suddenly there was a roar of thunder, and Lord Shiva manifested in a terrifying form at the sacrificial site. So terrifying was He that the king and the boy's parents fell dead on the spot.

Lord Shiva tenderly lifted the little boy and asked him, "Now, what else can I do for you? I have saved you from being sacrificed, and the king and your parents have died for their wickedness. Is there anything else that you want?"

The little boy said, "Lord, please resurrect the king and my parents."

Lord Shiva said, "But they were the ones who were going to kill you just a few minutes ago. Why should I spare them? They will become spirits and will be under my complete control; I will make sure that they pay for their crimes."

But the boy told Him, "No, it is because of the king and my parents that I could see you so easily. I might never have attained the intelligence to worship you, and even if I had I could never have achieved so quickly. So please revive them; I am thankful to them."

Lord Shiva smiled at the boy's discriminative power and revived the three corpses. But no one got the treasure, nor has anyone been able to locate it since; plenty have tried, and they all came to grief. One sadhu came and, thinking perhaps the treasure was underneath the temple, moved the Linga; another had sexual intercourse with a local girl near the temple. Such strictly forbidden activities earned these men the wrath of the community and made the villagers suspicious of all sadhus. There was even one sadhu who came to town wearing a solid silver loincloth, but in the end he too had to flee just like all the rest. It is said that human sacrifices have even been performed there, but they too were of no avail.

When I asked Vimalananda about this he told me, "There is a good reason why everyone has failed. The Shiva Linga in the temple is over 2600 years old. It was established there by Gahani Nath, a disciple of the Gorakh Nath, who does not want the place disturbed by a bunch of treasure-seekers. In spite of all the evil karmas which have occurred in the neighborhood it would be a very auspicious place to perform rituals because there we can tap the power of Gahani Nath, and through him Gorakh Nath. This is why proper worship there yields great benefit; worship of that Linga would give us the benefit of the penance of Naths."

I had heard of Gorakh Nath, vaguely, but before I could ask about the Naths he had gone on: "You know," he said, "this village is unique for other reasons besides Kubera's wealth. On the opposite side of the river from the village is a cave in which there is an image of *Ma* (the Mother Goddess). Now only bats go there, but in the past that image was regularly worshipped. There were some silver pots in the cave, and on the occasion of feasts or festivals the villagers would go to the temple and somehow the pots would be found full of food. No human would cook it; it would just appear. And no matter how many people were to be fed, there would always be enough food in the pots to feed everyone. This can happen only through the blessings of Annapurna, the goddess of food. This went on for many years until someone stole the pots from the cave. Then the goddess got angry, and since then no one has dared enter the cave. Greed always ruin things."

Undoubtedly the village knew the dangers of greed well, given the number of shady sadhus who had come and gone. Indian villagers, by and large, are extremely generous people, to strangers as well as to friends; but even under optimal conditions it is difficult to simply wander into a village and announce that you are going to dig a dozen fire pits and perform a Tantric ritual. I suspected that we would be met with less than open arms, and I was intensely curious to see how Vimalananda would extract permission from the headman for our work.

The few kilometers to the village passed slowly, for the monsoon had just ended and the road still bore the deep scars of recent downpours. We were of course the center of attention when we reached the village—a delegation of Bombayites, accompanied by a foreigner—and many of the villagers, especially the children, were literally open-mouthed in amazement. Soon enough the headman was located, and we sat down for a chat. Luckily for us he had spent many years in Bombay, since he and many of his neighbors grew flowers for sale in the markets there, so we felt that immediate camaraderie which Bombay-dwellers share.

As I had surmised neither he nor the residents of the village were anxious for a party of strangers to invade their temple because of the bitter experiences of the past. They were afraid we had come to try and unearth the money, and that our efforts would increase their misery. No one was thriving here; sickness was in every house, crops were scanty. People could see the spirits of the dead wandering about even during the daytime.

Vimalananda quickly took the situation under control. First, he assured them, we were not interested in the treasure; let it remain buried. We were interested only in worshipping God. Second, our homa would produce ash which could be used as medicine for the sick, and as a sort of potentiated super-fertilizer for the crops, which he had examined and found wanting during our approach. We would not try to do anything in secret, but would do everything in the open. Then he invited whoever wanted to to come and sit with us and watch our work, and if any of what we did was objectionable we would bid our farewells and not return.

Vimalananda was always a convincing speaker, and he underlined his remarks by using some of his "special" abilities to tell the headman some things which no one else but he knew. Soon we had the desired permission, and we sent to Alandi for a bullock-cart–load of wood. Meanwhile other members of our party dug fire pits, mixed offering materials, and brewed tea. A short while later Vimalananda called me to sit with him on the ground near the temple where the little boy had once so narrowly missed being sacrificed. I could see from his manner that he had some instructions for me, and I indicated by my manner that I was aware of this and was ready to listen.

He began, "Up until now you have done whatever you have been told with very little explanation. You have asked me many questions about homa, and I have told you as much as I thought you needed to know. Now I want you to know even more about what we are doing, and why we are doing it here.

"We are going to do our homa right down there on the riverbank, just below the temple, which is right across from that cave I was telling you about. It seems that where we will be sitting was once the village *smashan* (burning ground), which makes me feel right at home. Many corpses have been burned under the big banyan tree there in whose shadow our fire pits are located. This tree is immensely old; as you can see, by using its aerial roots it has created a second trunk some distance away from its first, and now it has 'walked' several feet to a third location. It does not look very happy, does it? It is not happy—or rather, the ethereal being who lives in it is not happy.

"One of our aims in doing this homa is to make this tree and its resident happy. It is our obligation to this village, when they have been so generous as to invite us to stay and perform our rituals here, that we do our best to make their lives happier. Properly performed, group homa harmonizes the atmosphere for miles around the place where it is done, and creates peace in those who live nearby, humans and ethereal beings alike. You are now part of our group, and you must do your job to the best of your ability. Now is a good time to learn, because when I am gone you will be on your own."

I started to protest that he would live for many years yet—I was still very young, and thought little of mortality—but he waved off my protestations and continued.

"You will notice that here, as elsewhere, we dig several fire pits, and that normally two people sit at each. Strictly speaking, each worshipper should have his or her own. When a man becomes an *agnihotri*, a fire worshipper in the Vedic sense, no one is allowed even to touch him, much less sit at the same fire with him, with the sole exception of his wife. But for convenience, and because when two sit together they can help one another out, we use this arrangement.

"Before we sit we salute Mother Earth, who supports us, and we ask Her to make our worship successful. Then, after remembering Ganesha (the elephant-headed son of Shiva) and asking him to remove any obstacles, we begin to prepare the fire pit. In the bottom of the fire pit goes the *yantra*." A yantra, I knew, is a sort of mystical diagram which is meant to control and contain the energy put into it by the ritual. The yantra also represents the deity invoked during the ceremony. "I normally use as a yantra a six-pointed star, which is composed of two triangles, one downward-pointing and one upward-pointing, superimposed on one another, because I am doing this sort of homa for the general good of all beings in the neighborhood, especially those involved in the ritual. The six-pointed star, the Star of David, is significant for us Indians as well as for the Jews.

Design and Construction of Fire Pits (Homa Kunda)

  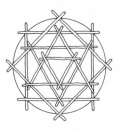

a.   b.   c.

a. Plan of a square fire pit used in rituals of peace and prosperity. The rim of the Kundra is built up in three steps of brick, at its base and facing east is the triangular Yoni (vulva) symbol. In the center of the fire pit is a six pointed yantra as used by Vimalanada.

b. Design of the Tripura Yantra commonly used in Devi (goddess) worship.

c. The placement and arrangement of the fire sticks above the Devi Yantra.

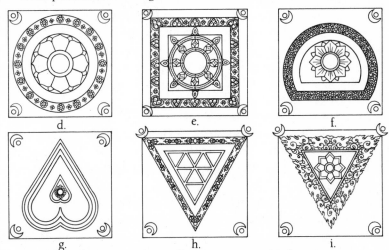

d.   e.   f.

g.   h.   i.

Yantras employed in the six Homa rituals of Tantra

d. Circular Yantra used in rituals of propitiation and peace.

e. Square Yantra used in rituals of prosperity.

f. Half moon Yantra used in rituals of subjugation.

g. Yoni shaped Yantra for conjuring forth.

h. Nine triangles used in rites of obstruction and causing hate.

i. Triangular fire yantra employed in rites of destruction and slaying.

"Have you noticed how important triangles are in life?" Vimalananda was fond of rhetorical questions, and I did not even try to answer this one. "Look at the human body. A man's pubic hair forms a triangle with the point upwards. A woman's pubic hair is triangular also, but with the point downwards. A woman's triangles point downwards because she is responsible for the creation of duality. From one she becomes two, when she bears a child. A man's triangle points upwards because he is meant to control and finally overcome duality. Only when the two come together is creation possible. When a man and a woman enjoy sex together the two triangles come together to form a six-pointed star. Don't you think there must be some significance in this?

"There are other triangles in the body also. A woman's two breasts and her vulva: downwards. A man's penis and testicles: upwards. The seminal vesicles and the penis—I could go on and on. Four triangles form a pyramid when fitted together, and pyramids have their own peculiar uses, as the ancient Egyptian, Incan and Mayan civilizations knew well. They are all yantras. An external yantra can always be lost or stolen, which is why you should make your body into a yantra; then there is no chance of losing your yantra as long as you live. And you can perform so many rituals, internally, without anyone ever knowing about them, like the Rishis do. Isn't that better?

"A flame is also in the form of an upward-pointing triangle. The flame converts all things into ash; all dualities become one reality when they are burned. We offer the fire duality—our offering material—and the fire transmutes it. The head of a human being also possesses an upward-pointing triangle: the three eyes. The lower two eyes see duality—the upper eye, nothing but unity. Therefore it is only logical to conclude that properly performed worship of the fire will help to open your third eye."

It seemed logical.

"Once the yantra is prepared it is time to worship Ma. Every fire pit must have a symbolic representation of the vulva attached to it. Some have them built in. I usually just make two parallel lines on the side of the fire pit with red powder. You must worship Shakti before you begin, because without Her none of your work can be done; there is no creation without the female principle. And since creation is the function of the genitals, they must be worshipped. Fire is Shaktiman, the Controller of Shakti, but ordinary fires have lost their Shakti; you have to return Shakti to the fire, so it can do your work for you. Shiva and Shakti are identical in the absolute sense, of course, in the same sense that fire and burning are identical; but practically they are different."

This was confusing, but Vimalananda was not to be interrupted when in such moods.

"Then the fire is ignited. Have you ever wondered how a sadhu deep in a jungle or out in a frozen Himalayan wasteland is able to build a fire? Even if he can locate dry fuel, where will he get a spark to enkindle it? He doesn't carry a box of matches around with him. The answer is in the proper use of the Vishnu Sudarshana Mantra."

"The Vishnu Sudarshana Mantra?" I had never heard of it, but I knew that Vishnu, the Preserver of the Cosmos, uses a discus for a weapon, the name of which is Sudarshana, which literally means "good sight." There seemed to be some esoteric significance to the name of this mantra, especially given the mention Vimalananda had just made of the third eye, and I was hoping for some further insight.

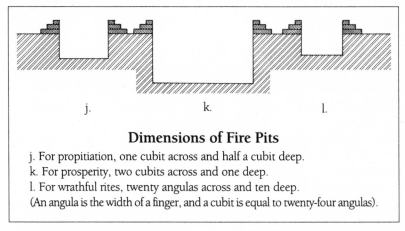

Dimensions of Fire Pits
j. For propitiation, one cubit across and half a cubit deep.
k. For prosperity, two cubits across and one deep.
l. For wrathful rites, twenty angulas across and ten deep.
(An angula is the width of a finger, and a cubit is equal to twenty-four angulas).

But Vimalananda said only, "Yes, when you repeat this mantra the fire automatically ignites and burns furiously no matter how wet the fuel. I have experimented with making funeral pyres burn brightly in pouring rain with this mantra."

Aha! I had been in Poona only a few weeks when I saw a front-page report in a local newspaper on a man who was able to create fire by repeating a mantra. Various eminent physicists had tested him for fraud and had had to conclude, scratching their collective head in amazement, that his was a legitimate power. But when he was asked how it was done, by people who wanted to learn that knack themselves, he replied that all prospective students should come with him to a secluded area in the mountains where they would stand on one leg for twelve years repeating the mantra, after which it would be energized sufficiently to work. He had no takers.

Because I had heard of such a thing, Vimalananda's claim did not strike me as implausible. He went on.

"Why is there creation? Because of friction. Without friction there is no creation. And wherever there is friction there is fire. Can you produce fire without friction? No, unless you take it directly from the sun, using a magnifying glass for instance. Fire is created for Vedic sacrifices by friction, by rubbing two sticks together, much as the American Indians used to do.

"Friction may possess an excess of any of the *Three Gunas*: Tamas, Rajas or Sattva." The Gunas are a crucial part of Sankhya philosophy that I knew well from my Ayurvedic studies; they are the three tendencies of consciousness as manifested through the mind. Sattva is equilibrium, Rajas activity, and Tamas inertia. The mind fluctuates among these three states continually until, by dint of sadhana, it is brought under control and focused on a single point.

"Tamasic friction is argument, discord between people. It creates fiery emotions like hatred, anger, revenge, and violent frenzy. Rajasic friction is sex, which is due to the Fire of Lust. The Upanishads explain that the woman is herself the fire, the penis is the fuel, and the pubic hair the smoke. The vulva embodies the flames, the friction is the coals, and the pleasure is the sparks. This is much better than Tamasic friction because the two people involved get some pleasure out of it. Not much, of course, and not for long. What is created? More lust, and a child. "Sattvic friction, which is sadhana, is the best of all. When you perform sadhana you are working against all your old tendencies and habits caused by the karmas of millions of births. This is bound to produce friction, and you will heat up. The word for penance, *tapas,* literally means heat. Have you noticed how often I apply ice to the top of my head?"

How could I have failed to do so?

"Enlightenment is achieved by the 'burning' of your karmas through tapas. When you do plenty of penance your mind heats up, and you become irritable. If you indulge in anger or lust their fire will burn away all the shakti you have accumulated, but if you follow through on your vows and control your temper and your passion the resultant enlightenment will make the whole thing worthwhile.

"Remember that fire's basic quality is to burn. Did you know that the fire which is in the tongue burns whatever it speaks? What this means to you is that you should always confess any bad karmas that you perform. This will free you from them; they will be burned up. And you should never speak about any good deeds you do, or about your spiritual experiences, because if you do they will be destroyed just as surely. Unfortunately this is Kali Yuga, and most people do exactly the opposite. They hide their sins down deep in their hearts where they can't be cleaned out, and they boast to everyone in sight about their accomplishments and spiritual achievements. I don't need to remind you of what would happen if you told anyone what mantra you repeat." This was one of the first warnings he had given me.

"If we wanted to show off for these people," he said, pointing at our hosts, "we too could light the fire by rubbing sticks together in the approved Vedic fashion; but neither do we want to show off, nor are we performing a yajna here that we need to maintain the same strict standards that are necessary for a Vedic sacrifice. Fire purifies whatever it burns, but it takes on some of the qualities of whatever is offered to it. As an Aghori I cannot afford to make any distinctions between a funeral pyre or a sacrificial fire; but as a householder I feel responsible for my spiritual 'children' who come to worship with me. Most of them are not yet ready to do homa on a funeral pyre. We settle for maintaining strict purity of our offerings, but we use matches to start the fire, for convenience."

The purity of offerings, I had already learned, extended to the wood used; someone inspected each piece to make sure it contained no insects that might be cremated when it began to burn. All the offering materials were also carefully sifted, screened and inspected to remove dirt and insects before they were combined together into the final offering mixture, the *samagri*.

"The choice of offerings in a homa depends on the work, both spiritual and mundane, that you have for the fire to do. In the homas I do with my 'children' we always offer clarified butter, barley, wheat, rice, sesame seeds, dry and fresh fruits, honey and sugar, combined together in a specific proportion. All are sweet because we want the fire to give us mundane prosperity as well as spiritual advancement. We add sugar cane also, which is very dear to elephants. This propitiates Ganesha, who must always be propitiated first whenever you do any sort of worship. In addition we add several medicinal herbs, which make the resulting ash medicinal.

"The homas that are done as part of the Six Rituals of Tantra—rituals performed to cause death, delusion, discord, hatred, obstruction, and enchantment—are quite different. Each ritual requires a specific set of mantras and even clothing, and worship materials like oil, salt, chilies, and other intense, spicy substances are used. Don't even experiment with these rituals; terrible karma is involved. And never try adding such substances to your own fire.

Since you don't know what you're doing you'll just be harming yourself. There is no limit to the good or evil which can be done through worship of fire."

"Why do such rituals exist at all," I inquired challengingly, "if Tantra is really a benign science?"

"I will explain that to you—eventually. But right now, since the Six Rituals are not part of our program, I would prefer for you to concentrate on what we *will* be doing."

I accepted this mild rebuke and signaled my deference. He continued.

"I begin my homa by remembering my mother: first my cosmic mother Smashan Tara, and then my physical mother. She is dead now, but even when she was alive I would think of her: 'Ma, because of you I am in this world. Thank you for giving me this opportunity to redeem myself.' Then I remember my family's Rishi, Bhrigu: 'These mantras originate in you and derive from you; and because I was born in your lineage, I salute you.' Then I salute the Seven Rishis as a group—Pulaha, Pulastya, Devala, Asita, Kratu, Bhrigu, and Angiras—and then four other Rishis whom I cannot name. Next, I salute various gods and goddesses, the planets, and all the demigods in charge of the village and the neighborhood, and of the home, if I'm performing my homa at somebody's house. Finally, I make offerings to all the other classes of ethereal beings: those who are relatively benign, like the Yakshas, Kinnaras, Gandharvas and Vidyadharas, as well as those who are more malevolent like the Brahma Rakshasas and other spirits of the dead.

"Finally, I turn to the fire and request it to enter me and enkindle my *Bhuta Agni*. The Bhuta Agni is the fire of the subtle body, the fire which must be ignited in order for spiritual progress to be made. One important reason for doing homa is to awaken Bhuta Agni. If I really want Fire to enter me, my 'I' must disappear; a spiritual vacuum must be created. To do that I offer my ears to the fire and ask for divine ears in return: clairaudience. When I get a positive response from the fire I then offer my eyes and ask for divine eyes: clairvoyance. When positive response comes to this offering I offer my tongue and ask for divine speech. Once Fire enters me I can proceed to do whatever work I have to do. You don't offer your physical ears, eyes, and tongue to the fire, except in Khanda Manda Yoga, which I will tell you about one of these days; in homa you offer your *senses* into the fire.

"After all these preliminaries I request my deity to be present in the pit, and I begin my offerings. As the homa proceeds the fire will sometimes crackle, hiss, or make other noises. This is the fire's way of trying to talk, which you can understand only if your perception is very subtle. The fire tries to communicate with you in other ways also; its color is especially significant."

"How so?"

"Modern science has itself proved that each different color of light has a different effect on the body and mind, by stimulating the pituitary, pineal and hypothalamus, which then influence the rest of the organism. One color may cause anger, another joy, and a third may improve concentration. When you get close to the fire and embrace it you offer yourself to it, and it enters you. Then the external fire acts as a barometer of the workings of the internal spiritual fire, the Bhuta Agni. You must bring Bhuta Agni under your control before you can completely control physical fire.

"When I am finished with the number of offerings I have planned to make, at the very end of my homa, I put a coconut into the fire. The coconut represents the worshipper's head, with its three eyes. Also, it is full of water, just as the head is full of blood, cerebrospinal fluid and glandular secretions. When I offer the coconut I offer my entire consciousness to the fire with a request that it be transmuted into a divine consciousness. I offer my own 'head' to get a divine head. Then I bow to the fire and request my deity to return to His or Her home, and my homa is completed. Then I sit by the fire for a while, after I am finished, and commune with it.

"Always remember this: fire is a living being. Once you bring it to life you are responsible for it. For example, you don't dare smother it any more than you would dare to smother any other living being. You must permit it to die out by itself. After you collect the ash you must wash the area thoroughly so that no one will step on any ash inadvertently, and any ash you don't use must be disposed of in water. That means put into a stream, or the ocean— not into a drainage ditch! And one other thing: if it seems like the fire is about to go out during your homa, never blow on it directly. Always blow on the palm of your hand first and let that air fall onto the fire. Why that is I will explain to you—eventually."

He fell silent for a few moments, to allow me to try to summarize and integrate what he had told me, and then continued: "Naturally, I don't expect you to remember everything perfectly this time; you will have many opportunities to practice homa and for me to correct your mistakes, while I am still alive and even afterwards. I have always said that half the enjoyment of enlightenment is the path you have to tread to get there. As your consciousness progresses from that of a limited human being to that of an unlimited being you will experience all sorts of things, wonderful and appalling alike. Don't ever become attached to any of these experiences;

they are only guideposts to tell you how far you have come and how far you have left to go. If you become attached you'll get stuck there and you'll quit making progress.

"My 'children' generally have good experiences as a result of doing homa. Because Nature is kind to me She is usually kind to my spiritual children also, especially if they come to me first and seek my permission before going out to do something. Once one of them had reached the end of his homa and was ready to offer some sweets to the fire and take some *prasad* in return." (Prasad is that portion of your offering which is returned to you for your consumption so that you can imbibe some of the vibrations of the deity you have worshipped.) "When he lifted the box of sweets all of them fell into the fire at once and began to burn. This fellow actually started to cry because he would have no prasad when suddenly one sweet fell out of the fire onto his leg.

"Another time a group of them finished their homa before using up all their samagri. Any such remainders must be properly disposed of, so since they were in a rural area they tried to give it to a cow, but no cow would touch it. Have you ever heard of a cow refusing to eat a mixture of rice, sesame, barley, honey and sugar liberally sprinkled with dried fruits and nuts? Not one but several cows did indeed refuse it. And a dog, who followed my boys all the way from the village, was ready to eat it but was not offered any of it.

"When they got back to Bombay I reminded these 'children' that Lord Shiva frequently comes to His devotees in the form of a dog. The cows in the place where they had done their homa refused to eat because the deity there, Lord Shiva, wanted them to continue their worship with that material, or at least wanted them to offer it to Him, in the dog form, instead of to the cows. When you begin to come near the deity you are worshipping, the deity will begin to play about with you. Everyone likes to play about.

"This is the way you should look after your spiritual 'children.' Children must be protected until they have progressed far enough to do things on their own. The Hindi word for child, in fact, is *baccha*, which comes from a word meaning 'to protect.'"

"So a child is 'that which is protected?'" I surmised.

"Precisely," he acknowledged. "For example, whenever my boys go out into the jungle, someone or another will bring them food and water when they need it. Ask them if you don't believe me. How does it happen? I don't know; all I know is that it happens. Once a group of them who were camping in the jungle began to be a little fearful around midnight. Suddenly a party of villagers with torches arrived, saying that they had suddenly got the desire to come spend the night out there.

"This does not mean that my 'children' are being handed everything on a silver platter, however" he hastened to add. "Whenever any of them tries to act smart the fire teaches them a lesson. Last time we went out for homa one of my 'children' got his hands burned so deeply they blistered; another scorched his foot very badly. It's dangerous to play with fire. Fire is a living being; to misuse it is to invite disaster upon yourself. As long as it loves you there is no problem, but the day you start fooling about you've had it. These two characters were full of jealousy because Freddy and Katyayani had come to perform homa with us. How dare they be envious! According to Indian tradition a guest is to be treated as God. Why shouldn't they suffer for being envious of God?"

Vimalananda never hesitated either to suffer himself or to make others suffer when he felt it was necessary.

"When people are envious of you and your achievements, like some of my boys are of you, as you well know, don't bother about it. Their jealousy will act as a wonderful fire to burn out all your bad karmas. You will find yourself getting lighter and lighter, and day by day they will be taking your karmas on themselves. Fire always burns, and if you worship it properly it will burn away all your bad karmas."

A year or two after our first homa there, after we had become fixtures in the community, Vimalananda and I were sitting near the temple early in the morning after a long night of fire worship. After our arrival, conditions in the village had gradually improved. Maybe it was coincidence or maybe it was, as Vimalananda had predicted, that our worship was affecting the villagers' lives positively. They certainly seemed happy with our homa; they would hover around the fire pits as soon as we arose, waiting patiently for the moment the ashes from the fires would cool off sufficiently to be collected. Some villagers used the ash as medicine—one woman healed a horrendous ulcer on her thigh simply by applying it regularly—and others just kept it in their houses for good luck. The farmers who used the ash on their fields reported bumper crops, and their prosperity allowed everyone to put a little money aside. The villagers were certain that this upturn in their fortunes was all due to our homa, and to the proper propitiation of their deities, and whenever we bade them farewell they begged us to come back again as soon as possible.

On this morning, as we watched them collecting their share of the ash— we kept some for ourselves for similar purposes—Vimalananda said to me, "Even the ethereal beings in the area enjoy our presence. They can't take the ash directly like the villagers do, so they just blow a little up into the air and inhale it. All you see is a puff of wind." He smiled.

"When we first came to the village our friend the tree did not look as if it would live long, did it? Now look at it: new leaves have sprouted, and it has recovered most of its vigor. This is because the ethereal being who lives there also enjoys our homa—the fragrance of the smoke and the resonance of the mantras. Her misery was ruining the villagers when she came, and now that she is happy again she looks after the locals and makes them thrive.

"There are other auspicious signs too that most people do not know how to interpret. Here is just one: Do you remember that pair of little owls that has come out to join us several times late at night when everyone is concentrating well on their homas? The ones who fly up and perch on the upper branches of this tree, chatter together for half an hour or so, and then depart?" I did indeed. "Owls generally do not come near light, but I think it is good for everyone involved that these two do.

"This is the right way to worship, the real yoga: not to perfect physical postures, but to make every home a happy home. If one hundred villages in India could be harmonized as this one has, the whole pattern of life in India would change. I can't do that, but perhaps my 'children' will be able to. A father lives for his children, not for himself, if he is a real father."

KUNDALINI

Vimalananda developed close personal relationships with his racehorses, visiting then regularly at the racing stables to feed them treats and love. He continued to call on his mares even after they had been retired to stud. It was on one such visit to a stud farm near Poona that the driver of the autorickshaw in which we were travelling abruptly refused to go any farther out of town, leaving us to trudge irately down the road during the heat of midday to cover the remaining half-mile.

A massive heart attack a few years previously had forced Vimalananda to carry with him pills to treat angina. Perhaps it was solely the combination of the heat, the exertion and his exasperation with the rickshaw driver that precipitated an attack that day, though there may also have been an internal reason to which I was never made privy. Whatever the cause, this particular attack was much more intense than ordinary angina, and the pills failed to relieve it. Despite his heart condition Vimalananda had continued to smoke, and I lit a cigarette for him as he stood stock still trying to minimize his anguish.

There we were on a deserted road, with no medicine other than the ineffectual pills, with no way to get Vimalananda to a doctor short of walking him there. As the pain had become too great for him even to walk, the only thing left to do was to move out of the road where we were standing, find a place to sit quietly in the nonexistent shade, and wait for destiny's gambit to unfold. As we headed toward a leafless thorn tree, Vimalananda flicked his cigarette butt despairingly into the air.

He sat on the ground beneath the tree and I stood behind him, reduced to wondering what would happen next, when some inspiration caused me to look up. There in the tree was his still-smoldering cigarette butt, precisely impaled on a long, sharp acacia thorn. My heart leapt into my throat: an omen! I shouted to Vimalananda to look, and when he saw it he smiled, then started to laugh and said, "Well, well, Robby, it looks as if I'm not going to die here after all. Nature hasn't deserted me yet!" Immediately his pain began to recede.

Vimalananda loved Nature, and Nature loved him. There is order in Nature, a grand rhythm called in Sanskrit *rtam* to which all the celestial bodies promenade. Because Vimalananda habitually moved in harmony with this cosmic rhythm the universe had become habituated to cooperate with him. When he tossed away his cigarette with a silent, desperate prayer to Nature, probably something like, "Don't let me die by the side of this road!" back came the answer in a sign from Nature: "Don't worry, you are still safe with Me!"

Dying cigarettes usually do not find their way to and impale themselves on acacia thorns. Perhaps a highly improbable coincidence chose to randomly occur there and then; but such "coincidences" happened day in and day out with Vimalananda, so a better explanation than "chance" is necessary. The unerring flight of that aerodynamically unsound projectile was an external reflection of the internal event which precipitated it: a cry for assistance in extremis. Vimalananda's prayer hit the cosmic bull's-eye with the same accuracy and force that his cigarette hit its bull's-eye; the latter event demonstrated, on the gross physical plane for all to see, the former event that was hidden within, like iron filings on a piece of paper conform to the lines of force projected by a magnet held beneath them.

The ancient Law of Microcosm and Macrocosm tells us there is no real difference between the vast external universe and the limited internal universe of the human body, except that the individual believes itself to be different. A human being is a living microcosm of the universe, and the universe is a living macrocosm of a human being. Each cosmos affects the other; the universe affects us, moment to moment, and each one of us by our actions influences the entire cosmos, for good or ill. The cosmos is the body of the Absolute, the vessel through which the Absolute expresses Itself. Every created thing in the universe contains at least a spark of the universal consciousness which is the Absolute, but most things cannot adequately express this consciousness.

Vimalananda explains:

"*Chit Shakti* (the power of consciousness or subjectivity) identifies with the Unmanifested Absolute, and *Maya Shakti* (the power of unconsciousness or objectivity) identifies with the world, the manifestation of the Absolute. These two Shaktis cannot exist without one another. Even in the grossest matter there is a spark of consciousness—this is why I say that even rocks are alive—and even in the highest states of consciousness there is a particle of Maya, as long as there is even the least sense of individuality. Once you learn the truth of the universe, you forget your own individuality, and remember your true nature; only then, when you no longer exist, does Maya no longer exist for you."

The One exists in the All, and the All defines the One; unity and duality both exist simultaneously. Wherever Chit Shakti is displayed there is intelligence and sensation; otherwise there is ignorance and insensibility. The human body is a vessel into which consciousness pours, according to individual capacity, filling the body via the nervous system. The spine and spinal cord extend consciousness from the brain, the pole of greatest awareness which is called Shiva, to the coccyx, the pole of greatest density. Each body cell expresses its own sort of consciousness according to its own capacity.

At the base of the subtle spinal cord in the subtle body lies the residual shakti of individuation, an energy which remains unavailable to the individual so long as his or her consciousness remains firmly entrenched in the mundane. This energy is our personal fragment of the cosmic power of self-identification. Thanks solely to this sense of I-ness called *ahamkara* (literally 'the I-causer') we exist as individuals. When Vimalananda spoke of the ego it was ahamkara that he meant, not the Freudian ego.

Just as discrimination is the chief characteristic of the intellect, ahamkara's chief characteristic is possessiveness, that proprietary overlordship of the organism which remembers your self-definition and allows you to hold your own in the world. Ahamkara self-identifies with every cell of your body from conception until death; you instantly die as soon as She ceases to self-identify with you. The more you identify with your individuality, your microcosm, the more She functions as your own personal Maya and the less She reflects the macrocosm; as you identify less with your individuality She is freed to reflect more of the macrocosm, to increase Her awareness of the One. Ahamkara and Kundalini are two names for the same power manifested in two different directions: ahamkara connotes Maya Shakti and Kundalini, Chit Shakti.

Maya Shakti keeps you awake to the world and asleep to the Absolute, while Chit Shakti awakens you to Reality and puts you to sleep with regard to worldly matters. Since the consciousness of a living being is conditioned by the matter in which it resides, the greatest Maya that we experience is the Maya of the matter which makes up our bodies. So long as we live the embodied life each one of us participates in the play of Nature, binding ourselves to the world by the "things" we accrete in our personalities. No incarnate being can be either wholly worldly or wholly spiritual; no matter how filled with light you may become, you never quite transcend your dark side fully so long as you remain embodied.

The expression of shakti in the physical body is *prana*, the life force, the power which keeps body, mind and spirit functioning together as a living unit. All parts of one's being require prana. Physical life, health and longevity require that ahamkara self-identify strongly with the individual organism so that sufficient prana will enliven the body, while spiritual health requires ahamkara to relinquish most of this attachment. Just as every plant requires just the proper amount of both sunshine and rain to flourish, so does a human being require just the right amounts of the sunlight of spiritual awareness and of the cloud cover of ego-attachment in order to thrive. Too much spirit burns the world out of you and makes it impossible for you to retain your body; too much attachment drowns your consciousness in worldliness.

In the ordinary human the ego is fully identified with the body and the limited personality, and all actions are centered around this temporary "self." Each microcosmic reality is influenced by every other; all of us are caught in each other's projections and are defined in large part by them. Our conscious personalities that we like to think of as stable and constant are in fact merely aggregates of ideas with which we temporarily self-identify. The conscious personality is a sort of museum whose curator—ahamkara—selects objects for display to others from the museum's warehouse, the subconscious. These objects are assembled into exhibits, the personality fragments which each act as if it were "the" personality while it operates. Popular exhibits enjoy a longer run, while less-patronized exhibits are changed more quickly. Eventually the museum goes out of business, at the moment of death when the ego completely forsakes the limited, limiting personality which it has supported for so many years.

Most people never notice the fluctuations of the ceaseless creation and destruction of their personalities any more than they notice the individual frames of film in a motion picture. This perpetual shifting of self-identification among all these personality pieces consumes tremendous amounts of energy and keeps ahamkara quite preoccupied. Only when some life-changing event forces the issue do you begin to wake from the sleep of contentment with Maya, like the Prodigal Son woke to find himself dining from the pig trough, and to take the first few toddling steps toward the light of Chit.

Kundalini will eventually awaken in every being in the universe. If you prefer to enjoy the vicissitudes of karma you can wait for that awakening to dawn; otherwise you can actively try to find your way to that state. Vimalananda outlined the choices:

"Whatever you desire will eventually come to you; this is the magnanimity of Nature. She will always eventually give you what you ask for; it is only a question of time. If your desire is the product of a controlled, coherent mind you will achieve it quickly. This is how the Rishi Vishwamitra created an entire parallel universe: the force of his austerities was so powerful that when he set his mind to it, it took shape immediately.

"If you desire God you will eventually get to God; about this there is not one iota of doubt. How long it takes you to get to God, how much of a gap there is between your desire and its achievement, depends on how much you want God. Once you become really anxious to locate God and your mind becomes focused on this desire you can achieve without much delay.

"Lord Krishna says, 'Bahunam janmanam ante': only after millions of births does an individual soul get the desire to return to God. Only after many, many rounds of physical existence does the soul finally say, 'Now I'm tired, Lord, tired of all this birth and death. Please take me away from all this.' As the soul becomes more and more desperate interiority develops, and if he keeps to it eventually he achieves.

"The first sutra of the Brahma Sutras is 'Atha ato brahma jijnasa,' which means, "'Now there is a sincere desire for knowledge of the Ultimate.' The Brahma Sutras have already existed for thousands of years, and will probably continue to exist for thousands more. The use of the word *atha* ('now') here indicates that there is no limitation of time when it comes to spiritual advancement. Whether it is today or ten thousand years into the past or one million years into the future, *atha* means 'whenever there is a sincere desire for spiritual knowledge.' 'Now' is thus different for everyone. Right now is the 'now' of the Brahma Sutras for all those of us who are trying to grope our way back to God in spite of the terrific Maya which assails us. "

The Maya which assails us is our own, of course, and that of our friends, neighbors and other co-conspirators who share a consensus reality. Most people do not want to rock the boat, much less go overboard, and many do not take kindly to the defection of their fellows. Vimalananda used to say, "Human beings are nothing but sheep. I used to be in the flock of sheep, but I ran away, so it's no surprise that everyone else, all the so-called normal people, thinks I'm insane or, at the least, abnormal. And I think the same about them. Only one of us can be right." (*Aghora*, p. 297)

Only those brave enough to disturb the somnolence of the world around them and shout that the Emperor is nude possess the strength to withstand the censure of the remaining sheep. Those who shout, "Beware of Maya!" malign Maya, for Ma always only gives us that which we ask for. When we call on the Goddess to ask Her for mundane boons, which bind us to limited forms, She appears to us as Maya; when we pray to Her power and energy She manifests as Shakti; and to those few who relate to Her maternally she reveals Herself as Ma, God the Mother. Those who remain stuck in Maya do so because they do not try to redirect their urge to individuation from Maya to Chit; they allow themselves to be carried along by the current of their lives, and of their neighbors' lives.

Aghoris never permit themselves to be passively defined by the external environment; they define themselves, and by so doing define their surroundings. Vimalananda's control of an awakened Kundalini gave his self-expression such accuracy and force that incidents which would be out of the ordinary for most of us, like that of the cigarette and the thorn, became commonplace in his life. He never hesitated to define his surroundings, even if doing so landed him in hot water:

"One day one of these people who call themselves 'Bhagavan' ('God') was having a big meeting down at Chowpatty (Bombay's downtown beach). They were charging Rs. 25 to get in. I didn't want to go in the first place, especially to see someone selling spirituality like that, but one of my friends insisted that I must see this 'great saint,' and he paid my way.

"Everyone who went to the saint was supposed to bring along a flower. I said to hell with that and didn't take along any flower or anything else. When we got there the so-called Bhagavan told everyone to take his or her ego, put it into the flower, and then put it at the 'guru's' feet. He called this the great 'Mohini Prayoga.'

"When it was my turn I went up to him, and he looked at me and made a gesture to say, 'Where is your flower?'

"I told him, 'Please let me know one thing. If I put my ego into a flower I will die *phat* right here; it is because of my ego that I am alive. My ego self-identifies with this body, and if it were to leave my body would immediately become limp and dead. And then how would I be talking to you here? So will you please explain to me how to do it? How to put my ego into a flower?'

"He looked at me in a peculiar way and then looked at one of his disciples who caught the cue and told me to get out. I thought I might be beaten, the way all his disciples gathered around us and threatened us. So we left. This was the same fellow who advises his disciples that they can go into samadhi by putting all their energy into the sex center, awakening Kundalini and having a great cosmic orgasm. What nonsense! Has Kundalini become so cheap? You know, in India you can get away with anything in the name of religion."

Ahamkara uses the body as ballast for the mind, that it may not drift away and be lost like a runaway balloon on a breezy day. When Kundalini awakens before death She will try to return to and unite with Her opposite pole, the pole of greatest awareness which is Shiva, by reversing the outward projection of energy which led to incarnation. While She slumbers She supports the body; once She is aroused and throws back the covers which bind Her down, the body-mind-spirit complex starts to unravel as the life force is released from its bondage to the organism.

If your awakening Kundalini unites totally with Her Shiva you will cease to exist, since nothing will remain to identify with your body. If She awakens slowly enough that you can "digest" the tremendous energies which are released as She lets go of everything that has been holding Her down, you will become a man or woman of God. If, however, She awakens too quickly to be controlled, and too slowly to kill you outright, you will be catapulted into the maelstrom of a "spiritual emergency," a Kundalini crisis.

Some modern writers inaccurately blame all human illness on such spiritual crises. While it is true that all disease is due, directly or indirectly, to ahamkara, to one's sense of ego and identity, all neuroses are not signs of incipient Kundalini arousal; and while a Kundalini crisis may produce a nervous breakdown, every nervous breakdown is not a spiritual emergency. Most of those who maintain that the awakening of Kundalini is the root cause of all their imbalances are merely experiencing the consequences of Her first stirrings from sleep; this is more a crisis of ahamkara than of Kundalini.

The "physio-Kundalini process," touted by some as a form of "natural stress release," is merely the preliminary purification of the ethereal nerves in which Kundalini will eventually move. The awakening of Kundalini is a "stress release" only in the sense that as the bonds of body and personality that hold Kundalini down are undone, the energy that had been used to self-identify with these "stresses" is released for the organism to otherwise allocate. The awakening of Kundalini releases all stresses, not merely those which produce neuroses; relief of neurosis is not regeneration of identity.

If Kundalini be triggered suddenly in an unprepared nervous system, the shock produced resembles that delivered to an unsuspecting toddler who grasps a live wire. When an unreconstructed personality tries to resist Kundalini, consciously or unconsciously, She may fry nerves and blow out endocrine fuses, shorting out the nervous system at its weakest point and blowing a hole in the victim's aura. Since the aura's job is to insulate us psychically from one another and from disembodied influences, holes in the aura permit all sorts of chaotic, negative mental vibrations, including even ethereal parasites, to enter the individual's field as they like and spread ruin.

If the individual remains functional, Kundalini may inflate and empower his or her limitations. That person into whose genitals Kundalini is diverted full force, for example, will begin to live, eat and breathe sex, and may misidentify as spiritual experiences the colossal lusts which arise. Or, should Kundalini become lodged in the digestive organs, insatiable hunger may supervene.

Even if overt calamity is avoided worse dangers await, for the ensuing catharsis can actually reinforce the limitations of the personality instead of releasing them. Those half-baked spiritual aspirants (called *ardha dagdha*, literally "half-burned," in Sanskrit) who permit the power to swell their heads, like gas inflating a balloon, may believe themselves to have achieved exalted states. Because the power of Kundalini that buoys them confers an aura of seeming truth to their words they may shoot up to the heights of self-confidence as pseudo-gurus, commanding others with confident persuasiveness to follow them until one day the pressure of temptation becomes too great and there is a cataclysmic fall.

Such self-inflation may proceed insidiously; as Gopi Krishna observes ". . . the desire for power, the yearning for mental conquest . . . often accompanies the activity of Kundalini in the intellectual center, causing a slight intoxicated condition of the brain too subtle to be noticed by the subject himself or by his uninformed companions, however erudite and intelligent they may be." (Gopi Krishna, p. 176) A spiritual aspirant may not intend to go wrong, but the power of even a half-awakened Kundalini often proves to be dangerous.

Which illustrates the great danger in the notion that all one's problems will be solved if one can just awaken Kundalini; problems are solved if and only if Kundalini awakens in a slow, controlled way. When She does awaken in a controlled way, She awakens slowly and reveals Herself gradually; only very rarely, as with Vimalananda, does She shine forth in nearly fully developed form almost from the start. What many people believe to be the culmination of their spiritual practices is thus really only the beginning, only a brief, tantalizing disengagement of Kundalini from Her normal self-identification with the mundane. Should this happen to you, you must then methodically follow up on it with measures to guide and channel Her if you hope to survive because Kundalini progressively unties every knot that binds the personality together.

Though I had been introduced to the idea of Kundalini before I met Vimalananda, She became real for me only after I began to glimpse Her peculiar path through his life. Because he was concerned to remove the idea of quick achievement from my mind, he never sat me down and said, "This is what Kundalini is all about." Instead he provided me with little bites of information from time to time, encouraging me to digest each morsel thoroughly and assimilate it efficiently. As he liked to say, "Never be in a hurry; start with a sip and end with the bottle." The long conversation reproduced below did not occur at one sitting; various snippets have been spliced together to provide an overall glimpse of his approach to Kundalini Yoga.

Self-Identification

"Actually there is no difference betwen the Kundalini Shakti and *Adya*, the original Shakti of the universe, except that the Kundalini Shakti has become individualized."

Vimalananda was not one to repeat himself; as soon as he began to speak about something of interest to me I was expected to drop whatever I was doing and listen. Usually he picked moments when I was engrossed in some mundane matter like reading the newspaper, since drawing my attention to his words would disengage my mind at least temporarily from its attachment to the mundane.

"That is why I call the Kundalini Shakti the ego. The ability to self-identify, to treat something as part of oneself, is ego. As long as the Kundalini Shakti self-identifies with the body She remains asleep. Once She awakens She searches for Her mate: Shiva, that fragment of the universal consciousness without which an individual cannot exist. When they merge that's it; the play is over. It's something like an electron finding its proton and merging with it.

"The Rishis, who are the only beings in our universe who can travel to the sun, have the full power of the Kundalini Shakti at their disposal. They can reach the sun in the instant they will themselves there, thanks to Her awesome might. Do you know the speed of the Kundalini Shakti? It's immeasurable, but since the Rishis can travel from here to the sun in less than one second its speed must be more than one hundred million miles per second."

I must have looked at him quizzically, for he emphasized, "Yes, I have been to college and have several degrees, so I know about the speed of light; but there is nothing faster than the speed of thought.

"The Kundalini Shakti is the highest possible expression of an individual's will power. When you have purified your will so totally that it can be directed to a single object at a time—coherent just like a laser beam—then the Kundalini Shakti is operating in you, not before. Anything travelling that fast must have tremendous force behind it, and very few people can handle such power. This is why I get so wild when I read about all those people in America who claim either to have had their own Kundalinis awakened painlessly, or to be awakening the Kundalinis of all and sundry effortlessly. Don't ask me to believe such drivel. If it were so all of America would have merged with the infinite by now."

Restraining his indignation with some effort, he continued.

"Why I am so outraged? Because the ordinary individual can at best, after long penances, become able to partially self-identify with the universe, or with a deity; whenever that self-identification becomes perfect the ego loses all concept of individuality and all contact with the body, which then disintegrates. Once you lose your ability to identify yourself with imperfection, how will you be able to continue to exist in our imperfect world? All the swamis and sadhus nowadays who talk about the awakening of Kundalini are really talking about Her partial awakening, whether they realize it or not. You may accidentally awaken your Kundalini partially, or a saint may partially awaken it for you, but that is not the end; it is only the beginning, which is why so many aspirants go astray."

A brief pause signified that this applied particularly to me.

"In an ordinary individual the ego resides at the lower end of the spinal cord because gravity has full power over Her. So long as She lies there sleeping the individual remains in ignorance. If you want to liberate the ego from Her restrictions you must create a force within your body to counteract the force of gravity; this can only be done by strenuous penance. The purpose of all spiritual practices in every religion is to disengage the ego from Her identification with the limited personality so that She may reunite with Her perennial personality.

"Whether you do it slowly or quickly, you have to rip your ego away from your nerves when you practice Kundalini Yoga, and this will come as quite a shock to your organism. The ego has such a strong grip on the body that it is impossible for most people to do this. In fact, some die of shock when Kundalini is awakened, and others become severely ill. Indiscriminate awakening of the Kundalini is very dangerous. Everyone is doomed to die, of course, but dying disoriented in pain and fear will ruin your chances for a good rebirth.

"If your nervous system is strong it can endure a great deal of shakti before disintegrating, which is why penance is required. If you do the practices your guru sets for you and control your tongue and your penis—"

"Or if you are a woman?"

"Or your clitoris, you can create nerves of steel. I'm sorry, but if you think you can dare to awaken Kundalini and survive while living in a body that has been weakened by dissipation you are living in a fool's paradise. How do you think Moses was able to withstand his experience with God? Only because of his long penances. Moses described a burning bush which burned but was not consumed. That bush was his own brain and nervous system, ignited by God.

"Kundalini has been described as *vidyut lata*, the "lightning creeper." Think of how a creeping vine clings to a tree; and then think of that vine as a lightning stroke, a bolt of billions of volts of energy which would splinter or incinerate any ordinary tree, or bush. But Moses was destined for greatness, and his nerves, though severely strained, were able to take the sudden flash of pure consciousness that God graced him with. How few are able to do this!

"If you could just for a moment experience the power of a fully awakened Kundalini Shakti you would know what bull is being put out by these phony Yogis who say that the Kundalini can be felt as a creepy feeling in the spine, or as a cool breeze in the palm. Creepy feeling, my foot! And to control Kundalini, do you think it is some sort of joke? Never! For an ordinary human to control Kundalini is impossible, or nearly so. Only immortals can properly control Her.

"No, raising Kundalini in an uncontrolled way is not the answer. You don't become enlightened or become a yogi just because your Kundalini is aroused. There is a great potential for abuse of this power. As long as it goes up it's fine, but when it falls, it falls like a thunderbolt."

"Like in the Bible where Jesus says, 'I saw the devil fall like lightning from Heaven?'"

"Yes. Jesus was talking about the devil of the uncontrolled ego, who tempts us to indulge in the pleasures of the mundane world. Isn't life in the mundane world really hell? And it is an endless torment, because we are reborn into it over and over again. To rise above all this misery you must raise your Kundalini, in a controlled way."

Coverings

"While Kundalini sleeps in the Muladhara Chakra at the base of the spine you are awake to the world and asleep to reality. When She awakes to unite with Her Shiva in your brain then you wake up to reality; you 'fall asleep' to the world. An ignorant person believes that he is in the world; his Kundalini self-identifies with the poison of Maya. A *jnani*, one who knows, says rather, 'The world is in me,' because his Kundalini self-identifies with Shiva.

"We say that Kundalini is 'sleeping' because She, the ego, is self-identifying with the individual's limited personality. Because of this self-identification She accepts its limits as Her limits. In Her pure form the ego is the purest of shaktis, but as long as She self-identifies with the body She lies under three coverings which prevent Her from remembering who She is and where She belongs. These three coverings are the Three Gunas (Sattva, Rajas and Tamas), the *Six Tastes* (sweet, sour, salty, bitter, pungent or spicy, and astringent), and the *Five Great Elements* (Earth, Water, Fire, Air and Ether).

"The Gunas control our minds, the Elements shape our bodies and the world around us, and the Tastes control our internal chemistry, which links our minds and bodies together. Together with the ten senses, the five we all know plus the tongue, hands, feet, anus and genitals, there are twenty-four limitations which distort the human consciousness.

"Externally the Universal Self is covered by *Maha Maya* (the Great Maya); internally Maya appears as these twenty-four limitations. The first step in Tantric spirituality is to work on the individual scale to uncover the ego and make Her reunite with Shiva, the true Self. Numerologically twenty-four means 2 + 4 = 6, the *Six Chakras* (energy centers). The Six Chakras are also manifestations of these twenty-four limitations, which means that only when you go beyond the chakras do you go beyond these limitations, and vice versa. Both are ultimately identical; it is all a question of perspective, of point of view.

"Now, what is the meaning of the word *Kundalini*? Kundala means a coiled earring, so Kundalini means 'the Goddess with a Kundala.' Here the coil is at the tip of the spinal cord; the ego is coiled because it is tightly constricted by the three coverings. So long as Kundalini lies sleeping in the Muladhara Chakra She is coiled up."

"And that is why She is sometimes called 'Kubjika' ('the Hunchback')?"

"Yes. Once She enters the Ajna Chakra, though, She completely loses Her coils and becomes straight and, unencumbered by the three coverings, She can express Herself fully. Conditioned knowledge is always slightly distorted; only unconditioned knowledge is truly straight.

"In Kundalini Yoga we usually begin with *Bhuta Shuddhi*, the purification of the Five Elements, to allow Kundalini to travel upwards through the chakras. Bhuta Shuddhi is really the essence of Tantra. The force of Her motion, if it is unimpeded, lifts the other coverings and eventually produces simple or ordinary spiritual wisdom: *jnana*."

"Jnana is *ordinary* spiritual wisdom?"

"Jnana is the knowledge that the entire cosmos is really One Great Being, in spite of the fact that we see multiplicity in the world: All-in-One, One-in-All. When you progress from ordinary jnana to the ability to influence the placement or the removal of these coverings on the cosmic scale—creation, preservation and destruction—you have practical spiritual knowledge, a higher stage, which is called *vijnana*. The 'vi' in vijnana means *vishesha* (special, extraordinary). You are then a *Siddha*, an immortal, because your own ego has become absolutely purified. Only Siddhas, and higher beings like Rishis, can possess this sort of practical or specialized knowledge; a *vijnani* is something quite different from an ordinary jnani.

"After the three coverings are removed from Kundalini your perception becomes quite different. It is the difference between capital 'I' and e-y-e 'eye.' The eye is symbolic of the world of sense objects. As long as the ego is covered, it knows nothing but the senses and their objects and is contented with them. But they are external, and therefore impermanent. The ego must be made to realize the capital 'I,' the Self, which lies within, and therefore, the first thing to be cultivated is interiority, withdrawal of the mind from external objects. Love, including orgasm, is internal. If you look for love externally, as most Westerners do, you will either become bored and perverted, or frustrated and desperate. Only interiority can give you bliss.

"Once you develop interiority your mind will gradually become quiet and perception will develop. Eventually you will realize that effect, instrument, and action are all one. You will see yourself in the goat being slaughtered, in the act of slaughtering, and in the one who slaughters. When you can see yourself in the butchered, the butchering, and the butcher, you will see that all are mere manifestations of the Self. All is His play, capital 'H.' When you see yourself everywhere, where is there any possibility of pity? This is jnana, ordinary spiritual knowledge.

"To go beyond this to vijnana you must go beyond the body, and to do that you must first understand the relationship between the body and the ego. The nerves of the body are the probes, the feelers of the ego. This is what Krishna meant when he talks in the Bhagavad Gita about the tree whose roots are above and whose branches are below: the roots of the nerves are in the brain, and the nerves themselves branch out to cover the whole body.

Nadis and Chakras

"The ego or ahamkara does not actually reside in the physical body, because the ego is not at all physical. It resides in the subtle body, and moves in the *nadis*, the ethereal nerves. The body's 72,000 nadis act as conduits for prana, which is closely related to the ego. Numerologically, 72,000 means $7 + 2 = 9$: the Nine Doors through which prana can enter or leave the body. Most of the nadis begin or terminate at these Doors, which are the sense organs: the two eyes, the two nostrils, the two ears, the mouth, the anus, and the genital organ. Prana, moving with the breaths, enkindles the body's fire, just as a bellows is used to ignite and inflame the fire in a forge, and the mind is carried out through these Doors by prana so that it can experience the world. Control of the nadis enables you to control the ego, the mind and the senses.

"Of these thousands of nadis three are most important: the Surya Nadi ('sun channel'), the Chandra Nadi ('moon channel'), and Sushumna (the 'fire channel'). The right nostril is related to the Surya Nadi, and the left nostril to the Chandra Nadi. Sushumna is closely associated with the spine and spinal cord."

"So, on the physical level there is a physical structure, and on the subtle level there is a nadi, and they more or less occupy the same space, so they influence one another; is that the idea?" I could visualize it, more or less.

"Yes, that is close. The sun heats things up, while the moon causes them to cool down. When your right nostril, also known as Ganga (the Ganges River), works more efficiently than does your left nostril your appetites for food and other enjoyments will increase. When your left nostril, also called Yamuna (the Ganga's main tributary), works more efficiently than your right nostril the opposite effect is produced: your body cools and relaxes, and your appetites decrease. If you take the trouble to observe your own body you'll find that each nostril works for about an hour and a half at a time."

I had not observed this before, but began to do so at that moment.

"Continuously throughout the day and night your body fluctuates from excitation to relaxation and back. Yogis control this fluctuation by performing pranayama. They make the left nostril work when they want to be submissive, when they worship God for example, and they make the right nostril work when they want to command. They also strive to create a balance between the left and right nostrils, because only when the Surya and Chandra Nadis work with equal force can prana be forced into the Sushumna Nadi to move Kundalini upward."

Pandit Gopi Krishna suffered for weeks from an intensely overheated system when the tornado of prana unleashed by his awakening Kundalini moved exclusively in his Surya Nadi; only when his Chandra Nadi finally opened and calmed him down again did he get relief.

"We must distinguish here between Bhuta Agni, the ethereal fire, and *Jathara Agni*, the digestive fire. Bhuta Agni is predominant; it is Bhuta Agni which causes Jathara Agni to become enkindled. Jathara Agni is in charge of physical digestion, and Bhuta Agni of mental digestion. When you take in new ideas you 'eat' them; Bhuta Agni 'digests' them so that you can comprehend them. A yogi who has good control over his digestive fire can afford to use his Surya Nadi in his sadhana because he will direct the energy to inflame Bhuta Agni alone, not Jathara Agni. Ordinary people who stimulate their systems with Surya Nadi will mainly increase Jathara Agni and weaken Bhuta Agni.

"The nadis meet and connect with one another at ethereal plexuses called chakras. The chakras exist only in the subtle body and are perceptible only to the enlightened mind, but nowadays everyone who reads a few books writes about the chakras, parroting the Tantric descriptions without understanding the inner significance. Very few people have any idea at all of what they are writing. They talk about the chakras' shapes and colors and speak knowingly about the Sanskrit letters which are present at each chakra, when in fact the only letters that exist at any chakra are the ones you create yourself.

"I can tell you this, though; if you start meditating on your chakras directly you run a great risk of exciting the nerves and nadis in the area where you have been told the chakra is. For example, suppose some guru tells you, 'My boy, meditate on the Muladhara Chakra, which is at the perineum.' If you have not been thoroughly taught about the Muladhara Chakra, if you have not been told what to expect when you get there, most probably you will never locate the chakra; you will merely inflame the nerves in the perineum and intensify the force of *Apana* (the downward-moving form of prana). This will probably turn you into a sex maniac, or some other sort of maniac."

There are five varieties of prana in the body: *Prana*, which takes things in; *Apana*, which throws things out; *Samana*, which assimilates; *Vyana*, which circulates and distributes; and *Udana*, which expresses, especially in speech. (In this book "prana" [lowercase] refers to the generic life force and "Prana" [capital] that variety of prana which ingests.) Each of these forms appears in a different part of the body: Udana in the head, Apana in the pelvic region, and so on. Any obstruction to the free flow of these five pranas causes imbalance and disease.

"This is why a good guru is so important. When Kundalini begins to awaken, a tremendous rush of energy is released. Unless the guru is strong enough to control it the disciple will be overwhelmed with desires and will become strongly attached to worldly things, precisely because the chakras are still blocked. If your sex centers are inflamed, for example, you may become so infatuated with a woman that you will create a jigsaw puzzle to prove that a *rnanubandhana* (bondage of karmic debt) exists between you and her. Probably it does exist, to have caused the attraction in the first place; but it is all imagination until you can remember your past lives, which allows you to actually know the karmic ties.

"This distortion can happen with any of the lower chakras. You know, I believe, that the Tibetans spend their lives reciting 'Om mani padme hum,' which is meant for the Manipura Chakra, the seat of the Fire Element. The

KUNDALINI

vast majority of Tibetans are not perfected yogis, so the main effect of this mantra is to inflame the fire in their physical bodies. This is good for them because they live in a cold country and have very little food to eat, so a strong internal fire helps keep them warm. Those who have plenty of food available to them however tend to develop an obsessive desire for food. Even some good lamas become gluttons, thanks to overstimulation of the solar plexus.

"If lamas, who do plenty of hard penances, can fall despite all their precautions, what do you think could happen to you if you concentrate on the Manipura Chakra in a hot country, or in a country where you have plenty to eat? Probably you would go berserk and eat everything in sight, which would just bind you down tighter to the *samsara*, the universe of manifested existence."

"I see what you mean," I inserted, excited with a sudden realization. "Some Westerners who practice Tibetan Buddhism swear that their religion requires them to eat meat, but Buddhism believes in nonviolence, so that doesn't seem likely to me."

"It is absolutely ridiculous. They are not talking; their inflamed appetites, which crave the heaviness of meat, are talking. When you arouse Kundalini before your mind is firmly under control, She will very likely self-identify even more strongly with your limitations, which can wreak havoc with your evolutionary progress. A good guru will close the doors to the lowest three chakras so that the Kundalini can never fall back into them. Then there is very little danger; otherwise the disciple will be most likely overwhelmed with the desire for food, sleep, or sex.

The Nine Chakras

"Most people will tell you there are six chakras. An Aghori will tell you there are nine. To understand this statement you must at least know the difference between a *nara* (man) and a *khara* (donkey). If you think this is a joking matter, it is because you are a khara yourself."

I had grinned at the comparison, and now I grinned at his affront. He snorted and went on.

"A khara believes only in the three lowest chakras, the chakras which are in charge of eating, procreating and excreting. The long penis of the donkey is a good symbol for those who have big appetites for worldly pleasure.

"When I told my Roshni (his foster daughter) that she needed to get married so that she could be well set in the world she told me in return, 'How can you say such a thing to me when you know that the world is filled with kharas? Would you give your daughter away to a donkey? If you can find a nara for me then I will marry, otherwise the game is not worth the risk.'

"I was so pleased with her answer that I said, 'All right, I will not even make you marry a nara; I will see that you marry Narayana directly.'

"A nara lives exclusively in the upper three chakras. Only a few naras exist in the world at any one time, and only a nara can become *Narayana*, God Himself, by going to the highest three chakras. The lower three chakras are for the mundane, the *adhibhautika*; the upper three are for the spiritual, the *adhyatmika*.

"The final three are for what is beyond both the physical and the spiritual. Some people call it the astral; in Sanskrit we call it the *adhidaivika*. These three chakras are within the head, and they permit the immortals to remain in their bodies, if they can retain Ma's grace. These chakras are secret and cannot be described in the way the other six are. They are only experienced, and they can only be experienced after the Kundalini is fully awakened. Until then there is no use in even discussing them, but I will tell you their names: *Golata*, *Lalata*, and *Lalana*.

"The first of the six chakras which can be described is the *Muladhara*, in the perineum. Then comes the *Svadhishthana* in the pubic region, the *Manipura* at the navel, the *Anahata* near the heart, the *Vishuddha* in the throat, and the *Ajna* in the center of the forehead. From the Ajna one moves into the *Sahasrara*, which is not a chakra at all. You have heard all of this before, I believe?"

"Yes, I have."

"So you know that each chakra has the form of a lotus of a particular color with a particular number of petals. Have you ever thought to ask, 'Why a lotus? Why not another flower, or something besides a flower?'"

He had me there. "No, I have not."

He smirked in triumph. "Well, the lotus is used as a symbol for purity because although it lives in mud it is not soiled by the mud but rises above it. Thus the analogy of the lotus of discrimination and the mud of Maya. But there is more.

"The lotus opens only when touched by the morning sun, and closes just as the sun sets. Likewise, the lotuses of the Six Chakras open only when the Kundalini Shakti is present within them; otherwise they remain closed. Also, even if the sun is shining a lotus will close if water is splashed on it.

You too must learn to be 'like the lotus in the water'; you must close your-self to external influences to prevent the Three Gunas from disturbing you. Try this when you are full of shakti and see how hard it is.

"Each chakra has a different number of petals—four, six, ten, twelve, six-teen and two, in ascending order—because of the different modes of dis-crimination which pertain to that chakra. Each petal is a separate *Bija Mantra* (seed sound) for that particular chakra. By performing the appropri-ate ritual with that Bija Mantra the knowledge of that mode of discrimina-tion is obtained.

"The Sahasrara, the 'Thousand-Petaled Lotus,' is at the top of the head. Although it is a lotus it is not really a chakra because there is no plexus of nadis there; there is only one nadi, which connects the Sahasrara with the Ajna Chakra."

"Sort of like the stem of the lotus."

"Indeed. The lotus of the Sahasrara has the largest number of petals. The next largest number of petals is in the Vishuddha Chakra, which has six-teen. All of its Bijas are vowels, since vowels are the basis of vocalization, which has its origins in the throat, the location of the Vishuddha Chakra.

"Kundalini lies coiled like a snake in the Muladhara Chakra. She has three and a half coils: the three refers to the Three Gunas, and the one-half to the cobra's mouth, the seat of ego. It is one-half because ego is Shakti, which is only half of Shiva, the Shaktiman or controller of Shakti. The purpose of Kundalini Yoga is to reunite Shiva and Shakti, to create the eternal form of Shiva, *Sadashiva*.

"Sadashiva's left side is female and right side is male; the two principles have united but have not merged. If they were to merge that would be the end of the play, and that would be no fun at all. Sadashiva exists on the cos-mic scale; in an individual this deity is called *Ardhanarishvara* ('the Lord Who is Half Female'). In order to manifest Sadashiva the Kundalini must be made to rise fully, because the highest manifestation of Shiva in the human being is in the head, the highest part of the body.

"In an ordinary person Kundalini is asleep at the base of the spine, and so Shiva is bereft of Shakti. Such a person is not Shiva but merely *shava* (corpse). I look at everyone I meet as a skeleton because that is what they are; until a person's Kundalini Shakti awakens and begins to dance on Her Shiva, that person is as good as dead."

The Nadis and Chakras

Ascending through the center of the subtle body is the median Nadi of Sushumna (fire), to the left and right of which ascend the Chandra (moon) and Surya (sun) Nadis respectively. These channels are described as being a thousandth of the thickness of a hair. The lunar and solar nadis enter or unite with the Sushumna in the Muladhara chakra and ascend to the region of the Anja chakra where they then descend to the left and right nostrils, while the Sushumna rises to the Sahasrara chakra. From the two nostrils extend the channels of prana which carry the breath to the distance of twelve finger widths.

At the base of the Sushumna is the Muladhara chakra (perineum), in which Kundalini lies coiled and sleeping with her head sealing the bulb (Kanda) or entrance to the Sushumna. The Muladhara chakra is described as having four petals (plexus of nadis) and sealed with the square yellow element of earth. Above this is the Svadhisthana chakra (pubic region), having six petals and sealed with the white half-moon of the water element. At the navel is the Manipura chakra of ten petals and sealed with the red triangle of fire. Near the heart is the Anahata chakra of twelve petals and sealed with the blue hexagram of air. At the throat is the Vishudda chakra of sixteen petals and sealed with the white circle of the element space. At the center of the forehead is the Ajna chakra with two petals and sealed with none of the five gross elements, but with the subtle essence of Mind. At the crown of the head is Sahasrara, the brilliant thousand petalled lotus.

Each of the chakras is described as having various deities and bija syllables at their centers and on each of their petals. (It need hardly be said that it is not supposed that there are any actual lotuses or letters engraved thereon. These and other terms are employed to represent realities of yoga experience.— Arthur Avalon).

The three secret chakras of Golata, Lalata and Lalana are said to be located on the uvula at the back of the throat, above the Ajna chakra, and within the soft upper palate. Their main inner yoga practice is in Khacari Mudra, although Vimalananda possibly refers to a practice even beyond this. In Khecari Mudra the linguæ under the tongue is progessively severed and the tongue is gradually lengthened by stretching until it can extend to a point between the eyes. The tongue is then turned inwards and upwards to press on and enter the duct of "the two headed snake and seal the tenth door" within the cranial cavity above the soft palate. The pressure of the tongue on the "*Ama Kala*"—the receptacle of lunar nectar, causes the lunar nectar (*amrita*; *soma*) to flow downwards abundantly and permeate the entire body with supreme bliss. Attainment of Khecari Siddhi confers a divine body of immortality which is free from aging, corruption and disease, endowed with the eight great magical siddhis.

The "two headed snake" is the channel that extends from the back of the throat to the "moon" just above the Ajna chakra. The "tenth-door" is the tenth orifice or aperture of the body. The "Ama-Kala" is the true philosopher's stone of immortality.

Raising Kundalini

I had to shake my head in appreciation and agreement, it was so true.

"To make Kundalini rise from the tip of the spine you must create enough pressure to force Her out of the Muladhara Chakra. The upward motion will continue only so long as the pressure remains; without it Kundalini drops back down to the bottom, due to gravity. Because humans stand erect, gravity acts only on the tip of the spinal cord, not on the whole thing as it does in other animals, whose spines are horizontal or nearly so. This is one reason why it is easier to awaken Kundalini in a human than in an animal."

I wanted to ask how one goes about awakening Kundalini in an animal, but he wouldn't let me get a word in.

"You might wonder how Kundalini, an ethereal force traveling in ethereal nerves, can be affected by gravity. Well, gravity must also have an ethereal form, mustn't it? All the Five Great Elements have ethereal forms, and gravity is mainly due to the Earth Element. Ethereal gravity is in fact more difficult to overcome than physical gravity. Besides that, as long as Kundalini is asleep She is completely self-identified with the body, which includes the nervous system, so the effect of physical gravity on the nervous system will disturb any attempt to pry Her away from physical consciousness.

"You will never be able to raise Kundalini until you can control the movements of the prana in your body. Kundalini can only leave the Muladhara Chakra when Prana, which ordinarily moves upwards, is made to move downwards and Apana, which usually moves downwards, is made to move upwards. Only when Prana and Apana meet and their 'mouths' touch can Kundalini's upward motion begin.

"And just because you begin to feel some upward movement from the Muladhara does not mean that that chakra has been fully opened! When Kundalini leaves the Muladhara Chakra for good, She throws off all connection with the Earth Element, all the accretions of millions and millions of births. These pass through your consciousness on their way out, and you learn all about the Earth Element. Actually, this is just a review of everything you have learned about Earth in all your previous lives. When you gain full knowledge of the Earth Element you can be sure that the Muladhara has become fully activated, not before. When you finally relinquish the Earth Element you must also let go of acquisitiveness and greed, the emotions which are based there. Earth is the only solid element, the only thing you can 'hold on to.' When you give up needing to hold on to anything you can progress.

"After the Muladhara Chakra comes the Svadhishthana, the seat of the Water Element and of procreation. When Kundalini leaves the Svadhishthana for good the *sadhaka* (anyone who practices sadhana) learns everything about the Water Element. In each chakra you obtain full knowledge of the Element it represents, as all the accretions of past experiences are dredged up from your causal body. You must conquer lust, the instinctual drive to procreate, before you can move beyond the Svadhishthana.

"From the Svadhishthana Chakra, Kundalini moves up to the Manipura Chakra, the seat of the Fire Element, where metabolism takes place. The lowest three chakras are meant for the mundane world, physical existence. When asked about their future prospects Indians frequently say that it all depends on what is written in their fate, pointing to their foreheads where fate is supposedly written. But fate is not written on the forehead. Fate is simply the sum of all your past karmas, good and bad, and it is written in your three lowest chakras. Rnanubandhana is strongest here, because these chakras pertain to the Earth, Water, and Fire Elements, which possess physical form. Rnanubandhana is not so strong with Air and Ether, which have no form.

"The Manipura Chakra is really crucial. There you learn the difference between Jathara Agni and Bhuta Agni. Whenever Bhuta Agni is strong Jathara Agni must be weak, and vice versa. You only have a certain amount of fire in your system, and you have to choose how it will be used. To progress at sadhana a sadhaka must progressively convert Jathara Agni into Bhuta Agni.

"It is very nice for you to learn new things," he said, looking pointedly at me, "but you must be in a position to digest what you learn. If you are not able to do so you will vomit back all the knowledge, which is shakti, and your last condition will be much worse than your first. When you try to take in too much energy before your Bhuta Agni becomes strong, much of that undigested energy gets converted into anger, the emotion that is characteristic of the Fire Element.

"The main reason for this indigestion is the element of doubt. Until your doubts are removed you will ask questions like, 'Why should it be like this instead of that?' whenever I tell you anything. Just experience it and you'll know about it; there's no other way. Without personal experience there just can't be firm understanding. This is another reason why I never teach anyone. How can I teach? People spend all their time trying to understand by asking questions, and most of them don't even know which questions to ask!"

I was on the point of asking a question, so I refrained.

"Why doesn't anyone ask about *Granthi Bhedana*, the Piercing of the Knots which obstruct the free movement of Kundalini in the nadis? There are three principal knots: the Brahma Granthi, the Rudra Granthi and the Vishnu Granthi. Kundalini cannot be completely awakened until She pierces these knots."

"Where are they?"

"Ah, *now* you ask!" He laughed. "We'll talk about it sometimes."

I suspected as much. "Some people blame almost all physical and mental diseases on 'blocked chakras,'" I continued, "Does that have anything to do with these knots?"

"It does, but not in the way they think. A little knowledge is a dangerous thing. The chakras exist in the subtle body, and their connection to the physical body is very subtle. It is true that both the physical and subtle plexuses may become blocked, but in most people the Kundalini is fast asleep in the Muladhara Chakra, and their chakras are absolutely closed and play no part in their day-to-day lives. It is because everyone's chakras are blocked that Kundalini Yoga is so necessary. As long as you are full of attachments to life your consciousness will never be able to get close enough to any chakra even to smell its fragrance, much less experience it.

"But in a way what these people say is true: if you try to take on too much shakti before removing these knots, the shakti will get blocked along the way, and then either your nervous system will overload and collapse, or all the energy will be 'vomited out' into your system and you will go berserk. Shakti magnifies and expands everything, including especially attachments. You need good guidance at every step of the way or down you will go, dive-bombing back into the samsara.

"Above the Manipura Chakra is the Anahata Chakra, the first of the upper three chakras which are meant only for spiritual activities, like sacrifice. The Vedas enjoin the performance of sacrifice, and today many priests loot in the name of the Vedas, performing sacrifices without knowing why, just to make money. The Sanskrit word for sacrifice is *yajna*, which is a word of two syllables: *ya* and *jna*. *Jna* of course stands for spiritual wisdom (jnana); 'yam' is one of the chief Bija Mantras for the Anahata Chakra. This suggests that a yajna involves ethereal worlds, which is very true. In fact, one of the main purposes of a yajna is to feed and satisfy various ethereal beings with the fragrance of the smoke from the various burnt offerings. It also suggests that Bhuta Agni rather than the Jathara Agni is to be used in a yajna, and that only a person whose Bhuta Agni is truly enkindled can properly perform a yajna.

"When you move into the Anahata Chakra, the chakra of the Air Element, you learn all about ethereal beings, the 'spirits of the air' which move about just like the wind does. Anahata means 'unstruck'; at the Anahata Chakra you begin to hear the *Anahata Nada*, the 'sound which does not arise by striking.' Associated with the Anahata Chakra, on the right side of the chest, there is a little organ referred to by its size: 'the thumb-sized person.' It is most useful; it acts as a universal translator. You can understand any language with its help because it provides a simultaneous translation into your own mother tongue. Language is sound, and sound moves in air; when you learn all about Air, you develop a comprehension which is good for all languages.

"From the Anahata Chakra the Kundalini moves into the Vishuddha Chakra. *Vishuddha* means 'especially pure,' and here you gain knowledge of the Ether Element, the subtlest and so purest of the Five Great Elements. You also go beyond the Six Tastes, since taste is only a permutation of the Five Elements in food. All that remains to obscure the Kundalini now are the Three Gunas. When Kundalini is in the Vishuddha Chakra your exhalation will move only two fingerbreadths beyond your nostrils, which indicates that your mind has become very calm. You've noticed, I presume, that in times of great anger, at the moment of orgasm, and in other intensely emotional situations your breathing becomes faster and more forceful, and your mind becomes more chaotic?"

I thought for a moment, and then said yes.

"Such breathing is useless for sadhana, for which you must have a conditioned mind. Yogis practice pranayama because they know that control of the breath causes control of the mind. The opposite is also true: whatever controls the mind controls the breathing.

"When your mind is well-conditioned, Kundalini will move from the Vishuddha Chakra into the Ajna Chakra, at the 'third eye.' Its lotus has only two petals, indicating only two Bija Mantras: one for Shakti and the other for Shiva. *Ajna* means 'command.' Here 'ajna' stands for 'guru ajna,' 'instructions from the guru.' Shiva is the world's guru, and at the Ajna Chakra He can be clearly perceived.

"Do you know how the tribe of immortal beings known as *Naths* address the Kundalini Shakti? 'Whore!' Yes, 'Whore!' They say, 'So, strumpet, You have been playing about with others! Now You come to me. You will never be allowed to flirt again!' They mean that their individual shakti, which has been busy self-identifying with all sorts of external sensory objects under the delusion that She is the body, must be forcibly brought up into the Ajna

Chakra where She will have only one to self-identify with: Her Grand Consort, Lord Shiva.

"At the Ajna Chakra the breathing is almost completely stopped, because here the *Shunya* state (emptiness, nothingness) begins. In the Shunya state all names and forms become extinct, and all you are aware of is your own individuality; otherwise only the Void remains. Everything in the universe is contained in the Shunya state, in unmanifested form; you can no longer perceive it. Although people call the Shunya state the Void, it is not empty; it is full.

"As long as Kundalini is still concentrated in the lower chakras, even the Vishuddha, there is still danger of self-identification with the body. Once Kundalini rises above the Vishuddha Chakra there is no possibility of any mundane thought because there is no longer any rnanubandhana, any bondage of karmic debt. How can there be? You have gone beyond the Five Elements which compose the physical universe; no physical tie remains.

"When Kundalini moves from the Ajna into the Sahasrara the final shreds of identity are lost and the sadhaka merges completely with the Universal Soul. In the Ajna Chakra there is still duality—the Ardhanarishvara or Sadashiva form, Shiva and Shakti united in one body—but in the Sahasrara they merge completely. All differentiation is lost, and the result is *Nirvikalpa Samadhi*, the *samadhi* (state of profound one-pointed consciousness) in which nothing is perceived except the Universal Soul. All determination and indecision drop away, all fluctuations of the mind disappear. You are finished! Gone to the land of no return!"

Samadhi

"I have always said that life is a memory. There are actually two types of memory: conscious and unconscious. The conscious memory is very fickle and inconstant; it is directed outwards towards mundane objects, which are temporary and transitory but seem eternal to the ignorant mind. The unconscious memory is permanent; it has been collecting all your karmas from tens of millions of births without any lapse or distortion. So the unconscious memory is actually conscious, since it perfectly records everything that happens to you, and the conscious memory is actually unconscious. People say, 'I did it because of the force of circumstance,' when what they mean is that they were not conscious enough to remember not to yield to the pressure of all the karmas encouraging them to do it.

"The result of the above is Maya. Through sadhana you can make the conscious memory truly conscious, and you can return the unconscious memory to unconsciousness. When these two merge, the result is the superconscious memory—the consciousness of reality—and in that state you exist in the causal body. Then you must go even further, from vijnana to *ananda*, the unlimited bliss of pure existence. When the last shred of ego is dissolved only awareness is left: Nirvikalpa Samadhi.

"Ordinarily no one ever comes back from Nirvikalpa Samadhi. Once the Kundalini Shakti enters the Muladhara Chakra the entire Earth Element must be transformed before She can move to the Svadhishthana Chakra. If even a tiny bit of Earth remains untransformed there will be no further rise. She can remain partly awakened, but She will be unable to awaken completely. This is true for every chakra. When Kundalini finally reaches the Sahasrara, therefore, She has relinquished all connection to the Five Elements, and the soul can no longer remain in the mundane world, where you must be imperfect in order to survive.

"You cannot last for more than twenty-one days in Nirvikalpa Samadhi; if you stay longer you can never return to your body. For the first twenty-one days you are in Nirvikalpa Samadhi your body does not decay. Not one hair falls, no animal bothers it, no insect disturbs it. After that it begins to decay because the causal body ceases to exist. Without a causal body how can the subtle and physical bodies continue to exist? You have become desireless.

"You can return to Earth from Nirvikalpa Samadhi only if Nature has a mission for you. If that is the case, or if you get permission to return to Earth to conduct your own research or just to play about, then you must select some karmas with which to self-identify to enable you to drop back into your body. They may be karmas from a tree, or a rock, or any sort of being; but there is no other way to return. You are like an insect that has escaped its cocoon, a cocoon of karmas. Once a worm becomes a butterfly it cannot return to wormhood unless it takes on new karmas, like Jesus did."

Kula Kundalini

"If you hope to continue to exist after Kundalini is awakened completely you must be able to make Her go from the Muladhara to the Sahasrara, and then in the reverse direction, downwards from the Sahasrara to the

Muladhara, under perfect control. Prana and Apana are then perfectly united. Apana is represented as a downward-pointing triangle, and Prana as an upward-pointing one. Their union forms a six-pointed star.

Kundalini Yantra

At the center of the yantra is the goddess Kundalini coiled around a linga within a downward pointing yoni triangle. This rests on two intersecting triangles placed over two intersecting squares, which represents the union of Kundalini Shakti with her Shiva. On the eight lotus petals are the six chakras, the Sahasrara and the yantra of Shiva and Shakti in union.

"We call this freed Kundalini by a special name: the *Kula Kundalini*. Like every Sanskrit word, the word *kula* has many different meanings. Its most important meaning here is 'Supreme Consciousness of the Universe.' It also refers to 'form,' because the job of the Kundalini Shakti, the Supreme Consciousness, is to finitize, to give form and limits.

Yantra of Shiva and Shakti

"In the astral sense kula means 'family.' The Kula Kundalini, the Kundalini once She is uncoiled and straightened out along the Six Chakras, takes the form of the Goddess Who is meant to be worshipped by the family into which you have been born. Kundalini is by herself formless and pure, but when She moves through the body She must be qualified, possessed of attributes, so She takes the form of one of the Great Goddesses and guides you. The particular form She takes is determined by your ancestry. Then you realize why you were born into a particular family, which allows you to understand your karmic debts, which in turn gives you knowledge of your past births.

"Take my own deity, Smashan Tara, for example. The word *tara* comes from a root, meaning among other things to swim. You know that when you swim you must remove all your clothes. To swim across the ocean of samsara you must remove all the 'clothes' of your attachments. This is one reason why Tara is always shown naked except for severed arms and heads, which represent the karmas and emotions that 'clothe' you, preventing you from seeing Her in Her full, unalloyed purity and beauty. Tara is meant to be worshipped only by the select few who need to worship Her to fulfill their destinies. Only they are fit to worship Her; only they can succeed.

"If this sounds complicated," and he could see that it did, "it is because it has a lot to do with your heredity and the state of your consciousness. As long as your ego self-identifies with your body your consciousness resides in your brain and is affected by the chemical environment there, which is influenced by the tastes in your diet and by the hormones produced by the brain cells. The hormonal pattern is determined by your genes and chromosomes, which are in turn determined by your ancestors.

"You told me a few days back that scientists have discovered a gene which produces a protein which causes depression. These scientists have a long way to go yet; they will find that many previously unsuspected things are included in our hereditary material. One of the main differences between ordinary humans and Rishis is that Rishis can play about with genes and chromosomes, and we humans cannot.

"Your genes and chromosomes determine which rasas you can manufacture yourself and which you have to imbibe from the world. When I say *rasa* (flavor) I mean both the physical tastes of your food and your emotional 'tastes' and tendencies. If your guru gives you the correct form of Ma to worship you can, by obtaining Her Shakti, perfect your personality, which involves bringing your brain chemistry into perfect balance. Then it becomes very easy to merge with the infinite."

"Does *Rasa Vidya* (Tantric alchemy), which I have been studying in Ayurveda, also help do this?"

"Of course! That is the whole purpose of Rasa Vidya. Rasa Vidya is a sadhana by means of which you gain control over your rasa, and transmute it into *Maha Rasa*, a transcendental flavor, within you."

Oh my. "No one talks about this at the Ayurvedic college," I complained.

"No one knows about the real Rasa Vidya over there, my boy," he said, and returned to making his point. "The followers of Tantra who perform this practice of making Kundalini into Kula Kundalini are called *Kaulas*. When the ordinary sadhaka's Kundalini is awakened the experience is so overwhelming that Nirvikalpa Samadhi is followed by cessation of individual existence. But with Ma's grace Kaulas deliberately come down to duality again and remain in those final three chakras that I mentioned earlier: Golata, Lalata, and Lalana. What they do there I can't tell you, but think about this: Krishna lived as a cowherd in Gokula—go + *kula*, the 'family of cows'—when He was young, and He herds the 'cows' (sense organs) of those of His devotees who reach Him in Goloka. The head is a Gokula itself, a 'family of sense organs.' Goloka cannot be described; it can only be experienced, in one of these chakras.

"After you become Kaula, *abhisheka* (ritual initiatory bath) is performed on you to make you *Maha Kaula*. But mind you, you become eligible for abhisheka only when you surrender yourself completely to your guru. Only when you are completely empty can you be filled with shakti. The liquid used for abhisheka is first charged with mantric energy, so this abhisheka is a kind of *Shaktipat Diksha*, initiation by transfer of shakti, and it permanently alters your personality. In India a king (*raja*) used to be given a Raja Abhisheka in order to fill him with sufficient shakti to govern well. This practice was not limited to India, mind you: Jesus's baptism by John the Baptist was a kind of abhisheka, as was the ancient Hebrew practice by which kings were anointed by prophets.

"When the Kundalini of a Maha Kaula is completely awakened he becomes *Maha Atharvan*. *Maha* means 'great,' 'immense,' 'cosmic'; Maha Atharvan is he who has gone beyond the limitations of the Atharva Veda, which is the source of Tantra. As I tell you constantly, the results you can achieve with the Vedas and Aghora are exactly the same; only the paths differ.

"In spite of all this explanation you may still wonder, 'Just what exactly is the Kundalini Shakti?' Shakti is shakti, whether it is the Kundalini Shakti,- Chit Shakti, Maya Shakti, or some other shakti. Energy is energy. Einstein tried for twenty-five years to prove it with a Unified Field Theory, but he couldn't do it because he didn't look deep enough. He was stuck in the physical universe. To fully understand the Kundalini Shakti, you must go beyond Her external manifestations, for which sadhana is necessary.

Comment

The Snake

As Joseph Campbell documents in his book *The Inner Reaches of Outer Space*, the force that the Tantras call Kundalini has been represented as a serpent in many world cultures, including the Sumerian, Chinese, ancient Irish, Aztec and Greek (the *caduceus*). Images of Kundalini as the Serpent Power predominantly reflect Her power of possessiveness, of Maya. Indian cosmology describes seven netherworlds beneath the surface of the earth in which dwell *asuras* (the "selfish" or "jealous" gods) and *nagas* (semi-divine snake beings). In the microcosm the 'surface of the earth' is the Muladhara Chakra; 'dwelling beneath the earth's surface' means living wholly in objective reality, within the realm of Maya, which is the skin of the universe.

So long as ahamkara predominates within you, Kundalini exists for you as a snake. After Kundalini has been awakened and controlled, the once deadly snake turns protector. Vimalananda explains:

"Snakes are usually poisonous, and as long as your ego, which is a fragment of the Kundalini Shakti, self-identifies with your body and your limited personality you will be full of the poison of the samsara, which is the poison of selfishness. Once Kundalini frees herself of all limitations, that poison is transmuted into *Amrita*, the nectar of immortality. The Jain religion talks about Twenty-Four *Tirthankaras*, or 'Ford-Makers.' A Tirthankara is one whose Kundalini has successfully passed through all Six Chakras (24 = 2 + 4), who learned how to ford the river of samsara, to pass over from imperfection to perfection, the other shore of existence.

"In Jain iconography some Tirthankaras are always represented with a serpent hooding their heads. That serpent is a symbol for Kundalini, the Serpent Power, and the fact that it is above their heads shows that their Kundalinis have entered the Sahasrara. The serpent acts as an umbrella for the Tirthankara; here, an umbrella indicates protection. Such beings are protected from pollution by reason of their fully awakened Kundalinis. The snake above the head of the Tirthankara has filled that Tirthankara with Amrita, and if you follow him you can obtain that same Amrita, as well as the bliss of Nirvikalpa Samadhi. Sometimes you see Buddha depicted with a snake as well; the meaning is the same. And Vishnu, of course, sleeps on Shesha Naga, the Cosmic Serpent."

Although the snake is regarded as demonic in the mainline Judeo-Christian tradition, the Gnostics believed that the serpent in the Garden of Eden was trying to free Adam and Eve from bondage to a limited world-god and to give them knowledge of the Absolute. Vimalananda, who refused to entertain the concept of Original Sin, also regarded the story of Adam and Eve as a Kundalini myth, a representation of the descent of consciousness into matter. Because Kundalini's self-identification with matter is essential for embodied life, Vimalananda argued that Adam and Eve first had to leave the Garden of Eden that they might eventually consciously return to the perfected state.

Jesus Himself used snake imagery when in conversation with Nicodemus (John 3:14) He likened Himself to the serpent of bronze elevated by Moses in the wilderness (Numbers 21:5–9), and Campbell's book reproduces a striking image, possibly originating from the 'ophitic' tradition (ophis = serpent in Greek), of Christ-as-Serpent on the cross flanked by the two thieves. It does not seem unreasonable to draw a parallel between this image and that of Sushumna, filled with Shakti, flanked by the Chandra and Surya Nadis.

Another implication of Kundalini as serpent: as long as She sleeps, you and your temporary personality can remain ignorant and healthy, but once you rouse Her from Her slumber you must either digest Her venom or die; there is no other alternative. Only if you are ready for such a jolt, as Moses was, will you survive Her. In Biblical times it is said that a priest would enter the Holy of Holies in Solomon's Temple in Jerusalem once yearly, bells on the hem of his robe and a rope tied around one leg. An unconsecrated priest would not survive; the bells would testify to this calamity, and his body would then be dragged out with the rope. Some would say that God killed him, when in fact he had killed himself by pouring God's Shakti into his unprepared nervous system.

The Chakras

Even though the chakras of the subtle body have been identified by other cultures, such as the ancient Egyptian and the Navajo, they have never been directly introduced into popular religion, for good reason. Having our Kundalinis unawakened and our chakras closed is a form of protection; existence is possible for embodied beings solely because their chakras are normally blocked. In fact, many Kundalini-generated disorders are due not to the blockage of a chakra but to the *lack* of blockage thereof. The delusion that the chakras are the cause of physiological imbalances stems from the confusion that exists between the chakras themselves and the other structures that exist in association with them. The chakras mentioned above, the Muladhara and the rest, function only when Kundalini moves within them; at all other times what functions are their corresponding but more superficial structures. Arthur Avalon comments that:

> . . . from an objective standpoint the subtle centres, or Cakras, vitalize and control the gross bodily tracts which are indicated by the various regions of the vertebral column and the ganglia, plexuses, nerves, arteries, and organs, situate in these respective regions. It is only therefore (if at all) in the sense of being the gross outer representatives of the spinal centres that we can connect the plexuses and so forth with the Cakras spoken of in the Yoga books. In this sense only the whole tract, which extends from the subtle centre to the periphery, with its corresponding bodily elements, may be regarded as the Cakra. (*The Serpent Power*, pp. 161–2)

The chakras are the knots that bind ahamkara into self-identification with the substances that make up the universe. Each of the lower five chakras is the place where ahamkara and one of the Elements meet and interact; the chakra plugs ahamkara into the frequency of that Element, in effect broadcasting that Element into the organism's consciousness.

Ahamkara continues to recognize and manipulate that Element within the body only as long as this connection remains intact. Conscious effort to open the chakras, such as visualizing them and repeating their Bija Mantras, may cause one or more of them to open prematurely, which will disrupt ahamkara's ability to manipulate that Element within the organism. Once these knots are untied it is as difficult to retie them while cosmic energy is flooding the system as it is to mend a hole in a dam while millions of tons of water are trying to flow out through it. It is always preferable for the chakras to open on their own when they are ready to open, which happens once Kundalini's three coverings have been removed through sadhana.

Kula Kundalini

The fourth, fifth and sixth chapters of the book of I Samuel describe the capture by the Philistines and the eventual return to Israel of the Ark of the

Covenant. While it is difficult to draw direct correlations between otherwise unrelated ancient cultures, it is striking to note that during the period that the Philistines possessed the Ark the idol of their god Dagon was mysteriously toppled and disfigured, and the entire population was struck low with hemorrhoids. It would certainly seem that neither the Philistines nor their god could digest the Ark's shakti. When they consulted their diviners they were told to return the Ark to Israel with a trespass offering consisting of five golden hemorrhoids and five mice, also made of gold. Is it a coincidence that hemorrhoids appear in the physical body near the location of the Muladhara Chakra, or that the mouse is the vehicle of Ganesha, the Lord of the Muladhara? Or does this imagery reflect similar subtle realities?

Siddhi means success at sadhana. While a "siddha" is technically anyone who succeeds at sadhana, Vimalananda used the word *Siddha* exclusively to mean one who has achieved immortality and supernatural powers as a result of sadhana. The freeing of Kula Kundalini is a sort of siddhi, though it may not necessarily make one immortal.

Kula, which also means "totality," "the giving up of egoism," and 'the road of Sushumna,' is Shakti, the manifested universe, while *Akula*, Shiva, is the Absolute Unmanifested. A Kaula maintains that since Shiva without Shakti is inert, and may not even exist, the two are perforce equal in our world. In the human body as in the universe, consciousness may come down from on high, but it must be manifested from the bottom up; Adam and Eve must leave the Garden if the world is to flourish. Creation occurs when Kundalini projects from Akula into Kula, and destruction when She returns to Akula. It is in this context that Kundalini is called a harlot, because She alternates between union with creation and union with Shiva. Unless your Kundalini is under your conscious control these two states fluctuate so fast that they seem to exist simultaneously.

Vimalananda's reference to "the family into which you have been born" is not limited to one's consanguinous family:

"Yoga is meant to make every home a happy home. When every family member is giving out his or her best to unite the family and make it a success, that is real Yoga. And I don't mean the family you were born into or married into, necessarily. Whoever you live with is your family. As we say in Sanskrit, '"vasudeva kutumbam"—we are all members of God's family.'" (*Aghora*, page 43)

The idea of a "kula" as a family of like-minded sadhakas who after reforming their errant Kundalinis follow similar paths toward Reality may have been inspired by the Vedic idea of *gotra*, or lineage. A gotra is a cowpen, a "protection for the cows"; because a group of families from a single lineage used to protect its cows together in a single pen, the word came to refer to the lineage itself. *Gotra* also means "protection for the senses"; each gotra originated from a Rishi, its members sharing genes and chromosomes which would enable them to easily succeed at a particular variety of sadhana. Perhaps as time passed it became more difficult to transmit one's spiritual lineage directly to one's child via the gotra system and so the kula system arose. Only a few genealogical families in India have preserved their spiritual lineages; most teachers, like Vimalananda, find that their spiritual children come to them from other biological parents.

PRELIMINARIES

Not long after I met him, Vimalananda suggested changes in my eating habits to address the dysentery which tormented me periodically ever since I had been in Africa. Once I had adjusted to a strict regimen limited primarily to milk—a diet which I was proud to share with the Masai—I realized that his purposes were not limited to the merely medical.

One day when he asked me how I was enjoying such fare I replied, "Just fine, thank you, and not so hungry as I was before."

He smiled knowingly.

"Was that," I went on, "part of the plan?"

Smiling more knowingly, he nodded corroboration.

"There are many ways to apply pressure to Kundalini to encourage Her to move upward," he began. "Certain *asanas* (Yoga postures), some of which you know—"

He paused and I interjected: "—and practice—"

He continued: "—can help, especially those in which the Muladhara Chakra is firmly pressed with the foot. You understand why, I think?"

"They prevent the downward movement of Apana."

"Exactly: they help Apana to rise. Since Apana is that form of prana which is in charge of excretion, however, constipation is likely to occur, which may unbalance your system. Have you noticed this?"

"I have, when I overdo those asanas," I replied sheepishly.

He smiled again. "Yes, like me you have a tendency to overdo things. To prevent disease, though, you must avoid doing anything that might aggravate Apana while you are trying to make Kundalini rise, especially because of your history of dysentery. By reducing your food you reduce the volume of urine and feces, and therefore limit the harmful effects of the constipation. By reducing or eliminating sex you prevent the discharge of semen or vaginal fluid, both of which requires strong downward movement of Apana." I was at that time sexually chaste.

"Reducing your sleep is also important. I had to learn the effects of sleeplessness when I was in training to become an Aghori. My guru sneered at me and said, 'You think you can stand the strain? Try it.' After two days without sleep *bandha koshtha*, the state of absolute constipation, began. I can't describe the agony. I started to bleed, and fissures developed. But I was obstinate and went beyond it.

"Ordinary Kundalini Yoga is difficult enough, but an Aghori makes it even more intense. Do you know how you feel when you are full of lust? You can't wait to enjoy sex; you will rip off your own clothes, and then rip the clothes off your partner. Likewise an Aghori, filled with the desire to experience Reality, rips the coverings, the clothes, off the universe when he wishes to love it. If you really want to progress at Kundalini Yoga you must forget your body, that thing which is clothing your consciousness, and to do that you must first forget food and water. After three days without water you begin to feel dizzy, your blood thickens, and so on. After five days you begin to gasp, and unless you are really dedicated you will decide you don't want to die, and you'll drink. Aghora is the fast, direct way, but it is too difficult for most people.

"If you don't want to force yourself to quit eating, and want to progress by stratagem instead, which is the way of the clever sadhaka, you must first understand the nature of food. To do this you must first thoroughly understand the nature of the Three Coverings of the universe, which are—?"

"The Three Gunas, the Six Tastes and the Five Great Elements."

"The Six Tastes are within the body, not outside. Have they taught you this yet in the Ayurvedic college?"

"They have alluded to it."

"Oh, they have *alluded* to it, have they? Anyway, if you want to do do without food and drink entirely and live only on air you must manufacture all the tastes within the body; then there is no need to take them from outside. Amrita, the 'nectar of immortality,' is a glandular substance created within the body which is necessary for this purpose."

That too had been alluded to in Ayurveda, with little explanation.

"We exist only because of the Three Gunas: Sattva, Rajas, and Tamas. Most people do not know that Sattva and Tamas are two sides of the same coin. Sattva is Amrita, which is of the essence of the Fire Element. The Amrita in your head, this glandular substance, is a physical manifestation of pure Sattva. Tamas is Visha, deadly poison, which is of the essence of Water Element. The metabolic toxins in your body poison both it and your mind. When you remove the bad qualities from poison it becomes nectar, and if you add bad qualities to nectar it will become poison. Ayurveda is full of examples of how poisonous plants and minerals can be used for medicine, and of how improperly used medicines act as poisons. I believe I am correct?"

"Yes, you are."

"Rajas is the bridge between the two. Rajas can transmute Tamas into Sattva, and it can degrade Sattva into Tamas. Rajas is pure shakti, energy, the very incarnation of illusion, of Maha Maya. Rajas does not know what it is doing; it just does it, so it must be well controlled. When Rajas is properly controlled almost anything can be achieved. And the only being Who knows how to control Shakti is Shaktiman: Lord Shiva.

"The name *Rudra*, which is another name for Lord Shiva, indicates the shedding of tears. Rudra brings you nothing but tears, but there is a big difference in ordinary and extraordinary tears. Before the Rudra Granthi is pierced the sadhaka sheds tears of misery, of Maya, because he cannot be sure of himself, or of the existence of God. This doubt continues until that Knot is pierced, when all doubt is removed. The glands of the body then begin to secrete Amrita; they 'shed tears.' This Amrita causes the devotee to shed tears of joy.

"Shiva drinks poison, but He converts it into Amrita. In order to do this you must know the relation between *visha*, which is poison, and *vishaya*, which means sense object. The world of sense objects is the true poison because it is impermanent. People fleetingly regard it as permanent, and this leads to delusion. During sex, for instance, a man feels, 'Oh! What bliss I am enjoying!' But suddenly, pfssst!—emission. Then he realizes, 'No, it is no longer there.' His dream construction of heaven has evaporated.

"Everything Shiva takes in is converted into Amrita, which is called Amrita because it is permanent, not transitory. And that is why it is connected only with Lord Shiva, Who is your real Self, your soul. As long as you are in the world your consciousness is connected with sense objects; it is the state of transience, of ignorance. Only when you come to Shiva can you find Amrita.

"To obtain Amrita the grace of your guru is also necessary, at the very end when you are just on the threshold of progress. It is like a Rishi's goat sacrifice. The Rishi who kills the goat will send it into a higher womb, but the goat doesn't know that and feels great pain at first. The sadhaka who wants to do without food also suffers, but a good guru is relentless, and finally the Amrita is obtained. The disciple goes beyond food and becomes a Siddha, an immortal."

Which of course was a secret ambition of mine at the time, as Vimalananda knew. I listened more carefully.

"This is the fast way of doing things, but even if the disciple is not tough enough to become an Aghori and do fast and terrible sadhanas he can still learn to do without food. First the guru will allow the boy to eat whatever he likes for a short time. When his major cravings have been placated his diet will be restricted. Naturally the boy will still occasionally feel hungry in spite of himself. Since this is not his fault, though, the guru will make him fall asleep, even for a few moments, when this happens. The disciple will be overpowered with an irresistible urge to sleep, and the sleep will make him forget his hunger."

Here he threw me such a mischievous sidelong glance that I burst out laughing. I have long been notorious for dozing off in any position, but during this stage in my life it had become almost a daily affair, and observers had been kidding me about it. So he was behind it all!

Vimalananda began to chuckle too, and then continued as soon as the mirth died away: "A hungry man usually cannot sleep; hunger and sleep are opposites, and opposites can be very useful. After a few days of occasionally uncontrollable sleep the disciple's system will adjust to the new diet. He will continue at that plateau for awhile until he is completely established in it, and then there will be further restrictions and further periods of adjustment. Finally the goal is reached."

I couldn't resist: "Am I going to be falling asleep at lunchtime for several years now?"

"It might take that long, you know. Success at this method is still far off, for you or anyone else, especially nowadays during Kali Yuga when almost all of our prana comes from food. There is another way: you continue to eat, but you lose all your taste for food. This is the way of Aghora.

"Actually, to do this you must lose your taste for all sense objects, because sense objects can disturb your consciousness. Because we are living in Kali Yuga, the age in which almost all of our prana comes from food, you cannot expect your mind to be pure if your food is impure. Your consciousness is a chemical phenomenon which exists at the mercy of the chemical composition of your diet.

"The food you eat can definitely disturb your sadhana; so can the water you drink, and the air you breathe. This is why Tantra lays such stress on the purification of the Elements that make up your body. Even if you have to start out with materials which are polluted by the desires and attachments of others, you can still use them safely after they have been purged of all these negative influences. This is why an Aghori can use either sewage or Ganges water for his rituals; he converts both into the same pure substance. How else do you think Telang Swami could dare to worship Kashi Vishwanatha with his own urine and feces?"

Good question. Vimalananda had already told me some stories about Telang Swami, the Pride of Benaras; some of these appear in *Aghora*.

"Other things beside food affect us, I suppose?"

"Everything affects us. Take my Roshni. She is very lucky to be able to wear my mother's bangles. My mother wore them for sixty-five years, during which all day long she would recite the mantra her guru had given her. It is no wonder that Roshni's mind has become so clear since she began to wear them, since bangles are worn on the wrist where certain important nadis are present. If I were to make Roshni wear her own mother's bangles you would see in a few days' time how her mind would become prejudiced and dull. I would caution you therefore not to wear any jewelry unless you know its antecedents."

Point taken. "Of course, the fact that the bangles are gold has some effect, doesn't it? I mean, if they had been made of steel she would not have got the same result, would she?"

"No," he replied, "they would have had a different effect. Wearing iron or steel bangles prevents you from being possessed by certain classes of lower spirits, but they also dull your mind. Anything you wear will affect your consciousness according to the innate qualities of the material it is composed of. But more important than the ornament itself are the vibrations attached to it. My mother recited mantras all day long, and the vibrations of those mantras penetrated her bangles through and through. *That* is why her bangles are valuable, not because they are made out of gold. They would be valuable if they were made out of clay. This goes for any ornament, any article of clothing, *anything* that you use, but the effect is more for food because the food goes inside you and becomes part of you.

"And that also applies to the place where the food is grown. Did you know that the very ground on which Bombay is built is cursed? Yes, the ground itself is cursed, which means that the very gravity of Bombay affects the minds of everyone who stays here. And since this curse is present in the ground, any food that is grown here and any water that is taken from here transmits those negative vibrations into anyone who consumes them. One effect of this curse is that everyone who comes to Bombay forgets all sense of morality and immediately thinks of how to earn money as fast as possible, even by selling his grandmother if necessary."

A thought-provoking concept. "And this effect is independent of what you mentioned before about the pollution that comes from the desire and attachment of others?"

Food

"Yes, that is a separate thing, but it is still the same principle: the food acts as a carrier, a via media, for whatever vibrations are added to it. Remember that Shaktipat Diksha can be given with water, or with some other substance that the disciple ingests. Every time you eat something, you are imbibing unaware all sorts of vibrations, all sorts of shaktis, some of which may be very unbalancing to your system.

"Old-timers in India complain about the quality of the food being produced in the country today, and there is a lot of truth in these complaints. In the past the grains of wheat, for example, were small but heavy, and one *roti* (whole-grain tortilla) would satisfy you more than three rotis made from today's over-fertilized large, light grains. Back then there was less food, true, but people ate better.

"There are at least six faults in the food we eat today. The first fault comes from the farmer who is greedy for a better price for his crop and so adds plenty of fertilizer, with results as we have noted. The grain acts as a vehicle to transmit his greed to us.

"This greed is compounded by the middleman who buys from the farmer. He cheats the farmer with adulterated weights—the second fault—and then adds chaff or filth to the product to increase his profit when he sells it to a merchant, which is the third fault. The shopkeeper himself is the cause of the fourth fault, because he cheats on his measures when he sells to the public.

"The fifth fault comes from the cook, who is in a hurry to go do something else and so does not approach the food with the proper reverence.

Eating home-cooked food is still better than eating in a restaurant, though; a restaurant cook is a paid hireling who cares nothing whatever about your health. If he is angry with his boss for low wages no one knows what he may add to your food!

"The sixth fault occurs when the eater of the food forgets to offer thanksgiving to the Creator of the food before it is eaten. With all these faults is it any wonder that food is no longer as nourishing as it once was? This is the effect of Kali Yuga."

This was a new idea to me, this idea that one's thoughts and desires project onto and "stick to" one's possessions, or the things one wants to possess. I did not quite understand why this should be so characteristic of Kali Yuga, but I knew Vimalananda would tell me about it eventually if I simply expressed the thought, so I did not interrupt his soliloquy.

"I always prefer simple food," he went on, "because you can taste it, or even look at it, and very easily know exactly what the cook was thinking about it when he or she was cooking it. So you immediately have some idea of what is going on in the household, because those thoughts are carried to you through the vehicle of the food. This is why it is so important to be choosy about whose food you are willing to share. You don't want nasty thoughts ruining your own consciousness, do you? Definitely not, if you are trying to perform some sadhana.

"This is one reason why it is generally best to be vegetarian if you want to do any serious sadhana; it makes your mind much clearer. The violence involved in killing animals gets transmitted to your consciousness when you eat their flesh. People who want to justify the murder of animals say, 'But plants are alive too. Don't you kill and eat them?' To which I answer, 'Yes, they are alive, and they feel pain when they are chopped for the pot.' Whenever I hold a cabbage in my hand I think, 'Oh, Ma, now I am going to cut you. Don't worry, it won't hurt for long, and I will take care of you.'"

I had to smile, for I had seen him do this so many times that I had also taken up the habit. Vimalananda's ready love and compassion for all things, even empty matchboxes and flaking paint, was so natural, so real and so sincere, that it was difficult not to follow his example.

"The point is that plants have less power of expression than animals, so less karma is involved in eating them. The curse that they give you for eating them is milder than the curse an animal gives you for killing it.

"Another problem with meat eating is that meat is flesh, after all, and when you make your Jathara Agni identify with flesh in order to digest it you encourage your ahamkara to self-identify more strongly with your own flesh, which will not help you in disentangling Kundalini from Her bindings. Plants at least provide less for ahamkara to self-identify with. Yes, meat is sometimes used in the Tantric ritual known as the Panchamakara Sadhana, but that is something different altogether."

"What is it?"

"It's something else entirely, which I will tell you about later. For now, think about food. The best way to avoid all the negative influences in our food is to do without it altogether. To do this you must proceed stepwise: first you become a vegetarian, then you limit yourself to roots and fruits, then to milk alone. Milk is freely offered by the cow, and it transmits some of her maternal love to the drinker; this is the real reason yogis like to drink milk. Eventually you move on to water alone, and finally to air. Those who live on air alone get their prana directly from the atmosphere. They do not use their mouths to eat; they eat with every pore of their bodies. But it is essential for them to get sunlight, just as it is for plants."

"Oh. Another reason why the Rishis worship the sun," I hazarded.

"Yes. A Rishi does Gayatri and exists on the energy of the sun alone. But that is too far ahead. Ordinary people like you and me must eat. And now I'm hungry, so let's eat!"

Vimalananda always preferred to cook his own food, to protect the purity of his consciousness. His food was always cooked to perfection, light and easy to digest, and a feast for the eyes as well as the stomach. Before long I was spending quite a lot of time in the kitchen. Soon he began to teach me to cook in his own unique style, although because of my dietary restrictions, only rarely did I eat anything that he or I cooked. Several of his officious friends made wailing noises about "how hungry poor Robby must be," but I like dairy products and did not miss eating ordinary food very much. Vimalananda would sometimes tell me, after such a busybody had left, "Such people go out of their way to show how much they care for you, but they don't really care; this is just a ploy to make you think more highly of them. It's all superficial, just a sophisticated frothy bubble." I knew he was right, so I ignored them and continued to relish my culinary duties.

One afternoon after tea, when the topic turned again to food and its faults, and I asked again how to prevent them from affecting me, hoping for a new angle on the subject, Vimalananda launched into an explanation of how to purify the Five Great Elements that make up the body. Characteristically he began by considering the most extreme of the purification methods: Panchamakara. As soon as he mentioned Panchamakara my ears awakened, for he had referred to it obliquely on more than one occasion without elaborating, knowing that I would be especially attentive when he did finally explain it to me.

Panchamakara

"You know, the whole purpose of Tantra is to free us from all limitations. The world is full of negative influences that limit our consciousnesses, and one of the greatest of these limitations is that of the Five Great Elements which make up the universe. If you can purify these Elements within you you can free yourself from their influence, and then your Kundalini will be free to rise unimpeded. As I have told you before, Bhuta Shuddhi is the essence of Tantra. All *puja* (ritual worship) is really Bhuta Shuddhi, and it is impossible to worship Shakti unless you use representatives of the Five Elements in some form or another to help purify those very Elements.

"The simplest possible puja, one which is performed by tens of millions of people daily, involves offering to God flowers, to represent the Ether Element, incense for the Air Element, a lamp for Fire, food for Water, and sandalwood paste, or another fragrant unguent, for Earth.

"Panchamakara also uses representatives of the Five Elements, but they are different from the ones that most people use. Panchamakara means 'the Five Ms': *mamsa*, *matsya*, *mudra*, *madira*, and *maithuna*. Normally these are translated meat, fish, parched grain, wine, and sexual union, and one of the reasons Tantra has a bad name today is that people have read or heard about this ritual and believe that you must be a drunken carnivorous libertine in order to be a Tantric. Ha!

"The people who babble on about such things don't understand what they are saying. It is so typical. Think of this: How many Catholics have ever considered that by eating Jesus' flesh and drinking His blood, as they say they do during their communion, they have become cannibals? If you love Jesus, can you ever think of eating his flesh and drinking His blood? Never!

Unless, of course, you are an Aghori, but none of these padres are Aghoris—far from it. This is why I say there are very few real Christians left. Almost all those who claim to be Christians just follow the ritual without any idea of what they are doing—like most Muslims, Hindus, Sikhs, Jains, Parsis and followers of all other religions who also perform their rituals mechanically. At least people should think of the implications of what they believe and practice.

"Each M of the Five Ms represents a different Element. Grain corresponds to Earth, fish to Water, alcohol to Fire, flesh to Air, and sex to Ether. In this way the universe itself is used as the articles of worship. This is why the Tantrics can say, 'Liberation is achieved by use of that which causes bondage.' Normally the use of meat, fish, other stimulating foods, alcohol or sex binds you down more tightly to the world, but if you use these same substances in the Tantric way they can be the source of your liberation from bondage, by stimulating the free movement of Kundalini. The key of course is to use them in the right way.

"In the physical type of Panchamakara most of the stimulation comes from the substances themselves. In small amounts alcohol increases appetite; it is a very hot substance, and hot things always stimulate the flow of blood in the body. Fish has a lot of phosphorus in it. When you remember that phosphorus burns whenever it is exposed to air you can imagine how hot it is. Phosphorus increases the appetite by increasing blood flow to all organs, including the brain. This appetite stimulation makes you hungry enough to eat the meat and the parched grain, which further increase this blood flow. All the extra circulating blood dilates the capillaries in the brain, filling its cells with extra energy. This makes the sex ten times better than normal, since full excitement is present. Full excitement improves satiation and helps turn the mind away from sex for its own sake. The sex itself of course increases the excitement even more. If you know what you are doing, all this excitement will help you awaken your Kundalini.

"Only a few people are fit to use these Five Ms," he concluded, delivering another blow to my spiritual ambitions. "Others can use substitutes, or better yet, if they are well advanced, they can perform the spiritual Panchamakara directly. Can you imagine how that might be?"

I shook my head no.

"In the spiritual Panchamakara *mamsa* is the tongue. You 'eat meat' by preserving silence. *Matsya* is the breath, and 'eating fish' means holding the breath via pranayama. *Mudra*, 'eating grain,' is the holding of the body in a certain posture to encourage free movement of Kundalini within it. *Madira* is the 'wine' of Amrita which drops from the glands within the head into the body, and *Maithuna* is the union of the Kundalini Shakti with Her Shiva in the Sahasrara.

"There is even an adhidaivika version of Panchamakara, but it is too advanced for you to even hear about right now. Suffice it to say that the Adhidaivika Panchamakara involves fiddling about with the genes and chromosomes. The world of the adhidaivika is very difficult for most humans to comprehend, because it is the world of the gods and goddesses, the embodiments of cosmic forces which have assumed personalities in order to interact with other beings.

"The puja in which Panchamakara is performed is called *Chakra Puja*. Chakra here means circle or ring, because during Chakra Puja the participants sit for worship in a large circle. There are Sattvic versions of Chakra Puja, like the Bhairavi Chakra, and there are also Rajasic and Tamasic versions. Most forms of Chakra Puja are varieties of the Panchamakara Sadhana."

"Does 'chakra' also refer to the chakras in the body?"

"Definitely. Such names are never chosen arbitrarily. I once wanted to go to the West and start a Chakra Puja cult, but of course my mentors would not permit me."

When he didn't want to answer a question he would change the subject.

"I really admire Westerners, and Americans in particular, for their practical attitude. They are the true Vedantins in this respect, not like our gasbag preachers of Vedanta here in India. Westerners, or at least a few of them, could learn how to do Panchamakara properly because thay are not as inhibited as today's Indians are. The only thing is, I'm not sure they could do without sex long enough to gain control over it, because sex has become so free and so common over there.

"The Tantras state that eating, excreting, sex, and sadhana all should be done strictly in private. Both the West and India have deviated from this ideal, but in different ways. Westerners believe in open sex, sex in any public place, but they are strict in insisting that you must eliminate your bodily wastes in private. Here in India, on the contrary, we don't care where you piss. What if you are an old man? You will be troubled if you have to hold your urine for very long. But we don't believe in open sex; we believe that love should be secret. We believe in getting rid of the filth within us, and Westerners believe in holding onto their filth and displaying their treasures in front of everyone where they can be stolen."

That was going too far, but I knew he was exaggerating for effect so I let it pass.

"The only way to progress, at least in the beginning, is to throw sex out completely. Forget even the existence of sex and you will be able to make progress; otherwise you will always be yielding to temptation, mentally if not physically. This is why most sadhakas who experiment with sexual sadhanas before they have become really firm inside succeed only in dissipating themselves. Sexual sadhana is one thing, and ordinary sex quite another; ordinary sex and sadhana just don't mix. If you try to both raise Kundalini and continue with ordinary sex at the same time you may develop a ravenous appetite for sex.

"I still believe that the best way to deal with the problem is to ignore the opposite sex in the beginning, until your consciousness is firm. Until I was in my twenties I never had anything to do with girls. I was a wrestler, and wrestlers are supposed to shun sex. Once I was going to have a bout with a wrestler named Imam Bux, so I went to an old man to get suggestions as to how to fight him. As soon as the old man saw me he said, 'This boy has never even seen a vagina, much less used one; how will Imam Bux be able to fight him?' And in fact I had no trouble defeating Imam Bux when I did fight him.

"The old man could say this because he knew that before you get caught up in this sex business you are completely innocent, and if you set your mind to something you can easily achieve it without any distraction. But once you see a vulva, or a penis if you are a female, it has such a queer effect on your mind that sometimes for no reason at all you will remember it and your concentration will be broken. This is true of everyone, not just you and me. Even a Rishi as powerful as Vishwamitra fell prey to an apsaras."

The *apsarases* are dancing girls in the court of Indra, the king of the gods. Famous for their bewitching beauty, they are powerful beings whom Indra sometimes sends down to Earth to delude sadhus into sexual excesses.

"Vishwamitra had been meditating with perfect concentration for ten thousand years when one day the Apsaras Menaka strolled by. Suddenly a gust of wind blew away the flimsy diaphanous garment she was wearing, exposing her full, firm, voluptuous body to his gaze. Without warning Vishwamitra's eyes led him astray, and he was overwhelmed with lust. He took Menaka aside to fornicate.

"Their sexual embrace lasted for thousands of years, until one day Vishwamitra told her, 'O beautiful woman, it has been pleasant dallying with you here for these few hours, but now I must prepare myself for the evening worship.'

"She told him, 'What are you saying, Maharaj? That afternoon when we

first met was centuries ago. Here is our daughter Shakuntala.' As Vishwamitra suddenly realized the depth of the Maya into which he had fallen
Menaka slipped quietly away, knowing how potent a Rishi's curse can be.

"Any fool can tell this story, but how many can, or will, explain its esoteric
meaning? Indra means *indriya*, sense organ; Indra is Lord of the Senses. An
apsaras, in the esoteric sense, is a particular mode of movement of prana in
a particular nadi which causes you to suddenly become sexually excited for
no reason at all. Once prana starts to move in that nadi it is hell to remove it.
Vishwamitra's mind never really recovered fully from being shaken by
Menaka, and eventually he married again. There was no need for him to
marry; he had been a king in his youth and had had plenty of wives whom
he had all given up for sadhana. But after renouncing sex and then being
reminded of women he could never quite forget them again. Forgetting sex
is really a chore.

"And what about Indra himself? He is described as having one thousand
eyes, but did you know that those one thousand eyes were once vulvas? He
was burdened with one thousand vaginas because he seduced Ahalya, the
wife of Gautama Rishi. Indra allowed his consciousness to be dragged away
by his sense organs, and was cursed by Gautama as a result. Indra became
extremely embarrassed when he found he was covered with vulvas, and so
he meekly propitiated the Rishi, who modified the curse, and the vulvas
were converted into eyes. Can you guess what this story means?"

I could not.

"Those one thousand vaginas represent the thousands of 'holes' you can
fall into, the thousands and millions of wombs which can trap you into
being reborn when you crave the enjoyment they offer. They became eyes
because you are usually led into temptation by your eyes."

He fell silent briefly to let this sink in, and then continued.

"This tendency to be tempted into sense pleasures has been with us from
the very beginning, of course, but it is much, much stronger during Kali
Yuga. You have probably heard about the Four Yugas?"

I had: "The Four *Yugas* are the Four Ages through which the world passes,
over and over again. Each one lasts for so many thousands or millions of
years. Kali Yuga, our current age, is supposed to last for 432,000 years. Are
these real calculations, or are these numbers mainly significant numerologically?"

"They are mainly numerological."

Joseph Campbell found that while the number 432 (4 x 108) is numerologically significant in Indian, Norse, Babylonian and Jewish myth it is also

significant in the world of physics. 432 results when one divides the 25,920 years in one cycle of zodiac progression by 60. A heart beating sixty times a minute beats 86,400 times a day (864 ÷ 2 = 432), and lungs breathing fifteen times a minute breathe 21,600 times a day (216 x 2 = 432). Even the Wilson Company, after long research, concluded that its golf ball should possess precisely 432 dimples for maximal flight.

"Each period of creation, or 'day' in the lifetime of the Creator, is called a *kalpa*. Each kalpa is named; our current kalpa is called the Sveta Varaha Kalpa, the White Boar Kalpa. Each kalpa lasts for billions of years, and is divided up into fourteen periods called *manvantaras* which are ruled by a *manu*, a being who is the progenitor of the races who live on the earth during that time. We are currently in the Vaivasvata Manvantara, the seventh manvantara of this Kalpa.

"Each manvantara is made up of about seventy cycles of the Four Yugas. The Four Ages are *Satya Yuga, Treta Yuga, Dvapara Yuga,* and our era, Kali Yuga. We are now living in the twenty-eighth Kali Yuga since the beginning of the current manvantara.

"At the end of each Kali Yuga there is a *pralaya,* a period when all societies and communities are destroyed, usually by natural calamities. Then there is a period of rest, and Satya Yuga begins again. At the end of each manvantara there is a more extensive destruction, and at the end of the kalpa the entire cosmos is temporarily resolved into its elements while the Creator 'sleeps.' When He wakes, the cosmos is again recreated by His thought. We are all actors in the Creator's dream.

"At the end of the Creator's life even He is resolved into the Absolute, and although He is currently in the second half of His life there is no need for concern since He will die trillions of our years into the future. Even after He dies another Creator will eventually be born and the cycle will continue. Creation and destruction, destruction and creation: time marches on.

"The influence of the time in which we live affects both our desire for God and our ability to fulfill this desire. As long as you are mortal you are subject to time, and you will be molded by whatever Yuga you take birth in. In Satya Yuga, which lasts at least four times as long as our present age, people have at least four times as much righteousness as they do today. There is nothing like religion during Satya Yuga; everyone worships by identifying the individual Self with the Universal Soul. During Satya Yuga (which is also known as Krta Yuga), people obtain everything they need by power of will. There is no disease, no discord, and nothing to interfere with your sadhana.

"In Treta Yuga one-fourth of this righteousness is lost. Sacrifices begin, and people get what they want through sacrifice. Then in Dvapara Yuga another fourth of righteousness disappears, and plenty of diseases and calamities arise, and so penances become necessary. People in Dvapara Yuga achieve their desires thanks to their austerities.

"Now, in Kali Yuga, only one-fourth of the normal amount of righteousness remains. Or maybe less, considering what I see going on in the world today. Everything is in flux and always changing, and you are likely to get contrary effects from any religious rituals you perform. But, the texts say that Kali Yuga is the best of all ages because it is the age in which everyone, regardless of caste or karma, can realize God. The problem is, most people are so overcome by Maya that they have no desire to know God.

"Kali Yuga eventually develops into the *Ghora* ('terrible') Kali Yuga, when things get really bad in the world, at which point the gutters are overflowing with filth. Nature then cleans out the gutters, by whatever means She sees fit to use, and Satya Yuga begins again."

"These yugas seem to be some sort of cosmic seasons," I interjected.

"Yes, they are, and just as each season has its own characteristics, so does each yuga. Even the types of beings which predominate in the universe differ according to yuga. During Satya Yuga the *devas* (literally, 'the shining ones') have a chance to exhibit their play. The devas or *suras* are what most people call gods. They are very high ethereal beings who like to help humans out if we request their help in the proper manner. They have an excess of Sattva in their natures, so they are very benevolent beings. But they are not pure Sattva, because we find that they are always getting into trouble in some way or other. Not only that, they are complacent. Once they have achieved something, they try to hold on to it; they don't want to progress further. Complacency is a characteristic of Tamas. Because of their complacency they are always getting conquered by the asuras.

"The asuras ('anti-suras') are also highly evolved spiritual beings, but they are jealous and selfish. They are creatures of Tamas; they are eternally plotting wars against the devas to challenge them for dominion of the universe. But they also possess some Sattva; if they didn't they could never get the idea to perform penance, and they can perform terrific penances, austerities which the devas could never dream of doing. Unfortunately, when they obtain shakti as a result of these austerities they always misuse it. For example, they have learned how to control the minds of other beings. If they were to use this power for good they could be very beneficial to the universe. But they use it only to delude.

"There is a big difference between Sattvic intellect and Tamasic intellect, between the intellect of the devas and that of the asuras. A Sattvic man who has an animal looks on it as a living toy and watches it enjoy its life. An asura, who has a Tamasic intellect, looks at such a toy and wants to crush it, kill it, and eat it. An ordinary American will look at a cow and think, 'Sirloin steak'! But an ordinary Indian will look at a cow and the way she feeds her calf and licks it clean and think, 'Mother!' Asuras have no use for that type of love. They are not fools; they are knaves. What does one do with a knave? You tell me. A fool one can forgive, but a knave? Better just to leave him and let him continue as he is. Why bother?"

"Would it be fair to say that *sura* means 'su' (good) + 'ra' (the Bija Mantra for the Fire Element), and that the devas have 'good fire,' while the asuras, the 'non-suras,' have 'bad fire'?"

"That is exactly what I just said. The devas have Sattvic intellect; their Bhuta Agni is strong, and they are not so dedicated to the physical existence as are the asuras, whose Jathara Agni is strong and whose brains are filled with Tamas. Asuras direct most of their energy into their bodies, not their consciousnesses."

"Which is why we don't worship the asuras," I added helpfully.

"There are some people who worship the asuras, but they usually regret it in the end."

"Couldn't the universe have done without them, and only had altruistic gods?"

"You can't have the one without the other. If only devas existed, the universe would stagnate and nothing would ever change because the devas believe in the status quo and change only when the asuras force them to change. Asuras believe in change; they are always willing to try something new, whereas the gods are stuck where they have always been. But if the asuras alone existed they would destroy the universe in no time because of their selfishness. Nature has created the two groups to balance one another. Which is natural; if there were no evil, could there be any such thing as good?

"The asuras get a chance to demonstrate their play in Kali Yuga. Satya Yuga lasts for millions of years and Kali Yuga for just a few thousand. Satya Yuga is slow-moving, nearly static, reflecting an almost complete absence of the power of the asuras. Because of that, if you want to reach God during Satya Yuga you must do penance for at least ten thousand years. Kali Yuga, on the other hand, shows the ascendance of asuric power: fast change that is very hard to maintain. You see, the basic difference between devas and asuras is that the devas have more awakened and far-reaching intellects. An asura will usually do exactly what he should not do, and he will not understand his mistake. Asuras are rather like children: they can be both very kind and very cruel.

"Asuras can achieve great things, but they also make great mistakes and cannot be trusted with authority. In their own ways they can become very good Siddhas. They can even become Naths and *Munis* (higher-ranking immortal beings), but never Rishis."

"Why not?" I was beginning to understand his concept of hierarchies among ethereal beings.

"How can he? The Rishis are in charge of the universe. If an asura were to become a Rishi then the whole world would be finished in no time. An asura can never change his nature to the extent of becoming a deva, even though he can merge with the Ultimate, which is nearly as good. Fortunately for us not all asuras are experts at sadhana. The majority of them are very, very foolish. For some time they will follow the rules and restrictions of sadhana nicely; then suddenly they will break it—eat meat, have sex, or what-have-you. This is because they have no inherent sense of purity.

"It is a great blessing to be a guru to a bunch of asuras, or to be their king, because then you are in a position to make them into true knowers of Reality! And that is beautiful. Unfortunately they tend to fall back into their old habits very easily, since their innate natures cannot change, and so even the guru of the asuras became tired of them after a while. I call most Americans, and many Indians, asuras; even when they have the desire for sadhana they have great difficulty ever succeeding, because they cannot persist in following the basic rules of discipline. And so I too have grown tired of them."

He fell silent for a moment, and I thought of a story from the Brhadaranyaka Upanishad: The men, gods and asuras came to their father Prajapati and asked him, "Please instruct us." Prajapati told the gods, "Da," and asked, "Have you understood?" Thinking that he meant the word *dama*, which means "restraint," they said, "Yes, we have. You are telling us to control ourselves." Prajapati said, "Yes, you have understood," for the devas are naturally unruly. Prajapati then told the men "Da," which they understood to mean *dana*, "give," for men are naturally avaricious. He also told the asuras "Da," which they interpreted as *daya*, "have compassion," as asuras are naturally cruel. The story ends by suggesting that a person should learn all three "Da-s," since unruliness, avarice and cruelty are present in everyone to some extent.

So I asked, "If the devas have Sattvic intellect and the asuras Tamasic intellect, I suppose humans must have Rajasic intellect?"

"Of course; our world is the world where things can change. This is why even the gods vie to be born down here, so that they can progress. Wherever there is change there is Rajas. Change occurs because of desire; the whole universe is created by desire, and each human is created as a result of sexual desire. If you follow the path of the devas, you go toward Sattva; if you follow the asuras, you develop more and more Tamas.

"This is all on the cosmic level. On the microcosmic level, your own personal devas are your good thoughts, your unselfish thoughts. Every selfish thought and attitude that you have are your asuras. We say that the asuras are so good at sadhana because most people who have selfish reasons for doing sadhana—who believe they will profit from it somehow—are really enthusiastic about doing it."

"Can everything that has been written about the devas and the asuras be interpreted internally?"

"Everything. I will give you some specific examples about the devas and the asuras another day; right now though, let us concentrate on the Yugas and their esoteric meaning—one thing at a time. Most people who talk about the Four Yugas do not realize that they also exist inside each of us, in our heads. Satya Yuga is the mind itself. Treta Yuga is formed by the three eyes, the two physical eyes and the hidden 'third eye'; *treta* means 'the third.' Dvapara Yuga is represented by the two nostrils; *dvapara* comes from the Sanskrit word meaning 'two.' Kali Yuga is the mouth.

"Now see why this is so. In Satya Yuga, the perfect mental age, no one bothers to talk because all communication is telepathic. Everything is mental in that age; there is no need to use any of the sense organs. People eat mentally, taking in prana, the life force, directly with their minds. Even reproduction is mental. In Satya Yuga a man can look at a woman with such intense affection that she will conceive, or he can make her conceive merely by wiping the sweat off his forehead and giving it to her. Such is the tremendous mental power available in those days that people can even create beings without bothering to use the womb.

"In Treta Yuga *trataka* is performed. Trataka is a form of meditation in which one stares fixedly at an object. If done properly trataka can open the third eye. In Treta Yuga people use trataka to obtain prana from the sun; they eat with their eyes. They communicate with glances and make romance with significant looks. This ability exists together with telepathy, which is only possible after the third eye is opened.

"The quality of time changes further in Dvapara Yuga, and it becomes more difficult to use your eyes alone for all your work. The people of Dvapara therefore begin to take in prana through the nose instead of through the eyes or the mind as before, and they practice pranayama as their primary sadhana. Some of this emphasis on the breath survives even today, as among the Eskimos and the Hawaiians where the traditional greeting is an exchange of breaths.

"In Kali Yuga we receive most of our nourishment from food, through the mouth. And what's more, we talk—no telepathy. And that is why they say that in Kali Yuga the best penance is repetition of the name of God, because it controls everything we do with our mouths, and purifies the prana we take in."

"Then why bother with things like Panchamakara?"

"Well, remember that I said that Panchamakara is not for everyone; it is only for those who can avoid being tainted by Kali Yuga."

"Just like Bombay is only for those who can avoid being tainted by it."

"Precisely. Even though Kali Yuga surrounds us everywhere, there is no need for Kali Yuga to exist on the inside. As long as you have your mind and sense organs, and you control and cultivate them by sadhana, you can create and live in whatever Yuga—Satya, Treta, Dvapara or even Kali—as you so desire, internally.

"This is how the Rishis did it when they lived on earth: They would begin before dawn by practicing samadhi, perfect equilibrium of consciousness in which the mind is utterly still and inactive, for three hours. This was equivalent to Satya Yuga. At dawn came three hours of *dhyana*, *dharana*, and *pratyahara*—meditation, concentration, and withdrawal of the senses—which represent Treta Yuga. For three hours until noon came Dvapara Yuga: pranayama and asana.

"The three hours just after noon were reserved for food, for conversation and for interacting with other beings according to the rules of good and bad conduct, *yama* and *niyama*. These last two are particularly necessary in Kali Yuga, when humans must live by regulation. At the evening twilight the Rishi would perform certain rituals, and after night fell he would take another meal, enjoy sexual intercourse, and sleep, all of which belong to Kali Yuga. Do you recognize all these practices?"

The eight limbs of the Ashtanga ('Eight-Limbed') Yoga of Patanjali, are those very eight practices, in reverse order: yama, niyama, asana, pranayama, pratyahara, dharana, dhyana, samadhi. Since he had already made clear to me his belief that Patanjali's method as it is commonly taught today is not appropriate for Kali Yuga, he was now stressing that he respected it when implemented in the proper way at the proper time.

"We who are not Rishis may not be able to perfectly imitate their lives, but we can learn from their examples. We must begin where we are, in Kali Yuga, and work our way back to Satya Yuga. The first step is to learn yama, external disciplines. Do you know the Five Yamas Patanjali mentions in his Yoga Sutras?"

Oops. "Uh . . . nonviolence, truth-speaking, refraining from theft, sexual continence, or if you are married, monogamy, and, uh, . . ."

"And noncovetousness. After you establish these disciplines to prevent bad habits, then you must introduce good habits, which are collectively called niyama. Patanjali's Five Niyamas are purity of body, mind and spirit; contentment with whatever one possesses; penance; study and recitation of sacred scriptures; and devotion to God.

"Niyama is a very meaningful word. 'Ni' represents constraint or control. Take the 'ni' away from niyama and what do you have left? Yama, life's essential restraints. *Yama* is also one of the names of Death, which means that if you take the control away from your sadhana you're heading for failure. No matter how hungry a lion may be he will never stoop to eating grass. He is a meat-eater, and he will eat meat and nothing else or he will die. It should be the same with you; when you follow your niyama you should follow it strictly. If one day you cannot get the food you are permitted to eat it is better to starve that day than break the rules. Ultimately you will find that it was all worth it."

I nodded thoughtfully; it made visceral sense to me.

"Do you know the story of Nachiketas?"

"Yes. His father performed a sacrifice in which he gave away as alms old, lean, hungry cows. Nachiketas was grieved by his father's miserliness, and asked him sadly, 'Father, to whom are you going to give me?' His father flew into a rage at his son's seeming impertinence and replied, 'I give you to Yama'!" I paused to let him pick up the thread and tell the rest of it; I loved to hear him talk.

"Yes. When he heard this, Nachiketas did not wait to be collected; he walked all the way to Yama's abode. Yama, who drags souls off to the afterworld, was out doing his work, and Nachiketas had to sit alone on the doorstep of Yama's home for three days and three nights without any food or water.

"When Yama finally did return home he was amazed that a human could have located his house. Then he became concerned about the bad karma involved in forcing a small Brahmana boy to suffer from hunger and thirst for three days. A guest is equal to God, after all. In recompense Yama offered to grant three boons, one for each day that Nachiketas had had to wait.

"For his first boon Nachiketas requested that his father should be pleased with him. His second boon was for the secrets of the fire which leads to heaven. Yama granted both these boons readily. The third boon was, 'Tell me the truth of the identity of the Self.' By asking for this Nachiketas was really asking the god of death, 'Who are you? Tell me your nature.' Yama knew that to answer such a question would be equivalent to giving Nachiketas full knowledge of birth and death, so he offered the boy all sorts of material benefits if he would withdraw it. But Nachiketas stood firm, however, saying, 'All that you have promised me is useless, because my sense organs are feeble, and my life is limited and will someday end. I have requested my boon.' Finally Yama had to answer the question, realizing that Nachiketas was a fit pupil. As a result of what he learned Nachiketas became immortal.

"Many people know this story, but few ever ask the obvious question: When Yama is able to take thousands of people and millions of animals every day all over the world, how was it that he could not even locate one little boy for three whole days? The answer is very simple: Nachiketas was following niyama. Anyone whose niyama is strong is always protected; Yama can never come to such a person. Nachiketas was practicing a particular type of sadhana to the exclusion of all others; that was his niyama, and he stuck to it. When you break your niyama it loses its first syllable, and then you once again become prey to Yama."

"That's not all there is to this story, is there? There must be some deep esoteric meaning to it."

"Of course there is." But he had no intention of talking about it at that moment.

"The hardest sadhanas and niyamas are often the simplest. The *Ajagara Sadhana*, for example, is easy to describe but very, very difficult to practice. 'Ajagara' means python. You know about pythons; they don't eat very often. If a python eats a big meal today it may not eat again for days, or even weeks. Whenever it is not eating it lies around peacefully, totally inert.

"In the Ajagara Sadhana you become just like a python. You are not allowed to move from where you lie. All your appetites—for food, sleep, sex, whatever—have to go; you must lose all desire to 'eat.' You are only allowed to eat when someone comes to you and takes pity on you and puts food into your mouth, and even then you can accept only what is offered without asking for anything more. Does this sound simple and easy to you? Oh, no! But Aghoris go even further. They learn not only not to move, like pythons, they learn how to melt their bones, so that they cannot move even if they want to. Of course such drastic niyamas are far away for most of us, because we have to allot a good portion of our attention just to remain in one piece."

"I can just imagine what would happen to me if I was to practice the Aja-gara Sadhana downstairs on the street in Bombay today."

We snickered at the thought of what would follow. "But there are many other niyamas that you can follow. For example, since today we are living in an age in which everyone you meet is ready to cheat you in some way or another, learning not to cheat in return is a fine niyama. What about our dhabawalas? They practice a true niyama, a niyama that is practical for today. They are an amazing illustration of the power of niyama."

"What about them?" The *dhabawalas* are men who bring hot home-cooked lunches to hundreds of thousands of workers in Bombay every day. Each morning they carry long racks of neatly stacked metal lunch pails by train from the suburbs to downtown Bombay, and then tote them on their heads from office to office, distributing them to their owners. Because most dhabawalas are illiterate the pails are identified with a complex series of symbols, but so well does the system work that almost never do mixups occur.

"What *about* them?" he retorted indignantly. "They live in Bombay, and yet they have not been affected by the curse which ruins everyone else's mind. They have never gone on strike; if they ever did Bombay would grind to a halt, because there would be no way for everyone to eat." That I knew for a fact.

"They have never been known to molest any lady, though they have plenty of chances to do so since they collect and return the lunchbox from the worker's home every day when only his wife and other female relatives are there. Dhabawalas don't even look lustfully at women. Compare this to America, where milkmen are well known for entering the house to enjoy the wife once the husband has gone to work. This never happens among our dhabawalas." OK; I nodded sagely to agree.

"Why is this?" he went on. "It is because they are all followers of our Jnan-eshwar Maharaj. They all worship Vishnu in the form of Vitthala, and to a worshipper of Vishnu everyone is a family member, a member of 'vasudeva kutumbam' ('Vishnu's family'). Who will such a person cheat, or have an affair with? The dhabawalas go on regular pilgrimages, and spend their time reading the Jnaneshwari and singing God's sweet name. I think these are the people to be respected, not all the priests and all the so-called saints and swamis who have sprung up everywhere. These dhabawalas have really put Krishna's teachings into practice: 'Do your work, and offer all the fruits of your work to Me.'"

As he fell silent we both traveled mentally to Jnaneshwar's shrine in Alandi and bowed to the saint who had such compassion that even after seven hundred years he was still guiding and inspiring whoever came to him.

"Eknath Maharaj, thanks to whom we have the Jnaneshwari, is another example. His fellow Brahmanas hated him because of his love for the common people. One day as Eknath was returning to his home after bathing in the sacred Godavari River one of these vicious Brahmanas spat on him. Eknath, saying nothing, turned around, walked back to the river, and bathed again. Again when he emerged the Brahmana spat on him; again he turned back to bathe. This happened many, many times; some versions of this story say that it happened as many as one hundred times. It went on until finally the spitter realized Eknath's greatness and fell at his feet begging for forgiveness. But Eknath said, 'My friend, I think that I should thank you, because it is thanks to you that I have had the blessing of bathing so many times in the sacred Godavari.'

"Eknath's control over his temper was something superb, the product of a powerful niyama. To dedicate yourself never to become angry no matter what the provocation is a terrific niyama, one which is not easy to keep. Although such control is essential nowadays in Kali Yuga it is very hard to achieve, unless you have help, like I do. I used to be a real firebrand; now, thanks to my mentors, I have cooled down considerably. Around here I think I need it."

I knew exactly what he meant.

"Although I have lived with Roshni's family for many years, Roshni's mother has never changed. She will not change, no matter what you tell her. If her mind was directed to God she would have been able to do unique sadhanas, but it is impossible. I have tried for decades, but I have had to give up; I am tired.

"The Ramayana says that you should always live near someone you can't get along with because they will help you remember God, and this lady certainly does help me remember God. You know very well that often I will expect that the preparations for lunch will be ready for me by a certain time, but when I ask I find that she has forgotten something. It happens time and again, and when I ask her about it all she will say is, 'I forgot.' Then what can I say? I have to keep quiet, and remember niyama.

"But I am fortunate, because whenever this happens, call it coincidence or whatever you like, I find that within fifteen minutes or so a knock will come on the door and there will stand someone who has brought some food to me, for no apparent reason. My Tara will not let me go hungry. You know this, Robby; you've seen it so many times."

Yes, I had, and I continued to see it. Once he and I were on a train going from Copenhagen to Paris, and I had forgotten to purchase any French money while in Denmark. It was Sunday; no banks were open; the vendors on the train refused to take any other currency. We were hungry. But then a lady got on the train in Namur, Belgium, and after a few miles opened her sack and offered each of us a Christmas cake. How good they were! In Tokyo, when everything was closed, the cook himself shouted to us from a restaurant and made us come in, and then all Vimalananda had to do was to look at the proprietress with a certain 'sweet gaze' in order to get vegetarian food even though it was not on the menu. Ma never let him down.

"This is all because of niyama. In Patanjali's system asanas were to be practiced only after yama and niyama were perfected. Here is another thing I get angry about: the people who have so debased Yoga that it is now simply a system of physical jerks. I agree that a flexible body is useful in sadhana; but you cannot become enlightened just by standing on your head. Asanas are for other purposes too.

"The word asana comes from the Sanskrit root meaning 'to sit.' To 'make your asana perfect' means to learn to be able to sit comfortably without squirming or fidgeting for at least three hours at a time. In the past, the real yoga gurus would tell their students, 'Go into that room and sit there for six months.' After sitting for that long the student's mind and nervous system would automatically become calmer, which would make the next step— pranayama—safer and easier."

Some years later I heard Baba Hari Dass tell of an old guru who used to test his disciples by making them sit in a cross-legged position and then fill their laps with dirt and plant grass seeds. When he returned a few days later to inspect the crops, only those students whose sprouts were rising straight and true passed the test; only they had obviously not moved. Those disciples whose sprouts sprawled every which way failed.

"I believe you have been taught *Shavasana*, the corpse posture, in your yoga classes?"

"I have."

"And I'm sure your teacher has taught you to do it at the end of an asana session in order to relax."

"He has."

"But was the corpse pose created just to help you relax? Of course not! It's another example of how superficial today's spiritual teaching has become. The purpose of Shavasana is to make you into a *shava*, a corpse, to make it easier for you to control your prana and disengage your mind from the outside world. When you do Shavasana you should become just like a corpse, not just with your muscles but also with your mind. In Aghora we believe in sitting on corpses, it is true; we believe in sitting on our *own* corpses. We say, 'Make your own body into a living corpse'; let the body live and perform its actions and you be away from it."

It made immense sense.

"Now think about pranayama, which means 'control of prana.' It is not necessary to hold your breath in order to control prana; if your mind is controlled your breath will slow and eventually stop automatically. Any method which slows the breathing is a form of pranayama. The purpose of pranayama is to slow the breathing as much as possible. Whenever your breathing is deep, slow and calm your mind is slow and calm; whenever your breathing is fast, shallow and agitated so is your mind.

"After pranayama comes pratyahara, which is detachment, withdrawal of the senses from their objects. The senses like to 'eat' things, to take in impressions from the outside world. Pratyahara (which can also be interpreted to mean 'against eating') occurs when the calmed mind stops craving sensory pleasures. Once your mind is disengaged from its cravings it is ready for dharana, dhyana, and samadhi: concentration, meditation, and that perfect equilibrium of consciousness which is the goal of ordinary sadhana.

"But perfect equilibrium of the consciousness is a difficult thing to achieve during Kali Yuga. There are so many distractions! Having sufficient time is not the problem; on the contrary, you can make very fast progress in Kali Yuga. In Satya Yuga it takes ten thousand years of penance to catch even a glimpse of God, because everyone in Satya Yuga is righteous and sincere in their worship, and God is in no hurry to appear before them; He tests them thoroughly. But in Kali Yuga the force of illusion is so powerful that only a few people want to worship God, and most of them don't know how to do it effectively. In Kali Yuga God feels so lonely that no one is remembering and loving Him that He will appear to you very easily. This is why Kali Yuga is the best Yuga of them all for sadhana. In Satya Yuga you have to sweep your guru's floor for years and years before he will deign to initiate you, much less teach you anything."

Another reference to my situation. I did appreciate his willingness to spend time to teach me, and I could not claim to be a worthy student.

"In fact, Kali Yuga is the time when all the experts in all fields are writing books and selling their knowledge, begging people to take it away from them. For just a pittance you can obtain knowledge that they have worked a lifetime for, and you don't even have to steal it from them. Read, Robby, read, keep on reading; you can never learn enough, because there are always new things to learn. Just remember that learning is also a form of Maya. It is very valuable, no doubt, but you can still become attached to it, just as you can to any form of Maya.

"The force of Maya is so strong during Kali Yuga that it is easy to get caught up in learning and forget to do anything with what you learn. This is where niyama comes in. As long as you make everything you do a sadhana, as long as you direct all your energy to achieving your goal, you will only want to learn those things which will help you progress, and you will use them to help improve your sadhana. If you want to practice Tantra sadhanas, you have to start with an unshakable niyama."

SADHANA

Khanda Manda Yoga

Natural potential for spiritual development becomes valuable only by careful cultivation. All spiritual practices are sadhanas, but all sadhanas are not created equal. Vimalananda explains:

"The Rishis, India's Seers, have understood our plight, and in their great magnanimity have created sadhanas by which we can extricate ourselves from our limitations and make progress. The Rishis have created many different sadhanas because there are so many different types of people, each of whom have special requirements. We Aghoris believe in using fast, terrifying methods of sadhana because we ache to return to God immediately; we cannot bear being separated from Him."

An Aghori meditates on burning corpses to force the consciousness beyond all limitations of the personality. The hardest concretions of identity are the most resistant, and steel-wool penances are needed to scour them away. Aghoris take no chances with potential ego-inflations; Aghora sadhanas destroy everything down to the ground of consciousness and rebuild from the bottom up. Then there is nothing to fear, because the new personality is engineered to be totally surrendered to the Will of God. Khanda Manda Yoga is a good illustration of Aghora's approach to personality development. Vimalananda described it thus:

"One of the most terrifying and difficult of all Aghora sadhanas is *Khanda Manda Yoga*. The practitioner of Khanda Manda Yoga cuts off his own arms and legs with a sharp cleaver, and throws them into a roaring fire. After twelve hours these limbs reemerge from the fire and rejoin his body. Some sadhus can do Eka Khanda Yoga, the cutting of one part of a single limb, like a foot; a few like Tailang Swami could do Tri Khanda Yoga, involving three parts, like the foot, the lower leg, and the thigh. But very, very few—perhaps only one or two up to now—can do Nava Khanda Yoga, using nine body parts, including the head.

"And beyond even Nava Khanda Yoga is Agni Khanda Yoga, in which a guru heats his firetongs white-hot, and then inserts them under his disciple's skin at the nape of the neck, running them down parallel to the spinal cord. A yogi who is really solid in his being will not even flinch when this happens.

"This is the physical Khanda Manda Yoga, and its benefits are many, including imperviousness to any weapon, and even physical immortality. It is really a wonderful sadhana, though I suspect you might faint at the sight of all the blood if you ever saw anyone perform it. Most people are very attached to their bodies, and don't like even the hint that some part of that body might be chopped off. Obviously you can only perform Khanda Manda Yoga once you have developed a certain objectivity about your body. But this is not so easy, you know; it is only possible once you have complete control over your Kundalini Shakti.

"The mental Khanda Manda Yoga is somewhat different; it has to do with thought. Did you know that *mandana* (creation) and *khandana* (destruction) of thoughts are going on continuously within you? For instance, if your lady love is not with you, you will emit from your heart incessant wishes to see her, be with her, embrace her, and so on. You continue to project these desires until you see the girl and fulfill your desires, at which point the projected forms are destroyed. This is a form of khandana, but it is imperfect. You will be rid of the desire only for a short time before it begins again because you are only projecting an image of how you want her to be, for your gratification. This image will always change because your desires are always changing, and because she is always changing.

"Most people never realize that these thoughts are simply temporary manifestations. They try to cling to them or avoid them, depending on whether they give pleasure or pain to the mind. True khandana would destroy that desire utterly. The true khandana is absolute and permanent destruction of your false personality, which is composed of all the desires, tastes, aversions, and what-not which have accumulated over millions of births. Only when all the imperfect projections are eliminated will you be able to see what is real. The other side of khandana is mandana, and the true mandana is projection of a permanent form, construction of a true personality. Mental khandana and mandana make up the real Khanda Manda Yoga.

"There are only two ways to perform khandana and mandana, just as there are only two types of medicine: external and internal. Either you get a doctor to treat you, or you cure yourself with your own force of will; there is no third way. Likewise, khandana can be external, by complete satiation of desire, or it can be internal, by complete control of desire. Suppression of desire will not work. Like a coiled spring a suppressed desire remains immobile only so long as it is pressed down. When the pressure eases up it will bounce with extra strength. The true mandana can only occur after your desire for limited, impermanent forms has dropped away, either through gratification or control."

After drilling the idea of niyama into my head, Vimalananda began his long-term lesson on sadhana, which was a sort of mental Khanda Manda for me, on a juvenile scale. After demolishing one of my preformed concepts about spiritual practices he would offer me little pieces of information, here and there, from which I was expected to synthesize a new concept. He would then test me periodically, without warning, to ensure that I had understood, for he believed that "the key to testing someone is to test them when they least expect it and are least prepared for it. Then you have an accurate idea of how much they really know." Only after he was convinced that I had learned something would he proceed to the next step.

Name and Form

Every month or two, when the mood possessed him, Vimalananda would take me and Roshni with him to the Lakshmi-Narayana temple in Central Bombay, to look upon the face of God. The images in this temple are carved from pure white marble, and their sweetness and sublimity effortlessly pierce the hearts of those who gaze at them in faith. All the humans there—the temple trustees, the priests, the watchmen—knew Vimalananda, and all were happy to see him arrive, all except the musicians, who were envious of his superior musical abilities. After making our offerings Vimalananda would sit down at the harmonium to play and sing for Narayana and Lakshmi. The sound of his voice, the incense's soft burning, and the transcendent equanimity permanently etched on the faces of the Lord and His Lady filled the hall with the palpable sweet ache of a devotee for his Beloved.

After one of these musicales, when we had returned home and I had poured a glass of Scotch for Vimalananda, he began to talk, tears glistening now and again in his eyes as emotion welled up and spilled over the banks of his everyday personality:

"Did you see how Narayana was dressed tonight? So *beau-tiful!* You know, you have the choice of worshipping God as a Formless Absolute or of worshipping God with form, and I have always recommended to everyone that they worship God with form. We are all human beings; God is supposed to have made us in His image; why not then make God in our image? It is so much easier to worship a God with a human form. Can you comprehend the immensity of the totality of the billions of universes? *No*, n-o. But you may be able to comprehend the compassionate eyes of Jesus, or the bewitching eyes of Krishna.

"There are so many different types of eyes in the world. Some are entrancing, some cruel and calculating, some innocent, some lifeless. But there have never been any eyes like the eyes of Krishna and Jesus. Their eyes make you go mad when you see them, mad with love. Krishna's eyes are bewitching; they are so full of sweetness that they turn you into a lunatic. And Jesus' eyes? His eyes are brimming over with divine compassion. Oh, my *God!* When I think of the eyes of Jesus I think of His chest. So broad it must have been, to gather everyone in to it and take over all their karmas—to be able to say, 'Come unto me.'"

"Something that I have been thinking about lately," I began hesitantly, averse to disturbing his mood, "is the fact that I was born and brought up a Christian, and now here I am involved in Aghora. I know that you are a great devotee of Jesus, but isn't there some contradiction in there somewhere?"

"Well, have you forgotten Jesus? Do you still love Him?" Vimalananda inquired gently.

"Yes, I do," I replied.

"Good. Because if you had told me otherwise, I would have told you to get out!" He smiled. "What is a deity after all? A deity is the One Consciousness expressed in a particular way, a certain aspect of reality which has a specific form. All deities are therefore limited to some degree. Jesus was a great being, but even He had some limitations. So did Rama and Krishna, so does

Shiva; any being that has a name and a form is limited, if only by that name and form."

"Doesn't Advaita Vedanta teach," I had to ask, "that while the Absolute is true, the Relative, which is the Manifested Universe of name and form, is inherently false, and so one should only worship the Highest?"

"Who says so?" he thundered. "Only one version of Advaita Vedanta teaches that, the version that Shankaracharya propagated. Other versions of Advaita Vedanta are not so limited. But it is true that the Highest is beyond all name and form, which is why I believe it is better not to worship the deities at all."

I tossed a confused look at him. He enjoyed catching me off guard; once a wrestler, always a wrestler.

"I believe that it is better to worship the One behind the deities, and to respect and appreciate the deities for how well they play the roles assigned to them. Do you see what I mean? There is a subtle difference. You love the deities, but you worship the Absolute that created Them and dwells within Them. Worship of a deity is a good way to get started on the spiritual path for so many reasons, but mainly because it is easier to love a form than it is to love the Formless. You may not choose to visualize the Universal Reality as Shiva; maybe you prefer Krishna, or Jesus. It doesn't matter; you will achieve God in whatever form you imagine Him or Her to be, so long as you worship with sincerity and love."

"So it is only when you distinguish one deity from another as if they were really different that there is a contradiction?"

"Exactly. You have worshipped Jesus since you were born. Can you forget Jesus now, even if you wanted to? Never! Jesus will never let go of your hand, even if you try to flee from Him; that is the depth of His compassion for you. But neither will He interfere, nor will He be upset, if you also want to worship God in another form. Jesus cares nothing for form; He cares only for pure love.

"You began by worshipping Jesus, and you must continue to worship Jesus. However, you personally can make faster progress if you perform certain Aghora sadhanas, because you have negative traits in your personality which need to be removed."

"This is like fighting fire with fire, I suppose? Using harsh measures to eliminate my own harshness?"

He nodded agreement as he sipped his drink. "You know, today's false swamis and other so-called experts go on and on about Satya Yuga, 'the Golden Age,' and Kali Yuga, 'the Iron Age.' Why can't they explain it directly without beating around the bush so much?" He was rapidly warming to his subject.

"It is just the difference between a gold sword and an iron sword. Both are used to cut through the *Ashta Pasha*, the Eight Snares which bind us to the world: lust, anger, greed, delusion, envy, shame, fear and disgust. A gold sword does not cut very well. Get into a swordfight with a gold sword and you'll soon see what I mean." We chuckled together over that image. "People in the Golden Age couldn't be good killers; they believed in mandana, not khandana. They believed that you should remove the Ashta Pasha by creating beneficial new *samskaras* (personality characteristics), which after taking root in the individual would eventually crowd out all his or her limitations.

"In Kali Yuga people believe in khandana. An iron sword will cut you very well, and aren't most people today killers? Either you become a killer or you get killed in today's world. The word *pashu* means 'he who is snared by a pasha.' Pashu also means an animal. As long as you are in the grips of one of the Eight Snares you are no better, and are probably worse, than an animal.

"All of us today are pashus, animals meant for sacrifice, trapped by the Eight Snares. The best way to get rid of the Ashta Pasha in Kali Yuga is to cut through them with Tantra and Aghora. If you can withstand the pain of having your personality ripped from you, then you can sacrifice yourself, and then when you are dead to the world new samskaras can be created. This is what Aghora is all about."

For a fleeting moment I felt sorry for myself, for being so profoundly snared that I could be redeemed only through butchery.

As usual, he caught my thought. "Do you think that only lechers, meat eaters and drug fiends are animals? Oh, no. The Tantras talk about spiritual pashus, who are just as animalistic as any other pashus but in a different way. Spiritual pashus are sectarian; they slander anyone who doesn't share their beliefs, or who worships a different deity. They are much more concerned with outer than with inner purity; they like to make a show of their worship. So many of the Brahmanas, the so-called spiritual caste, are the worst sort of pashu.

"Only a pashu, an animalistic human, will think of the deities as being fundamentally different from one another, and will be willing to kill for one god or another. Muslims have been notorious since the beginning for slaughtering as infidels anyone who did not believe as they do, but what did the Christians do for so many centuries? They fought and killed the Muslims as infidels, all right, but worse than that, the Protestants and Catholics slaughtered each other mercilessly. And for what? So that each could claim that they had a monopoly over the love of Jesus? Can anything be more ridiculous?"

"It is still happening even today, in Northern Ireland."

"Yes, it is still happening today, and not only among the Christians. Within Islam the Shias and the Sunnis still kill one another. Here in India it is not so bad—people kill each other for other reasons—but Hindus and Muslims still kill one another occasionally. And even among the Hindus some Krishna worshippers will abuse worshippers of Rama, and vice versa, and many worshippers of Vishnu think that worship of Shiva or the Goddess is nothing but piffle.

"All around the world the people who are really spiritual never look at the outer clothing of a person—what language they speak, what god they worship. They look only at the inner being. So I say, forget all this foolishness; leave the arguments to the pashus, and you worship God in whatever form you please."

"Provided that I know how to do so," I added, fishing for more guidance.

"Of course. You need to have at least a basic understanding of the process in order for it to proceed properly. If the blueprint is correct the structure is bound to be correct; that is my principle. I believe that the very first step in spirituality is to forget to merge your consciousness with external things. To keep aloof from the world, and especially from this sort of sectarianism, is to get closer to your deity. So long as you are attached to the world you are detached from God. Once you become attached to God it is inevitable that you will become detached from the world.

"Someone once told me that Rodin's famous sculpture *The Thinker* was a good example of detachment. I told him, '*The Thinker* is simply thinking. He has not gone so far into himself that he has become absolutely lost. If he had, there would be no need for him to be making such an effort to think. It is obvious that he is still stuck in his senses. In fact, I think he looks very much like a gorilla.'"

We chuckled again, and Vimalananda's tone intensified.

"Thinking about your limitations is no way to change them; in fact, if you think about them very much you will most likely reinforce them. This is why I have little use for most psychologists. They spend all their time making their patients remember all the bad things that happened to them, and never try to erase those bad memories and replace them with good samskaras, which is what you do when you visualize a deity."

"Freud once said, 'Neurosis is reminiscence.'"

"Unfortunately Freud himself was a neurotic; otherwise he would never have come up with some of the bull that he tried to pass off as knowledge. He thought he understood sex, but all he understood was sexual abnormality, and that not too thoroughly. But that particular saying of his is true: neurosis happens when you are trapped by your memories into perpetuating your limitations. This is why sadhana is so necessary, especially in Kali Yuga, when everyone has limitations to spare.

"I believe in the old Indian Law of Caterpillar and Butterfly, the Kita Bhramari Nyaya. Within the misshapen caterpillar is an image. Perhaps it is not a truly mental image, but is only present in the genes and chromosomes; but isn't that also an image? You are splitting hairs if you say it is not, because that image must exist somewhere in the caterpillar's consciousness for it to become a butterfly. It is there, at that rudimentary level, because of the ego. The caterpillar's ego continuously concentrates on its body, just as your ego is continuously self-identifying with your own body and your own personality. Otherwise you couldn't exist.

"But at some point the caterpillar's ego stops self-identifying exclusively with its caterpillar form and begins to self-identify with its butterfly form. It imagines itself to be a butterfly for so long that in the end it becomes a butterfly. Actually it always was a butterfly, and only time and concentration were necessary for cause to reveal itself in effect. Cause is effect concealed; effect is cause revealed. It's the same way with sadhana: Whatever you imagine you will most surely become. You might not achieve as fast as some do, unless you have already done a lot of sadhana in previous births and you have a powerful guru to initiate you into your mantra in this birth. But eventually you are bound to achieve, if you are patient and persistent. There is no instant payoff in worshipping God."

"So sadhana is basically just a matter of preventing Kundalini from identifying with a limited human personality so that She can identify with a cosmic personality?" I was becoming comfortable with the concept.

"Yes; in fact, if you identify with the new image strongly enough you will even start to look like the deity you worship. I knew a sadhu in Girnar who was a great devotee of Anjaneya—I like to call Hanuman 'Anjaneya' because it reminds me of His mother, Anjani. This sadhu concentrated on Anjaneya with such fervor that he actually grew a little tail! There was another who started to drink poison like Shiva does; he eventually became poison-proof! If you repeat "Coca-Cola, Coca-Cola" all the time you may not start to taste Coke, but eventually you will *become* Coke."

Hmm—another unusual image that interrupted the usual flow of my mind, as it made me suddenly realize that we have almost as many deities in the West are there are gods and goddesses in India. We have rock and roll stars, sports heroes, movie stars, cartoon characters—all sorts of images to imitate with appropriate mantras and hymns so that we can recreate ourselves in their image. Somehow I preferred the images Vimalananda was providing me.

"Visualization and repetition of mantras reinforce the new image being created within, then," I said.

"That's right. All the sacred books tell us that in Kali Yuga the greatest sadhana is to repeat God's name, but why? Always ask why! The reason is because name and form are identical; when you call the name you create the form. Each deity has a name because each name is a mantra, a way of creating the form of that deity.

"Mantra means 'man ki tarana': that which saves the mind from the perils of samsara. In Tantra and Aghora we believe in making use of the power of the mind to achieve the goal. Some Yogis say, 'Destroy the mind,' but I say, 'Why destroy something which can be of great use? Control the mind.' You should only destroy something that is dangerous and that you are afraid of, and the only people who are afraid of the mind are those who are not in control of it. So many of these 'yogis' are real hypocrites.

"Remember the words of John in his gospel: 'In the beginning was the Word, and the Word was with God, and the Word was God.' When you repeat God's name you actually create God's form within your consciousness, which gives your Kundalini Shakti something good to self-identify with. Repetition of the deity's name while visualizing His or Her form is the best sort of worship we have available to us.

The Soma Yaga

"If you are working to awaken your Kundalini and you try to do everything on your own, you only need to make one slip and you are gone; but if you worship and self-identify with a deity He or She will protect you when the energy becomes too strong for you to control. This is especially true if, like an Aghori, you are in a hurry to succeed, and you decide to practice dangerous sadhanas like Panchamakara. Meat, fish, wine, parched grain and sex are all intoxicants, and the purpose of intoxicants is to stimulate your nerves to be able to withstand the force of the Kundalini Shakti. You can use alcohol, sex and the rest to make fast spiritual progress only if you know how to use them properly; otherwise you just bind yourself down more tightly to the wheel of existence.

"If you do choose to use them, you must never lose your presence of mind. This is why I only permit one line of talk, one topic, during a session at which intoxicants are consumed."

"Like tonight," I said pleasantly.

"Like tonight. If you take intoxicants and then you switch from topic to topic your mind may wander; staying on one topic encourages control. Control is absolutely essential when you take intoxicants, no matter what anyone may tell you. If you hallucinate when you are intoxicated, it indicates that your system is not yet ready for that quantity of Shakti.

"I have used intoxicants for many years, and only once did I fail to finish a ritual because of them. That happened when someone fed me a tremendous quantity of marijuana without my knowing it. By the time I realized what was going on and took steps to counteract the effect I had missed my time for worship. I had to start the whole ritual over again, and this time I refused to accept any food from anyone's hand. I completed it successfully.

"Some years ago some people tried to poison the ears of my mother and father, telling them I was an alcoholic and spent all my nights drinking. I am a drunkard, as anyone can see," he said without pride or guilt, proffering his glass to me to be refilled, "but I am not an alcoholic; I am in perfect control of myself. So one evening I decided to demonstrate to my parents what I was doing with alcohol.

"After dinner I produced a bottle of Scotch and a glass, and started to drink the Scotch, neat. My father was annoyed, but he didn't say anything; he just glowered. My mother wanted to tell me that it was wrong to drink, and whatnot, but then I announced, 'Now let us discuss the Upanishads.'

"Now, the Vedas and the Upanishads were my father's pet subjects, and he used to take pride in his knowledge of them. But after I completed my discourse there were tears in his eyes, and he said, 'I never realized that you knew.' My mother said nothing at all, but the next time I visited them and we were sitting together after dinner she produced a bottle of Scotch and said, 'Here, son, take this and talk.' I'm proud that my parents appreciated my talks, and understood that I was not ruining myself with my drinking.

"The reason I am not ruining myself with my drinking," he continued, punctuating his words with a sip from his glass, "is that I perform a Soma Yaga, or Soma Sacrifice, when I drink."

People have been arguing over the meaning of the Vedic Soma Sacrifice for

SADHANA

many years, and many authorities have claimed to have discovered *the* plant from which the divinely intoxicating drink *Soma* was made. Vimalananda had no patience for such scholarly presumption, maintaining that the divine intoxication of Soma can be produced by a variety of substances, each of which can be made into Soma only in the context of a specific place, time and method of preparation and a particular consumer.

"The Soma Yaga has nothing to do with drinking the juice of some plant, although that external ritual still does exist in some places. I perform the Soma Yaga in quite a different way. When I drink alcohol I convert it into Soma with the help of a mantra. The mantra is necessary because Soma is full of Sattva and alcohol is full of Tamas. In addition to the karma of having crushed the life out of the yeast cells during the brewing process there are also powerful curses which must first be removed from the alcohol before you drink it. Alcohol has been thrice cursed: by Brahma the Creator; by Shukracharya (the planet Venus), the guru of the asuras; and by Lord Krishna Himself. If you drink without the proper mantra you will suffer from the effects of all three curses, and then you are sunk.

"Alcohol develops Sattva when all the miserable little yeast cells who gave up their lives in the brewing process are given jnana. When this is done they enter my body and instead of perverting my consciousness they begin to dance for joy. Then both they and I get some benefit out of drinking. This is only possible if I offer the drink into the fire of the Bhuta Agni, so that it can reach Smashan Tara. This is the sacrifice part; the alcohol is sacrificed to Her, and She takes the prana that all the wretched little yeast cells contributed to the alcohol and then saves those cells. What do I mean by 'save'? I mean that She fills them with jnana, and makes them be born again in higher wombs. This process is entirely internal, which is the best way to perform a yajna."

I had started to read Arthur Avalon, so I interpolated: "And this is why the Tantras call wine 'Tara Dravamayi,' the 'Savioress Herself in Liquid Form.'"

"Yes, and how wonderful it is, to feel Her dancing within you; I just can't describe it! Intoxicants are wonderful—but you can't just start with these things directly; you must do plenty of sadhana first, to make sure that your control is strong. I will repeat this again and again: unless you know this process you should not drink, because sooner or later the curses will come upon you, the alcohol will start to drink you, and you will be finished."

"Make Everything into a Sadhana"

"But I know you have said before that you don't have to renounce everything in order to achieve."

"No, you don't; but you do have to make everything into a sadhana. Offer every morsel of food to your deity; go to sleep at night remembering your deity. And as for sex, you don't need to know any complicated sexual rituals in order to offer a mantra with each stroke of the penis into the fire of the vagina. Always offer whatever you do to your deity, and He or She will always take care of you. However, how easy is it to remember to offer a mantra with each stroke of your penis once your sexual embrace becomes really intense? This is why I say that the more potential addictions you remove the faster will be your progress."

"From what I have learned, food at least has the potential to produce Sattva, sleep definitely creates Tamas, and sex generates tremendous Rajas," I added.

"And what I have learned is that any substance or activity can produce any of the Three Gunas, depending on how well you digest it. In the beginning you have to accumulate Sattva; this much is clear. When your consciousness is full of Sattva your power of discrimination becomes predominant, so you can judge easily what is good or bad for you. If you allow excess Rajas or Tamas to collect in your consciousness either your ego will run amok, or you will become a slave to your senses, or both.

"In the Sattvic Tantras you are given a mantra along with a description of its visual form for meditation. With that mental image you construct the deity in your astral body, and eventually that deity projects and shows Himself or Herself to you. Visualization is essential because of the primacy of the eyes. Not everyone is fit to visualize, but if you are you will eventually perceive the deity right before your eyes. What you will see is not the real deity; it is your own creation, from your own astral body. Do you know the Bimba-Pratibimba Nyaya?"

Let's see. . . "the Law of Image and Reflection?"

"Yes. When the moon rises over a still pond you see a perfect reflection of it on the water. It looks like the moon but is not. What you create within you by Tantric sadhana is only a reflection of the image you have of your deity. But since you have given that image all the powers of the deity that reflection can do your work for you, and eventually it will lead you to the real deity. This is the sure way; it takes a little time."

"In Aghora, which is purely Tamasic, you do not bother with sweetly inviting the deity to come to you. You demand that God come, and you catch God by the hair and drag Him or Her if necessary. Aghoris use intoxicants and other sorts of aids because they want a quick blitzkrieg process. But this results in excessive Rajas and Tamas, and if you make even the slightest miscue down you go, dive bombing. And do you think that God likes to be dragged by the hair? God will say, 'OK, if this guy thinks he is so great, let us see what happens when I give him a taste of his own medicine.' And then you had better be ready to endure God's Tamasic play, which is no joke. Aghora and Tantra are dangerous things to fool about with."

"So I should be patient," I said with a twinge of bitterness.

"You *have* to be patient. My case was different, I admit; quite different from most. I never intended anything to occur; from the beginning of my spiritual career until now I have never requested any specific sadhana from anyone. Jina Chandra Suri tricked me into sitting on that corpse (see *Aghora*), but had he not done so I would never have realized Ma so quickly. I have always had faith that Ma will teach me what I need to know, and so She has. Faith is the key, and the best way to gain faith is to repeat the sweet name of God, and turn your entire existence over to God. This is the essence of sadhana.

"One reason you will have to be patient is that deities don't like to come to you if They can avoid it. They are more like animals in that way. In the forest, will a deer come to you immediately, even if you call it with love? No, because deep down is the fear that one day you will come and catch its throat. Similarly, the deity is afraid that if He comes near you you will catch Him and give Him work to do. To overcome this fear you must know the likes and dislikes of your particular deity. You must offer Him that which He craves; then how will He be able to hold out? Deities love to play about, and may try some stunts on you in return. If you don't allow anything to affect you, you'll be OK. If you waver or fumble then you've had it.

"Deities are very simple, really; They're a lot like children. When They love you They love you without any restraint; but if you cheat or harass Them They'll never forget it. If you really want to become close to your deity, you have to become just like a little child. Remember the words of Jesus: 'Unless you become like a little child you will not be able to enter the Kingdom of Heaven.'

"You have to be able to say to your deity, in all sincerity, 'I'm so lonely; I don't have any other playmates. Please come and play with me.' But let me tell you, it is extremely difficult to forget your position and ego and what-have-you and become a child again. It takes years and years of hard work to reach this stage, the stage when you can say to your Beloved without an iota of cunning or craftiness, 'Look, I have this chocolate; if You will come to me I'll give it to You.' A child doesn't know how to bribe, so it's permissible. But you know, and you have to forget."

"And so one of the names for Shiva is *Smarahara*, 'the Killer of Memory.'"

"Yes. Only He can erase all your memories of who you are, which is how He kills you; He makes your Kundalini love Him so much that She forgets in that instant to self-identify with you."

"And if you do this willfully in sadhana—if you 'die while still alive'— then She can be made to identify with a new personality."

"Yes. One of the reasons saints love to remain in solitude is that they need time away from other humans to enable them to forget themselves. You know that to achieve success at Tantra you need strong virility; you must be powerful to perform sadhana. The more sadhana you do the more *ojas* you will create. Do I need to tell you what ojas is?"

"No." Ojas is an Ayurvedic concept; it is that essence of physical energy which produces your aura and your immunity to invasion by diseases or other unwelcome visitors.

"When you have plenty of ojas your aura becomes tremendously enhanced, which will attract plenty of people to you who will come and bother you. This happened to Ramakrishna Paramahamsa at one point. He actually had to ask Bhavatarini Ma to make him outwardly normal again, and to make him 'inwardly attractive' instead. Because he preserved all his ojas inside he was able to perfectly self-identify with Her; he dissolved into Her.

"Once you reach a certain stage in your love for God all you will be able to do is love, and you won't be able to express your love in words even if you want to. This sometimes happens between humans, too, if they really love one another. It can also be true of animals, which is why I like dogs. Dogs have pure, unselfish love for their masters, which is why I would like to become God's dog, totally devoted to Him alone."

Vimalananda's dog, Lizoo, an astute canine, overheard us discussing dogs, and jumped into his lap, as if to say, "And I am *your* dog, totally devoted to you!"

He petted her tenderly. "People frequently come and tell me, 'I am getting less and less peace the more I repeat my mantra.' Whenever troubles increase like that during sadhana you can be sure that you are getting closer to your deity. You cannot realize your deity until your consciousness becomes clear and clean, for which you have to burn off all your bad karmas. As you become firmer in your sadhana, more and more of your bad karmas from this life and from thousands of previous lives are liberated from your causal body. You are bound to be affected by this—everyone likes to spend, and no one likes to pay the bills—but don't let that stop you. Continue on, continue until you achieve; then you will understand that it was 100% worth it.

"This is Kali Yuga, though, and as soon as most people start getting this negative effect from the removal of their bad karmas they think that it is somehow the fault of the mantra and they quit their practice altogether, just at the point they should be doing it more vigorously. Is it any surprise that they never get any result from their sadhana?"

"It is no surprise," I echoed sardonically.

"There was once a man who did penance of Lord Shiva for one hundred years without every having any personal experience of Him. As this fellow lay dying he thought to himself, 'What is this? Is all my penance for nothing?' He should have remembered that just as matter is indestructible all action must bear its fruit; it is only a question of time. Time exists only for us mortals, not for the immortals. Nature's wheels turn very slowly, like those of the steam roller, but like the steam roller Nature crushes everything in Her path.

"The man was reborn as a bee. He forgot the mantra he was repeating, he forgot his ritual, he forgot everything, but at the back of his mind was the lingering tendency to worship Shiva; at least that much carried over from his previous life.

"It was probably this lingering tendency which led the bee to fly one day to Benaras, Shiva's chief city. He reached the garden of a merchant, and seeing the beautiful lotuses there began to suck their nectar. He had forgotten all about Shiva and everything else; he was thinking only of nectar. He became so drunk on nectar that he didn't notice that night fell and the lotuses closed while he was inside one of them. He was trapped. What to do? He had to wait until morning to escape.

"Next morning before dawn the merchant went out into his garden, cut the lotus that held the bee, took it into his worship-room, said, 'Bhole!' and put the lotus atop his image of Shiva.

"When the sun rose its rays fell onto the lotus, which opened and allowed the bee to exit. Lord Shiva, who knows past, present and future, said to Himself, 'Wah, wah! Here is a man who worships me and does penance for a hundred years and then dies and comes back as a bee to sit on my head!

Varam bruhi! (Ask for a boon!)'

"The bee said, 'What "varam bruhi!" now? That would have been useful when I was a man. Now make me like you are.' And immediately he became just like Shiva. In fact, he became one of Shiva's close attendants, an immortal."

At this point Lizoo jumped up and began to lick Vimalananda's face insistently, demanding immediate attention and so ending the conversation. This struck me as a sort of omen, a confirmation of all that Vimalananda had been saying, a reinforcement of his lesson.

The Sun, the Moon, and Fire

During the afternoons Vimalananda's conversation usually revolved around the racecourse, since most of the people who dropped by to see him at that time were interested in the hot tips which are the sustenance of those who gamble on horses. Those who were more interested in hearing him discuss spirituality would come in the evenings, when he would relax and let his mind focus on Reality. One night, after overhearing a couple of his spiritual "children" speaking knowingly of "devotion" and "knowledge," he felt a need to put the record straight:

"In sadhana, either there can be 'my wish' or there can be 'Thy wish.' If 'my wish' exists I follow the path of jnana, trying to become a jnani; if only 'Thy wish' exists I follow the path of bhakti (devotion), aiming to become a bhakta, a devotee. These are the only two possibilities. 'Our' wish cannot exist, because then duality is present. Duality is something in between, neither here nor there, and 'in between' is of no use in spirituality. You should either be 'here' or 'there.' If you are 'here,' worshipping the divine in your own being, then you are a jnani, and your wish exists. If you are 'there,' you worship an external form of the divine, and you are a bhakta. There is no third way.

"On the path of jnana the guru helps the disciple take out his astral body while his physical body is still alive. It hurts the disciple a little, because his astral body has completely forgotten its true nature. It self-identifies so completely with the physical body that it is hard to make it split off. But when it is finally done the disciple knows that it was worth it, because now he can enter his own causal body and choose the karmas he wants to pay off at his own pace on his own terms. All he has to do now is follow the *adesha* (commands, instructions) of the internal guru. Adesha means Adya Isha, the First Deity, the internal voice which tells the disciple what to do when.

"On the path of bhakti the guru arranges everything, and the disciple's only job is to maintain continuous devotion."

"Which is better?" asked a listener who came infrequently to Vimalananda's den.

"There is no better or worse; it depends entirely on the sadhaka and the guru. The result is the same. Once Jnaneshwar Maharaj was traveling on a pilgrimage with a group of other saints. It was very hot that day, and they were all thirsty. The only well they could find had no bucket. How to get the water?

"First Jnaneshwar's brother Nivritti Nath, who had taught Jnaneshwar the path of jnana, used his yogic powers to go down himself into the well and bring up water. Next Namdev, who had taught Jnaneshwar the path of bhakti, started to sing a song in praise of the Lord. His devotion was so profound that every living being in the neighborhood, even the trees and plants, became filled with the love of God. Soon even the water of the well began to overflow its rim out of sheer joy at hearing Namdev sing God's praises. Then Jnaneshwar realized that he had seen the end result of both the paths of knowledge and devotion, and he asked his beloved deity Vitthala for permission to leave his body, because there was nothing left for him to see in the world."

Silence descended for a moment as we all contemplated that scene, and then Vimalananda continued:

"Let's think about it in terms of the subtle body, the nadis and Kundalini. Bhakti and jnana are the two roads to the Ajna Chakra. Whoever follows the path of jnana must concentrate on the sun. The ancient Vedics all followed jnana, and they were all basically sun worshippers. What happens to a man who looks into the sun? He becomes blind; literally blind, if he looks literally at the sun, and blind to the world if he stares at the Sun of Jnana. When you become blind to all differentiation, all name and form, you can see nothing which is not the One Reality. A sun worshipper follows the Ganga, which here represents the right nostril, the Surya Nadi.

"The man who follows the path of bhakti uses in his rituals the left nostril, the Yamuna, which represents the moon. This takes a little longer than the path of jnana, and even in the external world the Yamuna River is longer than the Ganga; it meanders, whereas the Ganga is direct. Yama, the Messenger of Death Himself, who happens to be the brother of the river Yamuna, says that if one takes a bath in the Yamuna on Bhau Bija (Brother's

Day), then all one's karmas are washed away. So people flock to bathe in the Yamuna on that day, but they are fools. What Yama means is the Yamuna of the body, the left nostril."

After pausing briefly to let us gnaw on the idea of bathing oneself in a nadi, he shifted his tack:

"Of course, for a man to be overcome by bhakti is rare, though it is easy for a woman. A man must develop a waxen heart, a secret, internal love. What happens to someone who stares at luna, the moon? Lunacy, madness. When you achieve *Maha Bhava Samadhi*, emotional highlights, you go mad, mad with uncontrollable love and joy. The moon stands for the mind, and is cool. You get a delicious coolness and lunacy from the moon. It is this sweet madness that makes falling in love so wonderful. The sun also loves you, but the sun is so intense that it burns you to a crisp, without any interval of loveplay in between. The sun teaches you selflessness. Selfishness is your worst enemy, true, but without at least some selfishness there is no love.

"Rama, Perfection Encompassed (*Maryada Purushottama*), is of the solar race; His way is the way of penance. Krishna, Perfection Personified (*Purnatmaka Purushottama*), is of the lunar race; He loves to play hide-and-seek with His devotees, never letting them catch Him until the very end. The moon gets its light from the sun, but you can't look at the sun; you'll go blind. You can look at the moon, but you'll go mad. The choice is yours.

"Which is better therefore depends on you. But remember, if you choose to follow the path of jnana you will be using Surya Nadi, which will heat you up. The path of knowledge is dangerous nowadays because there are so many temptations. If your physical appetites are even slightly stimulated, it becomes most difficult to control them. So many good yogis have gone to the West and ruined themselves. They had good intentions, but did not realize, or perhaps forgot, that a yogi cannot be a *bhogi* (an enjoyer of sense pleasures) at the same time. Bhakti is much safer than jnana, because you use Chandra Nadi, which keeps you cool. It takes longer, but there is no danger of falling.

"It is because of these dangers on the path of jnana that Brahmanas, the priestly class, are supposed to wear their sacred thread, which is called a *jahnavi*, or *yajnopavita*. Jahnavi is also a name for the Ganga, which refers here to the internal Ganga, the Surya Nadi. The purpose of this sacred thread is to control and enhance the functioning of this 'sun channel,' which helps in the study of the Veda; the Veda is the path of jnana, and Brahmanas are supposed to be 'knowers of the Absolute.'

"I see that you are wearing a jahnavi," said Vimalananda to his visitor. "Do you know its significance?"

The man folded his hands in the universal Indian gesture of respect, and replied, in English, "Sir, I was born a Brahmana, and I have worn this for many years, but no one has ever explained it to me to my satisfaction. I hope you will please do so."

"Please don't call me 'sir'; I have not been knighted by the queen," said Vimalananda, also in English, laughing. "The jahnavi is always worn from the left shoulder down to the right waist, except when certain rituals like *Pitri Tarpana* (ancestor worship) are performed when it is worn opposite (right shoulder to left waist). Great people like kings, princes and generals usually wear their swords, bandoliers or sashes left to right as well. A sash creates both a mental and physical sense of command; a jahnavi creates a spiritual sense of command, which is necessary for the path of jnana. This is its effect on the mind.

"A true jahnavi is handwoven of raw cotton, not wool or silk, since these materials have a different electrical potential. It has three strands of thread, with three peculiar knots added. Very few people today know why this is so. It has to do with the body's three most important nadis and with the three principal knots which must be pierced if Kundalini is ever to be fully awakened.

"What specifically does a jahnavi do to the physical body? Well, it certainly makes the right, or masculine, side of the body predominant. By wearing it over the left shoulder it helps a man accumulate and harness shakti. A woman has no need whatsoever to wear a jahnavi, because she is the embodiment of shakti. Unfortunately, I will bet that the only time you even think about your jahnavi is when you gather it up and drape it around your right ear whenever you go to the toilet. Am I right?"

The man nodded, sheepishly and vigorously.

"This is necessary because of its connection with Apana, the downward-moving form of the body's shakti. What connection? We'll have to discuss that later.

"Back in the Vedic era the jahnavi was an integral part of sadhana. When a boy was ready to begin studying with a guru he would, on an auspicious day, undergo the *Upanayana* ceremony, the initiation into Vedic studies during which boys first put on a jahnavi. First he would strip naked and have his head shaved, and then he would appear before his guru, who would show him how to tie his loincloth, which was one long piece of cloth, not the sewn thing that people use today. It had to be properly tied so that it would press on a certain vertebra, and thus stimulate certain nadis. This signified the beginning of the period of the boy's life during which he would be a celibate student. Celibate, to prevent Kundalini from getting stuck in the sex center.

"Then the boy would do a full prostration to the guru, who would touch the boy's head and bless him. While holding the boy's head the guru would use phrenology to check out which parts of the brain were most fully developed, to determine which branch of knowledge the boy should pursue. A well-developed occiput would indicate a talent for mathematics, and so on.

"This was an opportune moment to test the boy's other capabilities as well. Suppose the guru wanted to know whether or not the boy could succeed at alchemy. He would pour mercury into the palm of the boy's hand, and tell him to pour it back into the bottle without spilling a drop. If he could do this, he was fit. He would be able to do this only if he had one long, straight line running across his palm, so this is a form of palmistry. Since the lines on the palm are created by certain genes, examination of the palm means examination of the genes. And since the genes are closely related to an individual's karmas, we will have a good idea of what will happen to him in the future.

"When the guru had decided what the boy was fit to study he would initiate him into that version of the Gayatri Mantra which was most suitable for him, and would make him wear the jahnavi. Then the boy's parents would beg for him to return home. If he really wanted to succeed, he would ignore them and stay with the guru. Those others, who did it only for show— everyone nowadays, since no one knows the process—would return with their parents, and in the course of time would forget the mantra and remove the loincloth. Then what would be the use of their continuing to wear the jahnavi?

"Many people wear jahnavis today, but most never know what they are meant for. How can you be a knower, a jnani, if you don't know anything about what you are practicing? No, it is always better today to follow the path of devotion."

Gayatri

"Do you believe," the visitor inquired, "that repeating Gayatri is a good thing?"

"I do smashan sadhana," Vimalananda replied, "because I am fit for it, and because it is fit for the age we live in. Some people, though, still try to perform sadhanas that were more appropriate for Satya Yuga. There are many people who claim to repeat the Gayatri Mantra, and claim to obtain all manner of believable and unbelievable benefits from it. They babble on about how 'A man who achieves success with the Gayatri Mantra attains to supreme realization,' and whatnot. But do they know that the mantra that they are reciting as Gayatri is not really the Gayatri Mantra? And that the form which they visualize as they do their *japa* (repetition of mantra) is not the real form of Gayatri?

"And do they know what will happen if they do too much japa of Gayatri? If you think I'm trying to be funny just try it sometime; your head will become overheated. Once a man came to me to learn the Gayatri mantra. I told him, 'Gayatri is certainly one of the most ancient and powerful of our mantras, but the mantra which is printed in the books is not the real Gayatri; it is the Savitri. You are not in a position to know the real Gayatri, so please don't try to do it. It is only meant for Rishis, not for you.'

"When he insisted, I gave him only one syllable of the real Gayatri and told him, 'You should not even try to do this, but because you insist I will give you a fragment of the real thing. You are not strong enough to handle the whole mantra.' I told him to repeat it only eleven times a day.

"Because he had already done plenty of sadhana he thought he was far beyond such a beginner's limit and he overdid it; he repeated it one hundred and eight times the first morning. That evening he suddenly told his wife, 'I am Narayana and you are my Lakshmi. Massage my legs!' As she did he repeated slowly, 'All in one, one in all.' Then he walked into the bathroom, complaining of a headache.

"When he didn't come out of the bathroom for quite a long time his wife panicked and called the neighbors to break down the door. They found him sitting with his head under the tap, trying to cool down the tremendous heat which had been created in his head. He did not survive long after that; he realized himself and threw off his 'earthly shackles.'

"Gayatri must always be performed in water. Since Gayatri is the power of the sun, the Surya Nadi works more strongly when it is repeated. It is not healthy for only one nadi to function continuously, so water, which is ruled by the moon, is recommended in order to encourage the Chandra Nadi to counteract any ill-effects of excessive solar influence. This keeps the sun and moon in equilibrium. If this man had repeated that single syllable only eleven times as he had been told to do, that excess of fire which did him in would never have happened."

[133]

A Gayatri Yantra

I thought again of Pandit Gopi Krishna and the sufferings his Surya Nadi caused him when it functioned continuously.

"When I first met my Junior Guru Maharaj he told me to repeat Gayatri, and to do it in water. I thought I would be clever and do it in my bathtub in the comfort of my own home, but he vetoed that idea and insisted that I do it in the ocean. Every night for more than three and a half years I would go down to the Arabian Sea around midnight and would finish by dawn. The currents would carry me several miles south during the night, and the waves were sometimes several meters high during the monsoon. But Smashan Tara was holding me in the palm of Her hand at all times and I never came to the least harm—not even a fish bite. I got into the routine so well that Guru Maharaj had to return to Bombay and order me to stop doing it. He didn't want me to go too far too fast.

"As for the benefits of doing Gayatri, well, you get the power of the sun. Let me put it this way: the great saint Samartha Ram Das, who lived right here in Maharashtra, did Gayatri for twelve years, and he could raise the dead. My Junior Guru Maharaj has been doing Gayatri for more than sixty years, a lot more. Think of what he must be able to do. He also worships the fire, but without any ostentation; he is too shrewd for that. He doesn't want anyone to know what he can do, or for that matter what he is doing.

"Gayatri is the only mantra repeated in Satya Yuga. As the Yugas advance all the other inferior mantras arise. Gayatri is the mother of all the Vedas. Only the Rishis, and no one else, know everything there is to know about Gayatri. There are twenty-eight types of Gayatri, and each Rishi specialized in one type; that is his special knowledge, his vijnana. For example, only one Rishi knows the full form of the Gayatri for creation, the Brahma— Gayatri. The Rishis obtain the power of the sun all because they repeat the Gayatri Mantra.

"I think you can see now that the Rishis were very advanced indeed in the spiritual line. A Rishi actually 'sees' the Truth. This perception of Truth spontaneously manifests in the form of mantras. Only a part of the Truth can ever be manifested here in our world, the World of Death, where things are imperfect and have to be imperfect in order to remain here. Each aspect of Truth has its own phonetic value, which is expressed in the vowels, consonants, rhythm, pitch, and intonation of the mantra. The mantras which were perceived in this way were collected in a coherent way to form the Vedas.

"They say that the Rishi Vasishtha composed a good number of mantras of the Rg Veda, and that Angiras composed so many for the Atharva Veda, and so on, but I do not believe that the Vedas are the product of many Rishis. I think that each Veda must be the product of only one Rishi. How could there be complete coherence in their subject matter if there were many different Rishis responsible for them, each of whom has his own individual vijnana, his own unique Gayatri? There must have originally been a Veda for every Rishi, because each Veda was an exposition of his own knowledge.

"What I am trying to make you understand is the essence of the Vedas and their fundamental teachings. The Vedas are a labyrinth to those who don't know the inner meanings of the mantras, and only a select few people know this now, or ever did. That is why certain junior Rishis had the duty to write Upanishads, as explanations of that essence. When people can no longer understand Truth directly, religions spring up to explain Truth to them. Some people then take advantage of the situation and become priests to extract benefits for themselves.

"A priest will not tell you that his purpose is to maintain control over the people, but he will tell you that he is an authorized intermediary between you and God, which is the same thing. When people have to go through priests to get to God, naturally the priests will become powerful. But that is all bull. You must forget all about priests and go looking for God on your own; you must carve out your own niche.

"But if you take on yourself the responsibility of carving out your own niche you have to follow the directions of your teacher to the letter. What happens when you don't follow instructions is what happened to this man to whom I taught Gayatri. I knew how much he could safely take, but he did not. Now he is happy, no doubt. Not happy—blissful! He is one with Narayana. But what about the weeping wife he left behind? Who is responsible for having made her a widow? I am. Now I no longer give people mantras. If people knew how dangerous it is to give out mantras they would think a hundred times before they ever did it.

"This applies to even 'harmless' mantras, like the one to control snakes, or the one for *Svapneshvari*, the goddess of dreams. Even Svapneshvari can be abused. You might send her to trouble someone else needlessly in their dreams, or you might tell her, 'Now I want to see Marilyn Monroe.' You will see her, but then if you say, 'Now I want to see her labia minora,' you will certainly see those too, but that will not be good for you in the end. A mantra is not a thing to use frivolously.

"Used properly, though, mantras can work wonders. For this we have the Rishis to thank, since all methods of sadhana have originated from them. You see, each Rishi is a scientist, with his own researches to conduct, and when he succeeds in his research the result is beneficial in so many different ways, like 'three-in-one oil.'

"For example, snakes possess different types of poisons. One poison paralyzes the nerves. Another thins out the blood so that internal hemorrhages occur. Some poison thickens the blood; it coagulates, clots form and the tissues are not properly nourished. Sometimes a clot might cause an embolism, which could kill the patient.

"Now, the ordinary man who learns a mantra against snakebite will use it only against snakebite. Maybe every year or two he will have a chance to use it and save someone's life. But someone whose intelligence is awakened will examine the mantra and discern its more general purpose. He may find that a particular mantra for snakebite thins out the blood and makes it rush through the blood vessels. Then he will realize that the same mantra can be used in every case where that effect is needed, such as an embolism, arteriosclerosis, and the like. And how many people suffer from these diseases? Millions.

"Such a man will be able to cure thousands of people with that mantra, whereas the ordinary man may help only ten or twenty in his entire life. This is the true knowledge of the mantra. If you know it, wherever you go you can hold your own against anyone, thanks to the Rishi who 'saw' the mantra."

He fell silent for a moment, and then turned to me.

"You know, Robby, all this mantra and tantra is very nice, but it is limited. There are things far beyond mantra, things the tongue cannot speak. And when you get to that point, there is no need for mantra. When you realize those things, you realize that mantra is just a toy. When you have the power of the sun at your beck and call, will you ever bother to use an Eveready battery? No, you won't, and the comparison is the same here. On the one hand, Gayatri and the power of the sun, the lore of the Rishis; on the other, Aghora."

"But until we get to that stage, we have to make use of mantra," I piped up.

"You have no choice," replied Vimalananda, and we all began to laugh.

Treasure Vase

The Five Elements

Earth (square); Water (circle); Fire (triangle); Air (crescent); Space (moon).

Shiva Linga

Mantra

"Once there was an Englishman, a District Collector (government administrator), who told his servant, 'When any great saint comes, tell me. I want to get jnana from him.'"

Vimalananda and I were sitting in Poona. It was mid-morning, breakfast was over, the preparations for lunch were under way, and he was in a good mood.

"One day a saint came to town with a large group of his followers, chanting the name of Krishna: 'Radheshyam, Radheshyam, Radheshyam.' When the Collector's servant saw this he immediately remembered his master and decided to tell him about the saint, hoping for a reward. When he heard that a saint had come the Collector said to his servant, 'Go and make arrangements for my visit. I am coming for jnana.'

"The servant returned to the place where the saint was doing his chanting and started getting everything ready for his boss's visit: a nice chair with a red sash in a prominent spot for him to sit on, and whatnot. When the saint asked the servant what was going on, the servant replied that a 'great man' was coming. The saint said, 'All right, but first remove that chair.' The servant said, 'If I do that, you don't know what sort of trouble you will be getting yourself into.' At that, the saint told his followers to ignore the fellow and start chanting again.

"When the Collector arrived he ordered everyone to stop singing and said, in Hindi, 'Look here, I have come for jnana.' The saint looked up at him and told him, also in Hindi, 'Dear boy, just repeat God's name,' and told his followers to resume chanting.

"The Collector asked a second time and received the same reply. He asked a third time, adding, 'I don't like this noise.' The saint looked at him and said in Hindi, 'Shut up, *sala!'*

"*Sala* means 'brother-in-law.' If I call someone my brother-in-law it means I am sleeping with his sister. This is a serious insult here in India.

"The Collector became absolutely wild on being called 'sala' and lost his temper. He shouted, 'Now you want to see who I am? Call the police,' he said to his servant, 'and have this man taken away!'

"The saint asked, 'What have I done?'

"The Collector answered, 'You have insulted me.'

"'And how was that?'

"'You called me sala.'

"Then the saint smiled and said, in fluent English, 'Now see what has happened to you: one little word has made you uncontrollably angry. And it is not even possible for me to be your sala because you have no sister! When one bad word can affect you so profoundly think of what a good effect you would get if you spent your time repeating God's name.'

"The Englishman was stunned. He had never dreamed that the saint knew English. Then suddenly he realized, 'How could this man know that I have no sister?' He immediately prostrated himself to the saint and said, 'I have received the wisdom I came for.' He went home, bequeathed everything to his servant, and without any delay became a sadhu. I know that this story is true; I met this man in Girnar. This shows you practical proof of the power of God's name."

He paused to light a cigarette. A troop of monkeys passed overhead heading for the nearby cemetery, as they did every Saturday.

"God's name produces results in any language in which you repeat it. Once you approach near to God and God begins to speak to you He will speak in your own mother tongue, the one in which you feel most at home. The priests of the various religions will tell you, 'No, God can speak only in Latin, or Sanskrit, or Arabic, or Hebrew, or Pahlavi,' but it isn't so. Who created all the languages? He did—capital H. So why can't He speak in any language that He pleases?

"And likewise you can speak to God in any language you like, and He will hear you, if you are sincere. Because each grouping of sounds has its own phonetic value, however, some languages are better than others for certain purposes. Arabic, for example, is very good for mundane magic. And Sanskrit is very good for creating deities. Each sound of the Sanskrit alphabet is a Bija Mantra. A Bija Mantra is a seed which when planted in the consciousness gives rise to a certain effect. Repetition of the appropriate Bija Mantra is a quick way to create the form of the deity you are worshipping because the vibrations of the sound itself produce the form."

"But of course this is applicable only to Indian deities," I interjected.

"Absolutely not!" he countered. "Someone who knows the phonetic value of various sounds can create a mantra that will be applicable for any deity. You have worshipped Jesus for many years; there is a Bija Mantra for Jesus also, and if you know it and know how to use it you can reach Jesus very quickly. Mantras can be very useful."

"If this is the case then why don't more Christians follow this path and get the result?" I inquired.

"Who bothers about these things?" he replied indignantly. "All the padres are too busy converting other people to worry about their own development. I say, forget about other people and worry about converting yourself. Convert yourself into the form of your deity; that is a *real* conversion. *That* is the beauty of Tantra.

Mantra Siddhi

"Many people talk about *Mantra Siddhi* (the manifestation of the deity inherent in the mantra), but I am afraid that most of them have missed the boat. Let's say that I want to locate you, and I know your name. But that alone is not enough. I must also know what you look like and where you live, because there may be many people with the same name. Only if I know your likes and dislikes, your temperament, all the facets of your character, do I really know you. Then I can locate you.

"It is the same in sadhana. When you call a particular deity with the help of a mantra, which is nothing but that deity's name, you must have a mental image of what He or She looks like. Day after day you call; where will your Beloved go? The deity must come to you, and will come as soon as you forget everything else. At first you will only be able to draw your deity to you occasionally. Then, as you get onto His or Her wavelength, you will be with that deity at all times. This stage is called *tanmayata*, or 'togetherness.'

"Eventually your own individuality becomes completely dissolved, and you and your deity become one consciousness. When you become identical with your deity you have reached the stage of *tadrupata*. At this stage there is *mantra chaitanya*: there is total union of your consciousness and your mantra. Every cell in your body becomes a resonator for your mantra; every pore becomes a mouth with which you speak God's name."

The Tantras maintain that the consciousness of a certain region of the physical body is its deity. Since every mantra is a deity, the entire human body is composed of mantras, and is a mantra itself. By repeating mantras you are continuously recreating yourself in a new image. Eventually, when you are truly purified, your original personality becomes totally effaced, and only the image of your deity remains. Vimalananda illustrated with a story:

"One day while traveling from place to place a wandering sadhu came upon a boy herding buffaloes. He was hungry, so he asked for some milk to drink, and the boy gave it to him readily. When he had drunk to his satisfaction the sadhu began to feel generous, and asked the herdsman, 'What would you like? I'm feeling so fine, I'll give it to you.'

"The boy chuckled and said, 'I really don't need anything. I do nothing all day long but herd my buffaloes, and I'm satisfied with that. Besides, Maharaj, you came to me as a beggar and I gave you alms. How can I expect anything from you in return? I am the giver, not you.'

"The sadhu was taken aback by this answer, and realized that this was no ordinary buffalo-herd. Then he thought he would do a good turn for the fellow anyway, and asked, 'What is it that you love most in the world?'

"'Why, this buffalo,' the boy replied innnocently, 'the one whose milk you just drank. She is the largest I have. She gives me more than ten gallons of milk a day, and she is so broad and strong, so loving and beautiful and well-behaved, that I love her best of all.'

"'All right,' said the sadhu, 'please do one thing. Go sit in that cave over there and imagine that you are this buffalo. Think of her; keep her picture with you in your mind. Completely self-identify with her; become her. As you sit repeat to yourself, "Bhaisoham, bhaisoham" ("I am a buffalo, I am a buffalo.") Don't worry about a thing; I'll look after your buffaloes.'

"The herdsman did as the sadhu instructed, and when after three days the sadhu entered the cave to check on the boy he found him sitting motionless with his eyes closed, repeating, 'Bhaisoham, bhaisoham.' Then the sadhu said, 'So, young buffalo-herd, how have you progressed? Come out now.'

"The herdsman answered, 'Don't call me a buffalo-herd! I am a buffalo. Can't you see that? Look at my broad back! How can I leave this cave? My horns are too broad to go through the entrance. Now don't be foolish; go away and leave me alone or I'll gore you and toss you out with these beautiful horns of mine.'

"But the sadhu persisted and said, 'Try to remember, my boy. I told you to sit and do this. Now, instead of repeating, "I am a buffalo, I am a buffalo," start to identify with Shiva. Repeat, "Shivoham, Shivoham" ("I am Shiva, I am Shiva").' The herdsman did that, and in about fifteen minutes he was in a deep trance. He realized his goal: the Universal Soul in the form of Lord Shiva.

"The sadhu was astonished. Tears came to his eyes and he said to himself, 'This fellow sits only three and a half days and achieves, and I have wandered around practicing without success for years and years.' Then he had to take that buffalo-herd as his guru, and finally he also realized.

"That the buffalo-herd could achieve so quickly is of course the result of preparation from previous births. The same thing happened to Ramakrishna Paramahansa. What it took his guru thirty years to achieve Ramakrishna achieved in a few days. Time is not the criterion; if the desire is strong enough the result must occur without delay. You must forget everything except the name and form of your deity; then you can achieve the highest."

"Is 'Soham' the same as 'Shivoham?" I asked.

"Not exactly. Many saints tell their disciples to repeat 'Soham,' which means 'Sa aham', 'I am He,' 'He' meaning the Universal Self in Its formless aspect. This is all very fine, except that it is not quite what is desired. It's not so easy to identify with the Universal Self, which is impossible to imagine, much less put into words. If the mantra is inversed, however, it becomes 'Hamsah,' which is the Bija Mantra of Sarasvati, the goddess of learning. Whoever repeats that mantra gets the benefit of Sarasvati's Shakti, which will lead the repeater step by step to Soham. It is always the Mother who shows the child the face of its Father, as Bhavatarini Ma did for Ramakrishna.

"The sadhu gave the boy a name and form on which to concentrate his mind because he had to do some preliminary work, no matter how minimal, with the help of a form. Both name and form are essential for worship. One part of the mind takes the shape of an object; that is form. Another part of the mind identifies and distinguishes it; that is name. To go directly to the highest type of samadhi is almost impossible. Even Ramakrishna had to worship Mother Bhavatarini for many years before his consciousness became one-pointed enough to achieve The Formless."

"Why a buffalo?"

"A buffalo was the logical choice for the buffalo-herd, because he lived around them, and loved them; he had a strong affinity for buffaloes. You may not choose a buffalo for your concentration, since after all a buffalo is the very embodiment of inertness and stupidity; it is Tamas personified. You will probably prefer to use a deity to prepare yourself, and that too one with whom you have an affinity."

Using Mantras

"How will I know which form I have an affinity for?"

"That is the job of your guru, to assign you the proper mantra and the proper form. He will know which mantras are appropriate for you. If you are of a very tender nature and you start to repeat a mantra for some terrifying deity like Smashan Tara you may scare yourself to death. If you are prone to greed and you worship Lakshmi, the goddess of wealth, you may simply enhance your greed, which will not help you progress. This is why a guru is necessary: to teach you what you need to learn. People are amazing nowadays; they tell the guru what they want to learn from him, instead of trying to find out from him what they need to know. Is there anything more ridiculous?

"You must also be sure that you have the proper form of the deity that goes with your mantra; otherwise you may waste years in fruitless effort. Most deities have many different forms. For example, it is possible to worship Krishna as a baby, a young boy, a handsome young man, a lover, a king, a warrior, Arjuna's friend, and so on. You can see Him in many different forms, including even His universal form. But name and form are identical, so each different form must have a different name, a different mantra. Without a guru's help, how will you know which is best for you? You can only know which is best for you if you have already understood both your own nature and the inherent nature of the deity.

"It may take ten years of hard penance for a man to achieve success with a mantra for Anjaneya, since most men relate to Anjaneya as the greatest of heroes; but a woman can satisfy Anjaneya in ten days. Most people will tell you that women should not worship Anjaneya since He is celibate, and this is true in the sense that romantic or erotic love is useless. But Anjaneya must respect and love one woman: His mother Anjani. So if a woman worships Anjaneya as if she were Anjani and He were a tiny baby monkey she can get results very quickly. It's wonderful, isn't it? People worship Lord Krishna in the same way, in the form of Lallu or Gopala, just as they worship the Baby Jesus. A man could do the same thing, but men are not innately motherly like women are; it may take a man years to develop real motherliness.

"Not only must you know the right form of the deity, but you must have perfect faith in that one aspect of the Godhead if you hope to succeed. One whom I've known for several years came to visit me recently and was boasting that he worships one deity, does japa for a second, prays to a third, and sometimes approaches others as well. How can he ever succeed in propitiating one when he divides himself among so many, like a prostitute?"

Another striking image: the spiritual harlot.

"And he is not alone; look in the worship-room of almost any Indian and you'll find pictures of images of fifteen or twenty gods, goddesses, saints, wonderworkers, and what-have-you. This is just a sign of a chaotic mind. If you ever hope to achieve you must select one form and stick to it; that is part of niyama. Look at the great poet-saint Tulsidas. When Lord Krishna came to him, he said, 'Lord, I know that you are nothing but Vishnu in a different form, and you are in no way any different from Lord Rama; in fact You are the Universal Self. But still I prefer to see the form dearest to my heart, my Raghuvira, my heroic Rama.' And Krishna smiled and showed it to him."

After a brief intermission, during which the rice was put on the fire to cook, Vimalananda continued.

"Even if you have been given an appropriate mantra, and know the correct form to visualize with it, and follow good niyama, you still cannot hope to succeed just by repeating your mantra without any discipline. It is always good to repeat God's name, and so it is good to repeat your mantra all day long, whether you are eating, sleeping, making love, or sitting on the toilet. But do not expect that this will be sufficient to achieve Mantra Siddhi. For that you need to follow a specific process called *purashcharana*.

"For one purashcharana you decide how many repetitions you can do in a year. You must do the same number every day. After you finish, ten percent of that amount must be offered as oblations, that is, as offerings into a homa fire. Then ten percent of the number of oblations must be offered with water; this is called *tarpana*. Ten percent of that number must be then recited as you sprinkle water about your body in a particular way; this is called *marjana*. Finally, ten percent of that number is offered as *bhojana*, gifts of food, usually to children. When all this is complete so is your purashcharana.

"In Kali Yuga they say that you need to do only three purashcharanas correctly to bring about a mantra's full effects. In truth, if you really desire God to come He can come in three days, or three hours, or even the minutest instant. But today Maya is so strong that very few can do even one purashcharana properly. Why do you think Maya tests everyone? Not because She wants to ruin us; oh, no! She is the Mother; She has given everything to us. It is because She has to know if our love is really meant for Her, or only for Her creations, that She tempts us; She loves us so much that She always wants us to get exactly what we want.

"Because a year is such a long time to follow strict discipline during Kali Yuga, God in his wisdom has established another, easier way of performing a purashcharana. According to this reckoning a purashcharana is made up of three anushthanas. One *anushthana* is made up of the minimum amount of japa required to perfect the mantra. Before you become so great as to do a full purashcharana you must first succeed at an anusthana.

"When we talk about 'perfecting' a mantra," he said pointedly to me as I furrowed my brow, attempting to understand, "we mean purifying it, and ourselves, so that it can exert its effects without any obstructions, so that its Shakti becomes available to us. The number of japas needed to perfect a mantra varies according to the mantra, but is often one hundred thousand or more."

"How many is it for the mantra I am repeating right now?" I had been repeating this particular mantra for many months, and a little voice was now telling me, "You haven't been paying attention to how many you've been repeating! How will you ever achieve this way?"

"For right now, assume that you are repeating a mantra for which one hundred thousand repetitions are necessary. Suppose you were to decide to do an anusthana, to repeat this mantra one hundred thousand times in a controlled, consistent way." I decided then and there to do so. "You can do them in as many days as you please, but you must do the same number each day. Then you must offer ten percent of that number, i.e., ten thousand, as homa. Ten percent of that, or one thousand, must be offered as tarpana, one hundred as marjana, and finally you must feed ten people. Each deity requires a different sort of human 'mouth'; for Anjaneya small boys are needed, for Ma little girls, and so on.

"So this is why I should keep track of how many oblations I offer at each homa," I said. "Should I do some of this tarpana and marjana, and feed people, after I do homa?"

"Of course you should! Then your worship will be complete. Each segment of a purashcharana or anusthana relates to one of the Elements. Japa purifies the Air and Ether Elements in you, homa the Fire Element, tarpana the Water Element, and marjana the Earth Element. Bhojana is your final offering to your deity, whom you see in all those people you feed. Unless you know how to apply this sort of knowledge you can never be successful with any mantra. This is practical Bhuta Shuddhi, purification of the Five Great Elements which make up the universe, which is the essence of Tantra. You are not yet ready for Panchamakara, so you can begin with this.

The Five S's

"Both anusthanas and purashcharanas require you to follow what we call in Sanskrit the path of the Five S's: *sthana, samaya, sankhya, samagri,* and *samyama.* The purpose of these rules is to achieve the *sa-guna* or manifested form of the deity. You know Sanskrit; translate these words."

"'Sthana' means location."

"So first you must stay in one location throughout the duration of your penance and not travel about. Moreover, you must sit in the same place each day, face in the same direction, and if possible sit in the same position."

"'Samaya' means time."

"Fix a time limit for your program—eleven days or forty days or whatever—and stick to it. Also, you must sit at the same time every day. Five minutes variation here or there is permissible, but no more. If you miss the time, you cannot count the repetitions you do that day in your total."

"'Sankhya' means number."

"You must decide the total number of repetitions you will do, and then divide that number by the number of days to determine how many you will do each day. And don't decide to do five hundred and then one day become busy and do only one hundred, and hope to make up for it by doing a thousand the next day. You must do the same minimum number every day; you can do more but you cannot do less, or you cannot count that day."

"'Samagri' means the materials used for worship."

"These must be the same every day; no substitutions permitted. And 'samyama'?"

"I'm not exactly sure, probably related to niyama?"

"Yes. Here samyama means complete control of the sexual organ; that means abstinence! Also, a woman cannot count the repetitions she does while she is menstruating. She should not even sit at her normal place of japa. In fact she should not even visualize intently, since that could imbalance the Prana and Apana in her body. Menstruation is a time for the body to purify itself; once it is over she can resume her previous routine.

"Only if all five of these S's are fulfilled can the performance give results. A sadhaka must be rigid about this. Also, you must concentrate on what you're doing when you do your japa. You cannot do a few repetitions and then start to worry about where your son is or whether your wife is cooking dinner or not. You must throw out all external attention and concentrate on interiority. And, you must be careful of your temper. While you are doing your japa your mind approaches God; if you become angry afterward all that you achieved in that department is immediately lost.

"There may be other restrictions too. For instance, a specific diet may be indicated. Whatever the diet you should not do japa for up to two hours after having a full meal. You should never even discuss mantras, astrology or any related subject for two hours after a meal. Why? Because your mind can only concentrate on one thing at a time, and if there is food in your stomach your mind will have to concentrate on that food in order to digest it."

"What about fruit or milk?" I asked, since that was my diet at the time.

"At least an hour after eating fruit, and at least half an hour after drinking milk or juice. You should even wait for fifteen minutes or more after you have drunk some water. Once you no longer need your mind in order to digest your food this restriction will no longer apply; but you have to be able to die while still alive in order to do that."

Ever the showman, he paused dramatically; but it was only a feint, for he then broke into a smile and said, "Now let us stop here and eat!" We went in to lunch.

Secrecy

Some days later when I was in Bombay I accompanied Vimalananda on an uneventful visit to K., one of his old friends. Afterward I noticed that Vimalananda was quieter than usual, so after we reached home and had tea I casually asked him, "Have you known that gentleman for very long?"

He replied, "There are many restrictions to follow if you really want to perfect a mantra. One of the most important is that you must never tell anyone which mantra you repeat. When you tell someone else your mantra you allow them access to the Shakti you are trying to accumulate, which is tantamount to giving them a blank check and asking them to clean out your bank account. Anyone who needs to know your mantra will be able to find out without asking you; whoever cannot find it out without asking does not need to know.

"About twenty years ago K. wanted me to give him a mantra to repeat. He pleaded with me so long and so insistently that finally, against my better judgment, I gave in. K. was proud of his new acquisition, and when my Junior Guru Maharaj came to Bombay in 1959 and K. came to pay his respects, Guru Maharaj asked him what kind of sadhana he was doing. K. told him, 'Vimalananda has given me a mantra which I am repeating regularly with great care.'

"Now, Guru Maharaj did not ask K. about his sadhana because he wanted to know about it. He already knew about it; finding out such things is child's play for him. He asked because he wanted to know how solid K.'s dedication to sadhana had become. When Guru Maharaj learned that his dedication was not at all solid he decided to teach K. a lesson."

"He knew it was not solid because K. was willing to speak about it, you mean?"

"That's it; he knew the rules. Anyway, Guru Maharaj got wild and told K., 'Who does Babuji'—meaning me; he always calls me Babuji—'who does Babuji think he is—God?—that he is giving out mantras? Besides, he has not told you the entire mantra. He is trying to keep something from you; he has left out one syllable.'

"K. became alarmed; if the mantra was incomplete he might repeat it for many years and nothing would happen! So he said, 'Oh, Maharaj, please take pity on me. Tell me the rest of it.'

"Guru Maharaj played his part well. At first he refused, but K. begged, pleaded and wheedled so sincerely that eventually Guru Maharaj took 'pity' on him and gave him the 'additional syllable.'

"The result? Since 1959 K. has repeated that mantra faithfully every day for ten to twelve hours. Ten to twelve hours! He passed the ten million mark long back, and is probably near the twenty million mark now—but there has been no concrete result whatsoever. That extra syllable changed the entire phonetic effect of the mantra's vibration. It didn't belong there, of course; Guru Maharaj added it just to teach K. a lesson. But what a lesson!

Twenty or thirty years of sadhana down the drain! To Guru Maharaj, of course, twenty or thirty years means nothing at all, but to us mortals it is our lives. It just serves K. right for speaking his mantra aloud."

I had heard stories of Guru Maharaj before, and after meeting him I found him to be as strict as Vimalananda portrayed him. At this stage in my life, however, such stories made me lose all interest in ever meeting Guru Maharaj myself, which is the effect Vimalananda intended. And he was right, of course; had I met Guru Maharaj then I would have been lucky to escape still wearing my skin.

"This is why people hate my Guru Maharaj," Vimalananda continued, noting my reaction with satisfaction. "When people come to him he sees to it that they have a good purge of bad karmas from their causal bodies. All that person knows is that he went to Guru Maharaj and suddenly everything started to go wrong, so Guru Maharaj is blamed. But he doesn't care. You can say he is just doing his job. He is very strict about doing his job, and rarely lets anyone escape if he finds out they are exceeding their limits. His lessons are really tough.

"Secrecy is always the best policy in sadhana. There is even a proverb to this effect: 'maunam sarvartha-sadhanam.' Translate please."

"Uh, 'silence accomplishes everything.'"

"Right. Consider this: whenever we are having a good discussion about spirituality some idiot always comes along to spoil it. Why? Because God does not like his secrets to be discussed so easily. How much more must He hate to have His mantras spoken?

"Knowing all these things I still allowed K. to have that mantra. Well, Guru Maharaj taught me a good lesson from this experience too: test an aspirant thoroughly before you teach him or her anything. If you give a monkey a razor, do you think he will shave himself or chop his neck? Very few people can understand the sort of play I have with my mentors."

I certainly didn't understand it.

"If I were to put my mind to it," he went on "no one, including you, would ever be able to get anything out of me. Once when I was living the life of a naked sadhu in Girnar some baba heard about me and came to me to see what sort of knowledge he could extract. He brought a 5-barrelled *chillum* (straight pipe) along with him, and filled each barrel with a different sort of intoxicant: one held marijuana, another hashish, a third opium, a fourth chendool, and I don't recall what was in the fifth. Chendool is certainly the worst; I don't know what its equivalent is in the West, but it is very, very addictive.

"The baba, who thought he was being very smart, didn't realize who he was dealing with. I smoked that chillum, and asked for more. He refilled it, I smoked it, and I asked for more. For the third pipeful all he had left was a piece of hashish the size of a walnut. I finished that too.

"After I was done I told him, 'All smoked up? I'm so sorry; what I had to tell you has been burned up by all this smoking. Now get out!' How did I do it? Well, that's my secret. But it has something to do with mantras."

Pronunciation

I could see that mantras were really very useful things.

"Telling your mantra to someone else is fatal, but there are other mistakes which can also ruin you. Mispronunciation is one of the worst. The way a word is pronounced has a lot to do with its meaning. For instance, when you come in and I say, 'Hello, Robby, how are you?' with a pleasant voice and a smiling face, how do you feel?"

"I feel like you're in a good mood."

"Naturally, and so your confidence grows and you ask me questions. But if I just say 'good morning' in a cold voice you would immediately think, 'Oh, he is off his mood today,' and you would keep quiet or leave. Isn't that it?"

"It is, most certainly; I have done that before."

"Yes, I know. Well, it is the same with mantras. When the mantra is pronounced precisely and correctly the result is inevitable. One mantra pronounced in two different ways will have two very different, and perhaps even entirely opposite, effects. That is why the Vedas lay such stress on prosody and intonation. You cannot get any benefit from the Veda unless it is pronounced perfectly without any error. No mortals today know how to do this properly, so while I like to listen to you and Freddy recite certain Vedic hymns I don't want you to recite most other portions of the Veda aloud. The game is not worth the risk."

He paused to permit me to demonstrate compliance with his request, which I did by saying, "I will remember that advice, and I will pass it on to Freddy."

"Good. I tell all my 'children' to always recite their mantras silently, mentally, and I want you to do the same thing. How many people can properly pronounce Sanskrit nowadays? Very few. Sanskrit is called a mantric language because each of its words can be used as a mantra. This is why Sanskrit is not to be taught to just everyone. It should be taught only to those who can pronounce it properly, because if the name is incorrect the form will also be wrong, and then everything will be in a mess.

"Long ago conditions were different. Sometimes two Rishis would meet and gather all their best disciples together. One Rishi would say, 'This boy has been reciting such-and-such a part of the Veda with such-and-such an intonation, and just look at the result!' Then that boy would recite and the result would be demonstrated. The other Rishi would then show, with one of his own pupils, how an entirely different result could be gained by using a different intonation for the same passage. This is how Rishis used to compete."

Four Levels of Speech

"Of course the Rishis and their disciples knew how to pronounce Sanskrit properly."

"Yes they did, and they knew other things as well, including how to best make use of all four levels of speech." As I racked my brain for any information I might have collected on that subject, he continued. "You know, speech is not a product of the mind; speech is an independent creative faculty, a sense which operates through the mind. Kundalini is the power of an individual's self-expression, which means that speech is simply the verbal expression of Kundalini. This is why the lotuses of the chakras have Bija Mantras for petals, and why mantras are so important for awakening Kundalini.

"What sort of speech you use will be determined by where your Kundalini happens to be when you speak. As long as Kundalini is still asleep, or predominantly so, you will speak mainly in gross verbal speech, the speech used habitually by so-called normal people. As She awakens, your speech becomes progressively subtle. The sort of manifestation you can generate with your mantra depends on the sort of speech you use when you repeat it. Whatever a Rishi speaks will come to pass, because Rishis speak divine words. God's Word is very different from your words or my words because God's ability to create is very different from yours or mine.

"The four levels of speech are, from lowest to highest, *Vaikhari*, *Madhyama*, *Pashyanti* and *Para*. Vaikhari, vocal speech, is only for mundane things; it is physical speech, which always has an external object. Dullards and ignoramuses like you and me use Vaikhari to communicate. Vaikhari is only useful for living beings; once you are dead you can no longer hear Vaikhari. You can hear the thoughts of those you left behind, but not their words, which is probably just as well, since so often humans say one thing when they really mean another.

"Madhyama, as its name suggests, is midway between the mundane and the spiritual. People who have good intentions use Madhyama, which is mental speech, so its object is internal. Pashyanti is only for spiritual things. Pashyanti means 'seeing'—seeing with the divine eye, clairvoyance. Actually, it is not seeing; it is perception, because the physical organ of sight plays no part or a very minor part in it. The eye acts only as a vehicle for this perception. Immortal beings like Naths and Munis who are aware of the significance of what they speak use Pashyanti. And Para is meant only for Rishis. It is beyond perception; it is telepathic speech, the highest.

"In Satya Yuga almost everyone communicates telepathically by using Para. Even in Satya Yuga, though, there are a few bad apples in the barrel, a few people whose consciousnesses are relatively impure, whose natures are more animalistic than the others'. These people use Pashyanti and Madhyama, which are still basically non-verbal forms of communication but are grosser than Para. When most people in the world can no longer communicate by Para you know that Satya Yuga is over. Satya Yuga is *satya*, truthful, because of Para, which can never be false. Satya Yuga lasts for eons because it is so full of truth.

"People can do better sadhana in Satya Yuga than we can now because they can speak in Para. Anything spoken in Para is millions of times more powerful than anything spoken in any other form of speech, especially Vaikhari. You should never express your love for anyone in Vaikhari; the fire in your tongue will only burn it. If you want to express love, whether for a person or a deity, always use at least Madhyama, if not Pashyanti or Para.

"This is why kissing is so wonderful. When kissing you cannot repeat your mantra in Vaikhari, and you may not remember to repeat it in Madhyama either; probably whatever you communicate will be in something higher. Just as in *Vajroli* (sexual yoga), give and take of energy is possible through kissing. Passing energy through a kiss is one hundred times easier than passing energy through Vajroli because much less energy is involved. If you have the intention to share your energy with someone when you kiss them, even if you have no idea of the technique, some transmission will occur, though it will be less efficient.

"Kissing with the lips still leads to loss of energy, however. Some energy does get transmitted, but most is lost because the attention gets trapped in the softness of the lips. In the past people used to kiss only on the forehead. As time went on they gradually moved down the face until they got to the lips. Kissing with the lips usually leads to sexual intercourse; the upper and lower lips are related. Kissing so that the underside of the tongue is involved stirs up the most energy because of the many nerves there. But what is the use of stirring up a lot of energy if you can't communicate well in Pashyanti or Para? Then very little of your energy will be successfully transmitted during intercourse; most of it will be burned off in passion. This is Kali Yuga, when Maya, including especially the Maya of the body, is very strong.

"Vaikhari, Madhyama and Pashyanti are predominated by Tamas, Rajas, and Sattva respectively. Since the world as we know it, Maya, is the result of these Three Gunas, the use of these three forms of speech is limited, imperfect, because they all exist within Maya. The state beyond the Gunas is the state beyond Maya. That state is perfect because it is absolute, and that is Para. There is no need for mantra in Para; mantras arise as the intent filters down into the grosser levels of existence.

"Look at it this way, with the help of the sacred syllable Om. The three and a half coils of the Kundalini represent the three and a half letters of the word Om: a, u, m, and *anusvara* (nasalization) at the end. But Om also has a *bindu* (orthographic dot) over the anusvara. Anusvara and bindu cannot exist without one another. Bindu is a point: position without dimension, as they define it in mathematics. Anusvara is pronounceable in Vaikhari and Madhyama, but bindu can be 'pronounced' only in Pashyanti and Para. How do you pronounce a dot? You can't; but the intention to pronounce it can be present.

"Intention counts for nothing in Vaikhari; a clever con artist can have you in tears while he is laughing inside over how easily he has duped you. Intention counts for something in Madhyama, and for a lot in Pashyanti. But intention counts for everything in Para. In fact, Para is nothing but intention: the purified intention of a purified ego, a Kundalini Shakti which has been magnified millions of times by intense penance. Bindu is used when the Kundalini moves from the Vishuddha Chakra into the Ajna Chakra, when Shunya begins. That is the very nature of bindu: emptiness, which is the source of all sound, the field from which sound arises."

It seemed complex, so Vimalananda provided me with an Ayurvedic image.

"Here is another way to look at it. What is the word for 'sweet' in Sanskrit?"

"Swadu, or madhura."

"Of all the sweet things in the world only honey is called *madhu*, because only honey can offer sweetness to the body without being digested first. This is because honey has already been digested by the bees. *Madhura* has an extra 'ra' in it; that 'ra' refers to the Fire Element. Anything that is madhura must first be digested before its sweetness can be released into the system. Of all forms of speech only Para is truly madhu. Para goes directly to its target and exerts its effect immediately, just as honey does in the body. All other speech must first be digested by the hearer before its effect can be felt. Pashyanti is always madhura, at least, and Madhyama usually is, which is why they are so useful. But Vaikhari is only sometimes sweet, because it is under the control of all Six Tastes. This is why sometimes we speak sweetly, and at other times our words are sharp, or bitter, or sour, or salty, or cold and hard."

The Four Classes

"And all this is due to the chemical composition of the speaker's consciousness," I volunteered, as I thought I knew which direction Vimalananda's discourse was heading.

He nodded his assent. "And this chemical composition determines what sort of sadhana is appropriate for you, what you can succeed at. There is no lack of people today who claim to have located the keys to the Vedas, and who claim that they are living a 'Vedic' life, and teaching their disciples 'Vedic' sadhanas. Most of them are gasbagging; they are talking out of their wits. Think, for a moment, about the caste system. India has been plagued by casteism for centuries, but the caste system started out as something quite different from what it has become.

"The Vedic literature talks of the body of society in this way: the *Brahmanas* or priestly class are the head, the *Kshatriyas* or ruling class the arms and chest, the *Vaishyas* or merchant class the abdomen, and the *Shudras* or laborers the feet. Some imperialist Brahmanas have used this description to justify their domination of everyone else, but the only reason for this classification was to illustrate the innate tendencies of each group.

"Suppose you want to teach a mantra to a 'child.' If the 'child' is a Brahmana he or she will use the mantra to gain knowledge; the head represents knowledge. A true Brahmana will use this knowledge for self-realization and to assist others to realize. Any Brahmana who uses knowledge to control others is a false Brahmana. 'Brahmam janati iti Brahmanah' (a Brahmana is he who knows the Absolute Reality), so how many true Brahmanas do we have today? Almost none!

"If you teach a mantra to a Kshatriya you can be sure that he will go out and use it. This is what the chest and arms are for, to do things. And because Kshatriyas are natural rulers they will tend to use the power they gain from austerities to conquer others. Kshatriyas can go much, much farther with penance than Brahmanas can because Kshatriyas have a natural immunity to pain, and an innate belief in 'kill or be killed'; succeed or die. Once a Kshatriya starts something either he will finish it or it will finish him. A Brahmana often tries to do ten things at once, motivated by intellectual curiosity. A Kshatriya does only one, but does a thorough job of that one.

"King Vishwamitra was easily defeated by the Rishi Vasistha's spiritual power when Vishwamitra and his army tried to steal Nandini, the wish-fulfilling cow, from Vasistha. This defeat made Vishwamitra realize that physical might was infinitely inferior to spiritual prowess, and he decided to perform austerities until Vasistha himself acknowledged him as a *Brahmarshi* (a 'god among Rishis'). Once he decided upon this course of action he forgot everything else, and concentrated on it alone.

"Vishwamitra performed terrific austerities, and was awarded various divine titles by various divine beings, but not the title he wanted. Eventually he decided to force Vasistha to give him what he wanted; he was born a king, after all, and kings are accustomed to getting what they want. Vishwamitra harried Vasistha mercilessly, but nothing seemed to affect Vasistha, not even the death of all of his many sons. Finally Vishwamitra became totally desperate, and crept up in the underbrush near Vasistha's ashram, holding a sharp knife with which to murder the Rishi who would not acknowledge his accomplishments. Just as he was getting ready to strike he heard Vasistha say to his wife Arundhati, 'Of all the Rishis today only one deserves the title of Brahmarshi, and that is Vishwamitra. I don't know why he is so much against me; how have I offended him?'

"When he heard these words Vishwamitra dropped his knife and ran to bow at Vasistha's feet, saying, 'Please forgive me.' Vasistha murmured, 'But, Brahmarshi, there is no need for forgiveness. I am honored at your visit.' And he blessed him. It was all Vasistha's play, after all; the play of the Rishis is something that is very difficult to fathom.

"A real Brahmana is too refined to be the kind of monomaniac that Vishwamitra became—but then, Vishwamitra achieved towering heights because of his one-pointed determination. Brahmanas are not better than Kshatriyas, nor Kshatriyas better than Brahmanas; they are different, that's all. A good Brahmana tends to develop Kshatriya fearlessness, and a good Kashtriya, as he accumulates knowledge, should become more like a Brahmana. A good king is never a good fighter; it is impossible. To fight, one must be willing to kill, and killing always introduces crudeness into your nature. A good king is always absolutely refined and sophisticated, and such people are absolutely no good on the battlefield.

"Anyone who is a Vaishya, a merchant by nature, will commercialize the knowledge he or she is given; he will sell it to fill his belly. Look at what is happening in America. Almost all Americans are born business people, and they have merchandized whatever jnana they have received. It is part of their nature. And Shudras? Shudras are people who slog. It is important to know all this, and to know how to recognize these classes of people. If you teach a mantra to a 'child' and he or she misuses it, part of the bad karma comes onto you, because you taught it, enabling him or her to abuse it thereby."

"You say that this business of caste depends on your own inherent nature. What about this business that you have to stay in the caste you are born in?"

"This is a more recent addition. Every human has a physical and a mental heredity. Your physical heredity is the inheritance of all your ancestors. If your forefathers have been warriors for the past several generations the genes which produce aggression will be reinforced in you, and you will most likely make good warrior material. This was the basis for the old caste system.

"Originally the caste system was not rigid; you could do whatever you liked with your life. But if you were born into a family whose traditional occupation had been business for many generations it is probable that the genes controlling the skills needed to do business would have been reinforced through each successive generation, and you would naturally take to business, like a fish takes to water. It would literally be 'in your blood,' in each cell, in your genes and chromosomes.

"Darwin understood a little bit about heredity, but he applied it too exclusively to physical characteristics. In fact, the principle of natural selection applies to society as well. If you are a businessman and you have three children, you will most likely leave the family concern to the child who shows the greatest aptitude for the business. And if this happens for fifteen or twenty or thirty generations in a row, the business genes will become stronger and stronger as a result of this 'natural selection.' This is what happened for centuries in my own family; we have been businessmen for more than fifteen generations.

"Because the Rishis understood all about genetics they inaugurated the gotra system. Each Rishi had a different field of expertise, and could manipulate the genes and chromosomes of his disciples to make them fit to receive the knowledge he wanted to pass down. Each disciple would get a different piece of knowledge. Because this genetic pattern would be passed from generation to generation, the children born into that family would develop tendencies which would make it easy for them to succeed in mastering that branch of the Veda which the Rishi had assigned the family.

"Suppose you want to use the Vedas for your own personal sadhana. First you must know your gotra, so you can know which branch of the Veda you should study. Then, you have to know the mantra and ritual which apply to your branch. But most people have forgotten this mantra and ritual, and so they wander around in the labyrinth, and fail to achieve. I know the truth of this; it happened to my own father. He was an authority on the four Vedas and their commentaries, but he did not know the mantra and ritual which are appropriate for our branch of the Veda. He did not even bother with the mantra for Bhrigu, the Rishi who began our gotra. He had his own guru and guru mantra, but if he had first achieved success with the mantra for Bhrigu Rishi, Bhrigu himself would have taken over and directed his entire progress from then on.

"This esoteric knowledge was never available to the masses, to whom gotras are important only in marriage negotiations. Marriages within gotras have always been forbidden, to prevent inbreeding; the Rishis understood eugenics long, long ago. But marriages within 'castes' were encouraged—Brahmanas marrying Brahmanas, Shudras wedding Shudras, and so on—so that the parents would have a clear idea of what their children would be fit for, and the children would find it easy to fit into the roles which they were destined to play due to the weight of their inherited karmas.

"But we live in Kali Yuga now, when everything is jumbled up. If Westerners are by and large innovative and clever, it is partly because they are 'mixed breeds': Vietnamese marrying Swedes, Nigerians marrying Scots, and so on. This allows new patterns of genes to develop, which tend to promote new ways of looking at things. It also causes lots of uncertainties and difficulties for the children, whose new pattern of genes and chromosomes may attract a spirit who has little affinity for the parents who conceived it. This lack of mental affinity may lead to the break-up of the family, since they cannot see eye-to-eye on many subjects. A child who becomes estranged from the family and who cannot find any other place to fit in may become delinquent, which then leads to the break-up of society. So the mixing up of genes has

[158]

both good and bad effects.

"Different from your physical heredity is your mental heredity, which you carry with you from birth to birth. Your physical body represents your past, the karmas which you have performed whose fruits you are now reaping. Your subtle or astral body, which is your mind, is your present condition, and how you use your mind to act in the world determines your future. Every action produces karmas, and all these karmas are stored in your causal body where they wait patiently for the right moment to project into your mind. If you have been a musician for many births you will be drawn to music in this birth as well, even if you have to become the son of a farmer, because of the weight of your karmas. This is what happened to me: I had no interest in business at all, only in spirituality, because of my work in previous births.

"This explains why the caste system fails nowadays. Originally those spirits who had affinity for business would naturally gravitate to the wombs of businessmen's families. Now stronger influences like the manubandhana between children and parents operate, which allow persons of differing tendencies to enter the same family. If you are born into a family of priests and you had been a priest often in your previous births, no problem; but if you are a spiritual type born into a family of materialists, or an artist born into a family of butchers, there will be conflict.

"People are reborn with limitations because of the weight of their bad karmas. Those who have accumulated good karmas get the opportunity to be reborn in a higher state. Any human who has more good karmas than bad will naturally be better able to shine out than someone who has more bad karmas than good. The Rishis never said that the lower classes of human were animals; they simply recognized that the animalistic nature is greater in those people who have more bad karmas. The Rishis always want everyone to make progress according to their own innate capabilities, which is only possible when everyone recognizes their limitations.

"So when I talk about Brahmanas, Kshatriyas, Vaishyas and Shudras, I don't necessarily mean those terms to mean castes. The Rishis, who believed in 'free love' and were more like today's hippies than like today's bigoted Brahmanas, never believed in castes, and neither do I. When I talk about Brahmanas or Shudras I mean the innate tendencies of a particular individual, which are determined both by the parents and by the previous births. This is why I call your friend Freddy a Brahmana; his Brahmanical tendencies are much greater than those of most so-called Brahmanas! A human being is by nature either a priest, a ruler, a merchant or a laborer, and it is very hard to change this nature. We see the importance of pedigree every day at the racecourse; you can't deny it. You cannot discount human heredity either, but you may be able to go beyond it."

"By sadhana."

"By sadhana, which is why having just the right sadhana is very important. Now, can you explain to me the difference between 'shuddha' and 'shudra'?"

I was stumped there. "They differ only in one Sanskrit letter."

"Yes, they do. *Shuddha*, which means pure, contains 'dha,' which is replaced by 'ra' in *shudra*. The Sanskrit letter 'dha' indicates firmness, the power of concentration. Concentration creates purity. You are a chemist; isn't that what chemistry is all about, purifying substances so that those substances may be used in concentration?"

"Yes, I guess so." A good play on words.

"'Ra,' as you well know, is the Bija Mantra for Fire. In this case 'ra' stands for Jathara Agni, the fire of physical digestion. A Shudra is anyone who is concerned more with feeding his belly rather than his mind. All food except milk was once a living being, and even milk is extracted from a living being. We deprive other beings of life in order to preserve our own lives. Is this not extremely selfish? The willingness to kill and eat epitomizes this selfish desire to feed at another's expense. This attitude alone is sufficient to disqualify such a person from studying the Vedas, but there is another more practical reason: when Jathara Agni is strong Bhuta Agni is weak, and Bhuta Agni is essential for spiritual progress.

"Everyone whose Jathara Agni is stronger than their Bhuta Agni is a Shudra, and such people are not fit to recite the Vedas because of the effect of Fire on what they speak. This is why I have told you and Freddy not to recite Vedic mantras. Eventually, if your Bhuta Agni becomes very strong, this will no longer be a problem. But for right now, remember that the effect of Fire on bindu and anusvara is always 'r + na = rna,' karmic debt. When the Fire Element in your body acts predominantly on food it becomes impure, and in that condition reciting powerful mantras will only add to your karmic debts."

"Shudras and mlecchas are different, right?"

"Correct. Shudras are not mlecchas. A Shudra lives a life of toil, bringing things to life and then killing them for profit, but still follows a sadhana and retains faith in Nature. Shudras are part of the Vedic system, but mlecchas are totally outside the pale of the Vedas. A *mleccha* is, by definition, anyone who loves filth, anyone who loves meat, alcohol, drugs, sex, gambling and other indulgent intoxications and has few redeeming qualities. Some big-oted Indians call all Westerners mlecchas because they have eaten beef; they are concerned only with outer, not inner, purity."

Vimalananda knew that I had already been called a 'mleccha' a few times. "They refuse to see how Westerners like you and Freddy have changed their ways, and they also ignore the fact that millions of Indians are adopting the worst of the West and are converting themselves into mlecchas.

"But why should anyone be trying to do Vedic sadhana at all during Kali Yuga? It's just not possible to do it properly, especially not today when everything has become polluted. Other sadhanas are more appropriate for Kali Yuga. In fact, Kali Yuga is the age in which Shudras are better equipped to realize God than even Brahmanas are. Shudras can get experiences of God which Brahmanas can never aspire to. If you were to meet God in person what would you do?"

"I'm not sure."

"You would, I hope, fall at His feet. You would not walk up to Him, squeeze His cheek and say, 'Hello there, God! I've come to love you.' No, you would prostrate yourself to Him. Shudras know how to be humble; anyone who serves someone else must learn humility. Until you possess sincere humility you are not fit to touch the feet of God, or even the feet of a good saint. Brahmanas have to overcome the pride they have in their learning, but anyone who is humble can say, 'Lord, I am stupid and I know it. You are my only hope. Save me!' And He will."

"Which of these four types are you?" I meant it playfully, but Vimalananda's visage solidified perceptibly, and his words became weighty.

"You want to know who I am? By birth I am a Vaishya, a merchant's son. By training I am more advanced than most of the Brahmanas we have in India today. When I do my austerities and rituals my determination is superior to that of most born Kshtriyas. And when I go to the smashan for sadhana I am much worse than a Shudra; what I do there no Shudra would dare to do. It is too horrible for the average person. But, then, this is Kali Yuga."

TANTRA

Time, Eclipses and Nights

In his youth Vimalananda had studied astrology with Jina Chandra Suri, and I frequently witnessed his amazing ability to cast an accurate horoscope from a visitor's face alone. Though astrology is a respected means of diagnosis in Ayurveda it is no longer taught in Ayurvedic colleges, and I held out some hope that Vimalananda would teach me himself. But every time I asked for instruction he would refuse, saying, "You have more important things to learn right now." He relented only with regard to those aspects of astrology which he felt would be materially beneficial to my sadhana.

"Do you remember the three wise men?" he began one day.

"Sure," I replied confidently, for I had learned their names in Sunday School: "Balthazar, Melchior, and Caspar."

"Right. One was an Egyptian, one an Assyrian, and one a Babylonian. They all followed the cult of the Magi, which originated in Babylon and was practiced in all three countries. It was a sort of Tantra. These three men performed their calculations independently, and when they met and exchanged notes they found that they had all independently reached the same conclusion: a prophet would be born. Then they set out to follow the star, and they found Jesus.

"This was a unique occasion, of course, but it shows the practical benefits of astrology. In fact, knowledge of time can pay dividends in all sorts of ways. Suppose you should find a rare white-flowering Flame of the Forest tree. This in itself is not so easy; I have found only two in the whole state of Maharashtra, and they are entwined together. If you can find one, though, and if you can take its wood during a certain astrological conjunction you can work wonders with it; you can even fly. But you must collect the wood at precisely the right moment. All of Tantra is based on time. If you do something at the right moment you get the result, otherwise, no.

"Do you remember that first night you came with me for homa?"

"Of course."

"Do you remember what we did with the cow dung?"

It took me a moment, but then it came to me: "We took some cow dung, mixed it in water, put it in a pan, and then balanced a pestle upright in it."

"And that pestle remained upright as long as the eclipse continued. As soon as the eclipse ended it fell, automatically. You saw it; how do you explain it? How will scientists explain it?"

"I have no idea."

"We explain it on the basis of the strange gravitational effects that eclipses cause. Eclipses are excellent for people like you and me because their gravitational effects multiply the effect of our sadhana. If you do one hundred repetitions of your mantra during an eclipse it is like doing one hundred thousand repetitions on an ordinary day. If you offer one oblation into the fire it is like a thousand oblations. And nothing beats this time for offering prayers and performing rites for your deceased ancestors.

"Of course any time period which is this powerful can have negative effects also, so some precautions are in order. Never look at an eclipse; the rays have a very disturbing effect on the mind. A pregnant woman should not even go outside during an eclipse, lest her child be affected. Take nothing internally, not even water, while the eclipse is going on, and for as long as possible, up to twelve hours, before and after. If you can follow this niyama you can make any eclipse work for you."

He had told me all this before. I waited patiently for him to get to his point.

"Eclipses happen irregularly, of course; you cannot rely on them. Fortunately, though, predictable moments for enhanced sadhana occur every year, in every season. India is such a wonderful place that even our festivals occur at those times when success at specific forms of worship will be easiest. The Rishis systematized these festivals in order to help sadhakas become clairaudient and clairvoyant.

For example, Ma, the Great Goddess, is worshipped during three periods of Nine Nights during the year because during those periods it is easiest to come into contact with Her.

"The Rishis, who created the universe, are well aware of the effects of the various Yugas on our minds. They also knew that these doctrines that we have been talking about are far too complex and subtle for the average individual, so they created seasonal festivals. When the common folk celebrate these festivals their minds become somewhat detached from the mundane and attached to the spiritual, while those who know the esoteric significance of the festivals use them to spur their spiritual progress.

"The festival season in the fall begins with Shravana, the month in which Shiva is worshipped, during which Krishna is born. Then comes the Ganesha festival, followed by the fortnight during which the ancestors are placated. Once both Ganesha and the ancestors are happy Kundalini can be safely raised, which happens during Nava Ratri, the Nine Nights which are sacred to the Goddess. Finally, we have Dipavali, the Festival of Lights, sacred to Vishnu in the form of Krishna, when each vertebra of the spinal column becomes a point of intense, pure light.

"The spring festival season is similar: it begins with Ganesha's birthday, followed by Maha Shiva Ratri, which is as you know the most important night of the year for Shiva worship. A fortnight later comes Hutashani, or Holi, a harvest festival which commemorates the burning of the demoness Holika, and after another fortnight another Nava Ratri begins, which culminates in the birth of Vishnu in the form of Rama. The birthday of Anjaneya, the monkey god who is an incarnation of Shiva, follows six days later.

"During these various festivals there are four important nights (*ratri*) which are ideal for ritualists like me because they are meant for specific practices. The first is *Maha Ratri*, the Great Night, which is Maha Shiva Ratri; it falls each year on the night before the new moon during the lunar month of Magha (February or March). The second is *Krura Ratri*, the Cruel Night, which is Holi, the next full moon after Maha Ratri. Then comes *Moha Ratri*, the Night of Delusion, which is Krishna's birth night. Krishna deluded everyone with His Maya! It falls in the month of Shravana, usually during August. The last is *Kala Ratri*, the Black Night, the night just before Dipavali, the new moon of the month of Ashvin. Dipavali occurs in October or November.

"On Maha Ratri people try to stay awake all night long, because it is said that Shiva will come, just for a moment, to anyone who does not sleep at all. But Shiva is too clever for us mortals, and almost everyone who tries this nods off for at least a minute or two just at the moment when Shiva is near them. He has to test those who want to see Him, doesn't He?"

"I suppose so." I had already tried this a few times, and had dozed off, as predicted, for a few moments each time.

"Krura Ratri commemorates the burning to death of the demoness Holika by her nephew Prahlada. Holika possessed a magic cloak which would incinerate anyone who wore it. Her brother Hiranyakashipu, Prahlada's father, ordered her to kill Prahlada by throwing the cloak over his shoulders. When Holika took Prahlada on her lap he realized what she was going to do and slipped out from under the cape as she unfurled it. The cape fell on her and burned her alive.

"It took great power to destroy Holika, and that sort of power is obtained most easily at this time of year. Krura Ratri is useless for anything auspicious, but it is excellent for practitioners of black magic, especially the *Shat Prayoga*, the Six Rituals which cause death, delusion, discord, hatred, obstruction, and enchantment.

"Moha Ratri is meant for worship of Krishna, and Kala Ratri is best for sadhanas meant for obtaining control over spirits. A number of things can be accomplished on that day, like Munda Sadhana."

Munda means "skull."

"You require five human skulls for Munda Sadhana. Four are placed in the corners of a square and one in the middle. In between each pair of human skulls you put the skull of an animal. Which animals you use depends on the specific ritual you are doing and the result you want to obtain. When all the skulls have been properly placed and aligned in the proper direction you cover the whole thing carefully and sit on top of it. Then you begin your japa. Do not try this on your own! When I want you to do Munda Sadhana I will tell you."

Though Munda Sadhana interested me, I knew it would be useless to try to press him for details and so another question formed in my mind. Vimalananda answered it before I could speak.

"You have more than once asked me why, if Tantra is such a wonderful thing, the Six Rituals exist at all. This is a good question that has more than one answer. One reason they exist is to protect society. A priest has the responsibility to help defend the kingdom in which he lives, and these Six Rituals can be used to kill enemies of the state, to sow discord among foes, or to entice wavering rulers into alliances. They thus become agents of policy. They are also used in romance, business, and so on, but with less justification.

The Panchamamsa Sacrament

Central to many tantric texts are the rites of Panchamamsa—the five M's, and the Panchamamsa—the five great spiced meats. Since these passages in the tantras are written in symbolic "twilight" language they present several layers of outer, inner and secret meaning. The drawing shows the homa rite of the five great meats which are compounded to produce pills that confer various siddhis. The drawing shows the five meats of a man, cow, elephant, horse and dog, boiling in a Brahmin's skull with the five ambrosias of fat, faeces, urine, blood and semen. The skull rests upon a firepit of human heads above a downward pointing triangular fire mandala and an upward pointing wind mandala. The rite of Panchamamsa has a direct resonance with the practice of Munda Sadhana.

"More important than any political use, however, is their use in sadhana. Suppose you want to make use of enchantment. If you perform the prescribed ritual correctly, the first effect will be that all the women in your neighborhood will begin to find you irresistably attractive." I had read about this; one text says, in fact, that they will rush to you 'oozing copiously from their swelling, dangling vaginal lips,' meaning that the desire created in them by this ritual will completely overcome their modesty and discrimination

"So," I interrupted, "this is some sort of super-duper aphrodisiac?"

"No; it is not essential that women become sexually excited when they are exposed to this effect; but because most people strongly self-identify with the body most women will inevitably experience this attraction sexually.

"Attracting the women is not so difficult; the difficult part comes after they have been enchanted. If your mind is firm you will not be tempted at all by these excited women; you will continue with your ritual, knowing that you are making progress. Soon the enticement will extend to other female beings, especially those in the ethereal realms. If you can resist all the temptations they will offer, then you will eventually attract the attention of a female deity. If you are sure of yourself you may request Her to teach you like a Bhairavi; if not, you should regard Her as a mother and not permit sex to have anything to do with the relationship. Then you are made."

Wow.

"So I think you will agree that the Six Rituals can be quite useful." Indeed I did. "Enticement is certainly one way to achieve; but in my experience it is not as good a way as pure, selfless love. It is not easy to preserve your balance of mind when a passionate *Yakshini* (demigoddess) or *Naga Kanya* (serpent princess) entwines herself around your body; but there is no danger of falling when you can say to God, honestly, 'Make me an ugly prostitute for thousands of births, if You want to, but always keep me near You.' When you can honestly say this, you are ready to become a true devotee.

"You must begin all sadhana with niyama, but you do not have to practice niyama forever. There will come a time when you will be so absorbed that you will remember the deity at all times. At that stage you won't be able to remember how many repetitions of your mantra you are doing, much less any niyama. Finally you'll forget even to repeat the mantra. But that is a much higher stage.

"Hazrat Bulleh Shah, who eventually became a great saint, was very conscientious early in his career about following a strict niyama, and about keeping track of how much japa he would do. He counted his japa one by one on his *japamala* (rosary) until one day he overheard the milkmaid who brought him his milk talking to her best friend.

"The milkmaid was in the habit of giving milk away free to her lover, and the friend asked her, 'Don't you keep track of how much milk he is drinking? How else can you know how much he is eating into your profits?'

"The milkmaid replied, 'Can there be any acccounting in love? My profit is the love he gives me.'

"Hazrat Bulleh Shah sat stock still when he heard this. Then he looked at his rosary and thought, 'This milkmaid has taught me something today. If I really love God, can I do any kind of accounting with Him? What a fool I've been!' He threw the rosary away at once, and never used one again.

"In the beginning a rosary is useful, and strict attention to time is essential. Once you become devoted, however, limitations lose their meaning; in devotion, just as in romance, there is no such thing as the limitation of time or space. If you can remember what time it is, you have no capacity for love."

Nyasa

"But since right now I do know what time it is," I said, "all these anusthanas and so on will not only help awaken my mantra but will also help me develop my devotion."

"That's right."

"Are there other practices I should know about?" I asked, knowing well that he expected me to continue asking even if I did not know what to ask.

"Well, there is *nyasa*. Very few people talk about nyasa, because so few people know about it. But without nyasa there is no Tantra."

'Nyasa' was another word that no one had been able to explain to me clearly and accurately, so I began to pay even closer attention.

"'Nyasa,' which comes from the Sanskrit root meaning 'to place,' helps infuse your being with the power of the deity you are worshipping, by placing that deity in your body. If you have already purified yourself to some extent by removing a good bit of the heavy overlay of filth in your consciousness, you have dissolved part of your old being. This is a type of khandana. Now the deity's ethereal body can be invoked into you, and His or Her limbs will take the place of the ethereal limbs which you have dissolved or chopped and burned by your sadhana.

"Nyasa is important because it enables you to identify yourself with your deity. The more you think of and visualize your deity the subtler your consciousness becomes. When your thoughts have been perfectly transformed, so that there is no khandana of projected desires, then your being is transformed. Nyasa also helps you by balancing the energy in your physical body and making it steady, which makes your worship steady.

"Steadiness is always best in sadhana. This is why I encourage all my children to repeat their mantras mentally. Mental recitation is best because of the problem of pronunciation, and also because it enhances the firmness of your consciousness. When you recite a mantra nothing in your body should wag: not your limbs, not your cock, not even your tongue—nothing. Only when you are absolutely still and stable can the mantra's shakti fill you; any movement will distort the effect and weaken it."

"What about the people who claim that when you recite your mantra your body will automatically begin to move into strange contortions, which proves you are making progress?" I knew what his answer would be.

"It's all just so much bull. If you are singing *kirtans* and *bhajans* (devotional songs) you may be so overwhelmed with devotion that you will begin to dance. That is a good thing; it shows that your kirtan is doing what it should. *Kirtana* actually means *kartana* (cutting) of karmas; the 'i' indicates that it is done musically. As your karmas are cut and you feel lighter, won't you dance? But this has nothing to do with mantra sadhana, for which your body must be firm.

"When you do it properly nyasa can be very powerful. Once in the jungle I met an old sadhu, whom I saluted respectfully. He got wild: 'Why don't you touch my feet to show respect to me like you know you should, you insolent young fool?'

"I told him, 'Maharaj, I am happy to do that, but I have been busy practicing my nyasa. If I touch your feet you will be finished, which I don't want to happen. That is why I do not touch your feet. If you insist, give me your wooden sandals and I will salute those.'

"When he did I touched them, and they turned to powder. He got the shock of his lifetime, and realized what kind of force he was dealing with. I don't claim that I am so great and powerful," he added, seeing a certain glint in my eye, "this is just the result you get when you do these practices correctly."

"I remember your telling me that each syllable of the Vedas is supposed to be pronounced with emphasis on a different part of the body; is this is a sort of nyasa?"

"Yes. There are so many things that are only hinted at in the texts, that most people never even suspect their hidden meanings. Always remember that both the Vedas and the Tantras are interested in the external mainly as a symbol of what is going on internally. Consider this: that aspect of pranayama which is concerned with holding your breath is called *kumbhaka*, from the word *kumbha*, which means pot. But which pot?"

I had no idea, which seemed to irritate him a little; since I had been studying Yoga I suppose he expected me to know. But no one had yet explained it to me, so how was I to know?

"Here the pot they mean is the pot of the torso, the chest and abdomen, in which you can store prana. You have seen how a potter makes pots; here you 'make' a pot by making your body completely steady. Once this happens you can proceed to the stage of kevala kumbhaka, when there is a cessation of breathing for minutes at a time. Only when there is kevala kumbhaka can your mind become completely firm, and your worship will only be as steady as your mind is."

"So this is what pranayama is for?"

"Pranayama is for what its name suggests: control of prana. Most of the people teaching Yoga think that this means you should achieve control over your prana by holding your breath. But kumbhaka does not mean actively holding your breath; it means the balancing of your inhalation and exhalation so that they cancel each other out. For kumbhaka to be of any value to you, it must be effortless; you must learn how to forget to breathe."

I had never told him the details of how I had strained myself by trying to hold my breath in the 'approved' Yogic way, but I knew that he knew anyway. Suddenly I became aware of how little most people who try to teach Yoga really know about it.

"So as far as pranayama is concerned, the 'pot' means the body. But don't assume that pots always represent the body! Oh, no! What meaning a pot, or anything else, has depends on the specific practice. Every part of a Tantric ritual is significant, but you can't just do guesswork about it; you have to know its precise meaning.

"You probably have seen that in formal ritual worship there is always worship of a pot. During Nava Ratri, when we worship Ma, a pot is the central focus of attention. The pot, here called *ghata*, is infused with shakti in the procedure known as *Ghata Sthapana* (The Establishing of the Pot). Now, what do you think the 'pot' represents here?"

I didn't hazard any guesswork.

"Here the pot is the pot of the head, filled with Amrita and other 'juices' or hormones, just as during the ritual the pot is filled with water before shakti is invoked into it. We worship the pot to make our minds firm, and to fill our minds with energy so that our worship during the Nine Nights will be totally steady."

"Which will help to awaken Kundalini in a controlled way."

"Exactly. As soon as you learn to control your Kundalini Shakti She will be at your disposal. But remember: only one who knows Shakti can control Her. If you hang a sword on your wall it may injure a child who tries to play with it or a servant who comes to dust it. As long as it exists, even for thousands of years, a sword retains its inherent nature, which is to slice, to sever. This is the true test of shakti: there should be no limitation of time."

"Another reason why it is difficult to control Kundalini."

"You should say, 'why it is almost impossible,' because the average person's personality is simply not strong enough to deal with cosmic energy. Which is why I say, over and over again, that the only safe way to awaken and raise Kundalini is to personify Her. Convert Her into a goddess and worship Her, love Her like your Mother, and then you will be safe.

"I always prefer to call Lord Shiva's Grand Consort Uma, instead of 'Parvati' or one of Her other names because 'Uma" is made up of the same letters which make up the word 'Om,' which is actually 'Aum.' Uma is not inherently different from Aum any more than Shakti is different from Shiva; they differ only in form. 'U' stands for Vishnu, the Preserver. 'Uma' is therefore 'U' + 'Ma,' 'the Mother Who Always Protects,' who shields the child from any danger or calamity. What can be higher than that? You can achieve Uma if you can learn how to love her.

"And if you want to learn how to love Ma you need to learn how to love Her creations. Every being has its own variety of love, some of which we humans can't even comprehend. I personally think rocks have the best form of love, because they are so stable, so firm. Once they love you they never change. A rock has its own forms of expression that you may not be able to understand. Suppose you heat it. After a certain temperature it starts to flow; it makes an offering of heat and light to you. How many people understand how to love a rock? Very few, but those who do, know something of how to love Ma."

He left me with that thought to think about until our next conversation, at the end of the next Nava Ratri.

Vimalananda usually went into retreat during Nava Ratri, fasting and repeating mantras, requesting his beloved Tara to enter and enliven him. I loved to meet him on the day he finished his worship, for he was quite a sight to see. His entire countenance would be filled with an intense other-worldly radiance, and the talks he would give in the expansiveness of that mood were particularly pleasing.

On this occasion he began: "Even yogis and sadhus are not spared the poison of ahamkara. One day someone was reciting some verse from Tulsidas, and suddenly my friend Chotu said, 'Why are you repeating what those fellows used to say as if it were because of them that they had written it? If they were really sincere in their absorption in God why should they have added their own names to so many of their verses? Was it necessary for them to write so often "Kabir says" or "Raidas believes" or "in Tulsi's opinion"? Why should that ahamkara of name be there? Why should they worry about whether future generations will praise them as the authors? If their words are really *prasadika vani* [words gifted from God], then how can the poets be considered the authors at all?' The other fellow didn't know what to answer. What could he answer? Chotu was right. Sometimes Chotu says the most amazing things."

"So even doing intense sadhana and developing great devotion, as all these saints did, is no guarantee that ahamkara will be totally kept in check," I suggested.

"It is no guarantee at all. So long as you retain your individual existence ahamkara must identify with your personality, even to a very tiny extent—and even a single thought of 'me' and 'mine' is enough to ruin everything."

"What is the answer, then?" I asked, despairingly.

"The answer? You know the answer: Throw yourself at God's feet. Offer everything you have to God, including your very existence. If your donation is honest, God will accept it, and will direct your path from then on, so long as you always remember Him or Her. The moment you forget God, 'you' return. I have told you many times, and I still maintain, that it is much easier to surrender to a personal God than it is to surrender to some cosmic form. It is all well and good to appreciate the vastness of the cosmos, but how can you grab hold of it to love it? You can't; but you can grab hold of Krishna, or Ma, or Whoever, though, and love Them.

Mental Worship

"Now, although there are many different ways to worship, I have always believed it is best to worship mentally, if you can. Physical worship is always limited, especially now during Kali Yuga, when not even the experts are always able to do their physical worship properly. Even the most proficient devotee must occasionally make a mistake in his or her ritual; even the best trained mouth must sometimes mispronounce a mantra. And in some sadhanas if you make even a minor mistake you are gone. To avoid all possibility of error it is always better to worship mentally instead of physically. There is nothing to misplace, nothing to spill, and no fear of mistake. This is what the Tantras mean when they call for 'internal sacrificial rites.' Do you think this is so easy? In almost every case nowadays only the show remains; the internal techniques have been lost, except to the chosen few.

"You can do any sort of worship internally. I have taught you to perform homa, no doubt, but homa is an external form of worship, and its limitations are those of all other external forms of worship. It is often easier to do external worship in the beginning so that you do not have to visualize everything you are offering, but everyone must eventually progress from external to internal worship. The special value of homa is that it purifies the Fire Element, which controls the sense of sight. As the Fire Element in your body becomes purer and your Bhuta Agni increases, your ability to visualize, which is utterly essential for internal worship, will improve. You are going to learn quite a lot about internal worship by the time I am through with you.

"Let's start with fire worship. Even if you cannot perform homa with an external fire every day—and how many people can nowadays?—you can still do homa every day and get benefit from it if you offer to your digestive fire everything you put into your mouth. Yes, it is not so pure as a well-tended external fire, but it is always ignited, always ready to accept offerings. You don't even need any special mantras; just offer each bite with the mantra you repeat daily, and see the result. This is a form of internal worship.

"Orthodox people go to temples, but I believe that the true temple is inside the mind. Why waste time worshipping physical objects when you have everything you need inside your own mind? Your concentration will be much better if you perform internal worship, because you do not have the distractions that trouble a person performing external rituals: the constant worries of obtaining the right substance at the right time, misplacing something, spilling something else. It is much easier to self-identify when your mind is not distracted by external things, even if they are your articles of worship. On the inside, everything is always ready for your use, if you make the effort to locate it.

"It is useful to worship in a temple that is filled with Shakti, true; but how many of those are there nowadays? A temple will be useful to you only if its *Prana Pratishtha* has been properly performed. Prana Pratishtha is the rite by which life-force is infused into the image, making it live. Every temple has had a Prana Pratishtha done for the image which is worshipped therein, but if the Prana Pratishtha is not done properly the image will not come to life. You can test this at the very end of the Prana Pratishtha ceremony when a mirror is offered to the image, so that deity which has been invoked into the image can see itself. If the job has been properly done, the mirror will shatter. Only then can you say the image has any power, not before.

"Even if an image has no power it can still act as a focus for your mind to concentrate on, of course. The only disadvantage of mental worship is that the mind has no such focus until you create one."

"This is a big disadvantage for most people."

"Yes it is. Many people come to me and claim to meditate for one and two hours at a time. I always tell them, 'First learn to concentrate and then you can meditate.' Try to concentrate on one thing for even three minutes and you will find that it is impossible unless you have had long practice in that department. Then try to imagine keeping all your articles of worship fixed in your mind for an hour or more, and you have an idea of the effort required for real mental worship. But it is definitely worth it.

"Once there was a poor man by the name of Bulaki Das who worked as a farm laborer for a big landlord just so he could get something to eat. He got into the habit of taking a half-hour break before his lunch and performing mental worship. After some time he found it so enjoyable that he began to sit for an hour, then two hours, three hours, and sometimes longer. The other laborers had no idea what he was doing, of course, and became indignant about it. They told the landlord, who came out to the field one day to see for himself.

"Back then landlords could do anything they pleased to their workmen, and in this case when the landlord saw that Bulaki Das was not working he gave him a good kick. Bulaki Das awoke from his trance and said, 'Oh my, look what you've done. I was giving food to all my saints, and only the yogurt was remaining; but now you've disturbed all that.' Then he opened his hand to show that the yogurt which had been in his palm had fallen to the ground. Bulaki Das's concentration had been so intense that the yogurt was actually created, in the physical world, as a result of his mental worship.

"When the landlord saw the little mound of yogurt on the ground near Bulaki Das's hand he immediately realized his mistake, bowed to him, and took him as his guru. They both became saints; they belonged to the Sant Sampradaya, like Dadu and Rajab.

"There is nothing higher than perfection in mental worship. You can actually create whatever articles you offer mentally, just like Bulaki Das did. You do run the danger of becoming totally useless to the world, of course, because the joy you get from your mental play is far more intense than any physical joy you might experience. When you advance far enough into mental worship your deity will come and play with you, and then you get yourself absolutely lost in that play. Beautiful!"

"It almost sounds too simple," I said suspiciously.

"Well, let's put it this way. Even a pashu can somehow or another perform ordinary physical, adhibhautika worship; but Kundalini must be at least partially awakened if you hope to perform internal, adhyatmika worship, since only when Kundalini is awakened does Bhuta Agni become truly ignited, and without a strong Bhuta Agni you will never be able to create a firm image in your astral body. But there is another form of worship also: the astral, or adhidaivika.

"Let's assume you are worshipping Ganesha. Externally you can offer things dear to Ganesha, such as sugar cane, into a physical fire with an appropriate mantra. Internally you offer your mantra of Ganesha into the fire of your Bhuta Agni. You must make use of your own personal goddess, your Kula Kundalini, in order to perform the adhidaivika worship. Kula Kundalini is essential to adhidaivika worship because only Kula Kundalini knows how to locate Ganesha.

"If you want to do adhidaivika worship, first make your Kundalini Shakti descend to the Muladhara Chakra where you make Her self-identify with Ganesha, the presiding deity of that chakra. Kundalini can self-identify with anything; by Her perfect self-identification with Ganesha She actually becomes Ganesha, and then Ganesha Himself performs the worship. Only when the deity exists within your own body can you do perfect worship. Then you know exactly how to propitiate Him or Her, because you have *become* Him or Her."

"And so the Tantras say, 'First become Shiva, and then worship Shiva.'"

"How else can you comprehend Shiva, unless you have become Him?"

Hmm. Just as I was about to proceed with this line of questioning some guests arrived, and Vimalananda deftly changed the flavor of the conversation. Clearly he expected me to work on this for awhile.

Ganesha

Vimalananda delivered the next in this series of musings at a Ganesha temple. I can no longer recall which temple it was, for he was very fond of Ganesha and we paid regular visits to several images of the elephant-headed god. The area around Poona has been associated with Ganesha worship for centuries, and Ganesha is still one of the most beloved of deities of that region.

After we had finished our worship and were relaxing, he began to address me thus:

"You have to be able to deal with all sorts of temptations when you start to raise Kundalini, because your prana will try to move in unusual ways. This is why sadhana of Ganesha is so important. Ganesha is 'Gana' + 'Isha,' 'Lord of the Attendants.' Usually people think of the ganas as spirits who are Shiva's attendants, but in Kundalini Yoga the ganas are the sense organs. Ganesha is Lord of the Senses; He is also called the Remover of Obstacles, because if He becomes pleased with you He will remove all obstacles from Kundalini's path as She rises.

Shiva Yantra   **Ganesha Yantra**

"The Muladhara, where Kundalini sleeps, which is the seat of the Earth Element, of gross physicality, is ruled by Ganesha. This is why you must worship Ganesha before you worship any other deity. You must request Ganesha to permit you to go beyond your physical nature, to admit your consciousness into the astral regions. Ganesha's blessing is essential for Kundalini to be able to leave the Muladhara Chakra. You know the story of Ganesha's birth, I think?"

I did. "Parvati, Lord Shiva's Grand Consort, created Ganesha from the dirt on Her body to protect Her privacy while She bathed. Ganesha was on guard when Lord Shiva arrived and wanted to go in to His wife. Ganesha prevented Him from doing so, and since Shiva did not know who Ganesha was, a battle ensued, during which Shiva slew the boy. When Parvati came to know of this She became so enraged at the loss of Her child that She threatened to destroy the entire universe, and would have done so had Shiva not placated Her by replacing Ganesha's severed head with the head of an elephant. Then She calmed down."

"And now what about the esoteric meaning?"

"I'm not sure."

"Ask me about it. The name 'Parvati' means 'She Who is born from the mountains'—in this case, the chain of 'mountains' known as the spine, within which resides the spinal cord. Parvati is the Kundalini Shakti. 'Chain' is a good word to use here: until you awaken and free Kundalini, the spine acts as a chain to bind you down to earthly existence. Ganesha was created from the dirt on Her body—the Earth Element, the Element associated with the Muladhara Chakra. Shiva, the individual's consciousness, tries to break through to the dormant Kundalini by force, but this threatens to be the end of the sadhaka, because the Muladhara is the 'root support' of the body. When Shiva realizes this He regenerates the Muladhara with the help of an elephant, a beast known for its intelligence.

"If you want to awaken Kundalini, therefore, it is best to allow this intelligence to direct the awakening, instead of barging in like a bull in a china shop and wreaking havoc on yourself. Instead of meditating on the Muladhara Chakra and trying to forcibly open it, it is wiser to transform it, with Ganesha's help.

"Now here's a question for you: how did it happen that Lord Shiva, Who knows past, present, and future, Who is Parvati's husband—how did it happen that He could not even recognize His own son?"

A good question. I couldn't open my mouth.

"Think about it for a while. You know, Ganesha is one of the gentlest of gods, if properly approached, most helpful and very sweet. But He can also get upset. He is a small child, and you know how children can be when they become angry. And think of how wild elephants can be when they become angry! When Ganesha does lose His temper He changes in a moment from the Remover of Obstacles to the Creator of Obstacles—and then you are in real trouble.

"Once I gave a man a Ganesha mantra and told him that after forty days of repeating it Ganesha would come and stand in front of him."

I knew this story well, but Vimalananda's tone of intense seriousness alerted me to his strong desire for me to listen to it yet again.

"Unfortunately something happened to break his niyama before the forty days were up, so I ordered him to start all over again. Finally, after he completed forty days, nothing happened. I told him, 'You are very close now; don't stop. Continue it for just a few days more.'

"The man said, 'Look, this is all foolishness, there is nothing behind it. I can't stand being away from my wife. I am going home now to have some good sex.'

"I warned him, 'You've gone too far for that now. Ganesha will become very angry if you do that, and I won't be able to save you. Just do it for three more days and I guarantee that you'll succeed.'

"What more could he have wanted? It was only a question of three days. But Mahakala, the God of Death, must have already grabbed hold of him. He told me, 'No, I'm through listening to you. I've really got to have some sex. Good-bye!'

"At first his wife tried to prevent him from climbing on top of her, but he forced his way into her anyway and enjoyed her, twice. Satisfied with his labors he fell asleep.

"In a dream he saw an enraged elephant charging at him. He tried to run but it was useless. When the tusker caught up with him he gave the man a solid blow to the jaw with his trunk. The next morning the man's entire face, jaw and all, was swollen to twice its normal size. He was taken to the hospital. The doctors couldn't find out what was wrong with him. I went to the hospital too, and he asked me, from his hospital bed, if I could rescue him. But there was nothing I could do, because his nervous system was blown to shreds. It was too late; he had gone too far. He died that night. After that experience I decided I would only assist people in their own sadhanas, and never suggest new sadhanas to anyone.

"Iron discipline is necessary whenever you commit to a sadhana; without it something is sure to go wrong. So don't start trying for this kind of perfection of a mantra unless you are so obstinate that you will finish it. If you decide that you must have meat for a few days, or that you must have drinks or sex, then you are ruined. Not only will you never succeed, but you will have to suffer for trying to act smart. If you know your willpower is limited it is better not to do anything at all. To break your vow and then say, 'Oh, I'll ask forgiveness of God and He will look the other way,' is only cheating yourself, no one else. Once you commit yourself to a sadhana you are really at risk unless you finish it off properly."

"Do you mean that God will not forgive any mistakes?"

"Of course not! God is always ready to forgive, if you go to him with humility. But there is nothing humble about this sort of sadhana; you are demanding attention from God. You are saying, 'Come on; I want to play with you on your terms.' If you tell God that, then you had better be ready for whatever God wants to dish out."

MUSIC

Teaching me about, and getting me involved in, the worship of Ganesha was part of Vimalananda's grand design for my development. As he explained, "Our method is very systematic: first you worship Ganesha, at the Muladhara Chakra; then He gives you the permission, and the know-how, to worship His mother, Ma, Who takes form with the help of your Kundalini Shakti. Ma teaches you how to worship Her Grand Consort, Lord Shiva, at the Ajna Chakra, and once you achieve Shiva He will take you to Vishnu in one of His forms: Jesus, Rama, Narayana or, if you want it and you are destined for it, Krishna, in Goloka."

Vimalananda was an expert musician, both vocal and instrumental, and many mornings I sat quietly for hours listening to him practice, sometimes accompanying him on the tanpura. Once or twice a week Narayanrao Indurkar, a reputed tabla player, would come to accompany him, and after the practice was over I would serve them tea while they told stories of the old maestros. It was in the aftermath of one of these sessions that, following Narayanrao's departure, Vimalananda introduced me to music as a sadhana.

"What is music?" he asked rhetorically as I lit him a cigarette. "People have been trying since the beginning of time to find out. What is that thing which can please us with its harmony? Sound, when it becomes music, is the only thing which can so possess people that they drop all their inhibitions and, just for a moment in this precious life, they dance! *That* is the real music. 'If music be the food of love, play on!': Shakespeare, *Twelfth Night*. I think I remember my Shakespeare."

"You certainly do."

"Real music has emotion in it, and this is why real saints love music so much; it helps them do their work. Shiva is rhythm, the father of music, and His Shakti is the mother, the sounds or notes. The child is Ganesha, the song: Rhythm + Notes = Song. Ganesha has an elephant's head, so he never forgets; he remembers everything, just as through song you can remember your true personality. And the musician? He is the bee who carries the pollen from flower to flower, giving rise to creation. And it is he who really enjoys the bliss of this creation. The gods, and especially the avataras, are those celestials who create and who enjoy the music of the spheres."

I had read that scientists have learned that the sun is ringing, just like a bell; probably one component of the physical aspect of the "music of the spheres," I thought to myself.

"The greatest music is written by *gandharvas*, celestial musicians who incarnate on earth. When a gandharva comes down to Earth he can't remember his previous state, but subconsciously longs to return to it. Gandharvas find it as hard to relate to ordinary humans as humans find it hard to relate to animals, and most gandharvas lead miserable, misunderstood lives. Many of the great Western musicians were gandharvas, like Beethoven, Brahms and Mozart. Even Strauss was a gandharva, but he was lucky; he had a son to follow him, someone who could understand him.

"All this emotion comes out in the music. A gandharva will be a prodigy, a musician right from the beginning, and anything he produces will be good, no matter what variety of music he might learn in this lifetime. Think of Beethoven, who composed some of his greatest work after he became deaf! What concentration he must have had, and what innate talent!

"Gopal Naik was a gandharva; music flowed from the very pores of his body. Unfortunately he lived in the time of the Emperor Akbar, and Tansen, Akbar's chief musician, became so jealous of his prowess that he conspired to have him killed. Gopal's body was dumped in the deep jungle.

"When Gopal Naik's mother learned of her son's murder she set out to find his bones so that she could burn them. When people asked her, 'How will you know whether or not the bones you find are his?' she would tell them, 'He had music right down to his bones; I will know them.' As she wandered through the forests of North India she would hold up to her ear every human bone that she found, and would listen to it intently.

"Finally one day she heard faint music coming from one of the bones she

[182]

held up to her ear, and then she said, 'These are my Gopal's bones.' She collected them and cremated them."

This story may well be apocryphal, but Vimalananda cared nothing for historical accuracy. He was interested only in "emotional accuracy," that attention to emotional detail which enables a tale to so possess a person that he drops all his inhibitions and, just for a moment in this precious life, he weeps from the fullness of his heart.

"Jim Reeves was a gandharva; that's why I love his songs. Like many gandharvas, he had an untimely death. He died in a plane crash; he 'fell to Earth.' What a rich baritone voice he had! And the wordings to some of his songs are really beautiful.

"My favorite song of his is 'You Love Me Daddy.' I don't know why, but I always cry when I hear that song. It's about a little boy who doesn't always do what his daddy wants him to do but whose daddy loves him anyway, because the little boy is his own son. No matter how naughty a child is its parents always love it. Whenever I hear this song I think of my own Big Daddy, my mentor. No matter how much I have disobeyed my mentor he has still loved me, in a way in which no one else has ever loved me. I don't think anyone else will ever be able to love me in the same way; certainly not a human.

"In fact, why don't you turn on the cassette player and let me hear 'You Love Me Daddy' right now?"

I did so, and the song brought tears to all four eyes in the room, as we both knew it would. After it was over Vimalananda was silent for several minutes while the wave of emotion swelled, broke, and receded, and then he spoke again.

"The right kind of music acts as a way of bringing light into one's consciousness. Music is a manifestation of sound, and sound exists wherever there is energy, which means heat, which means light. When a Siddha hears music he can self-identify with it, and with his astral body he can go to wherever the music is. When a sadhu hears music he is so overwhelmed with emotion that from an exuberance of joy things begin to happen.

"And it doesn't matter if it is recorded or live music. Whenever I hear 'La Paloma' I am always reminded of my guru and the fun we had together. After I hear it a few times the work just gets done on its own. You've seen it happen, Robby; you know. People have made millions out of me by playing 'La Paloma.'"

He looked at me sideways for a moment, and then said, almost in the tone a child would use to beg candy from a well-meaning but uncomprehending adult, "Would you play 'La Paloma' for me, just once?"

He knew that, after his heart attack, intense emotion would not do that organ any good. He also knew that Roshni, his foster daughter, was stricter in enforcing this sort of restriction than was I. I knew that he could perfectly well turn the stereo on himself, so I acquiesced and turned on his current favorite of the many versions of 'La Paloma' in his tape collection.

This time he did not weep; his face became calmer and clearer, and when he spoke again he did so resolutely.

"My Senior Guru Maharaj is the shrewdest possible person. Normally no one can get anything out of him. But if you give him the right type of music he will experience such intense emotional bliss that he will give away the results of years or decades of penance without knowing it. Only when the emotion leaves him will he realize what he has done.

"Once he and I and a Mr. Bilimoria hosted Acchan Maharaj, a descendent of the court musicians of Nawab Wajid Ali Shah of Oudh. Wajid Ali Shah was a ruler who had been a gandharva. On Earth, he became a great devotee of Krishna, though he was a Muslim by birth. When his musicians Kalika Prasad and Bindadin played for him he would go into Bhava Samadhi, emotional highlights, and Krishna would enter his body and dance. Wajid Ali Shah was an expert at the variety of dance known as Kathak, and this expertise was passed down to Acchan Maharaj. His son Birju Maharaj is today the greatest Kathak dancer in all of India.

"So Acchan Maharaj had a good pedigree, and we were all looking forward to his dance. When he arrived, he sat down and drank one and a half bottles of whisky—alone. After quite some time had passed we asked him if he would kindly consent to show us a little of his artistry, but he snarled, 'Who can play percussion for me?' While we were thinking of how to deal with this problem he drank the last half of the second bottle of whisky—straight from the bottle.

"Suddenly my Senior Guru Maharaj took me aside and told me to prepare my car for a drive. We drove to a lamppost in south Bombay under which a Muslim man was standing. The man never said anything, and never looked up, but just got into the car. We returned to the house, and when Acchan Maharaj was shown his accompanist he snorted, 'No one has yet been born who can accompany me.'

"To make a long story short, not only did that Muslim fellow accompany Acchan Maharaj, he began to make Acchan Maharaj dance to his own 'tune.' And when a percussionist can do that, well, he is something. We all watched amazed, entranced both by the artistry of Acchan Maharaj, who was indeed great, and by the wizardry of that Muslim on the tabla. My Senior Guru Maharaj, music-lover that he is, was ecstatic. Finally tears came out in Acchan Maharaj's eyes and he said, 'I'll pay anything to have this man as my permanent accompanist.' But my Senior Guru Maharaj said, 'He doesn't play for money.'

"All this time the tabla player had said nothing, nor had he looked up. Nor did he look up when I dropped him off in front of the same lamppost from which I had picked him up. I doubt that he was a human being, the way he was playing. What a night!"

Silence descended for a few moments, and then lifted again.

"If music can affect its listeners so powerfully think what it must do for its players. A real musician becomes completely devoted to his or her music. There was one *sarangi* (Indian fiddle) player I knew who used to carry a bamboo with him everywhere he went. Even when he went to buy vegetables, he would haggle about the price and pay with one hand while constantly practicing fingerings on the bamboo, as if it were the neck of his sarangi, with the other. This is real dedication to music, the kind of dedication that is necessary in sadhana also.

"Music should not be an end in itself for you; it should be a sadhana, a means of getting to your goal. Mantras are one way in which to make use of sound in sadhana; music is another. The Vedas are mantras set to music, but the Vedas are too far away for most of us, while music is available to everyone. If you are lucky, meaning if you have worked hard in previous lives and God is kind to you, your music can be sufficient to draw God to you."

"Regardless of whether it is Western-style or Indian-style music," I interrupted.

"Of course. Western religious music is very good, but it is limited; it can only make you realize the love of a servant for his master, or of a child for its father. Indian music can make you realize your deity in any relationship: as servant or father, and also as lover, spouse, or friend; as your own child, as your mother.

"The greatness of Western music is that many musicians together can cooperate to create a tone poem. An Indian musician paints his complete musical picture with one instrument only. Indians are good solo artists, but large ensembles and orchestras don't thrive here. But then, after all, sadhana should be done alone.

"In Indian music each *raga* (melodic scale) has a specific picture which must be visualized as you play or sing it. If you do it right the true image of that raga will manifest. For the Raga *Megha* (the Cloud Melody), for instance, you must imagine a cloudy sky and all its background. If you want rain you play Megha in a certain way and rain will come.

"If you play Darbari Kannada Raga properly, you will see the court of Akbar the Great, Emperor of India. He will be there smoking a little hookah; then he lifts a flower to his nose. Tansen wrote that raga by using the raga called Kannada and changing it slightly. If you play Kannada you won't get the same effect, because the tonal patterns are different."

"Isn't it true that one of the meanings of the word *raga* is 'passion'?"

"And that is what music should be: a matter of passion. Tansen had so thoroughly mastered the Raga *Deepaka* (the Kindling or Igniting Melody) that when he sang it at dusk all the lamps in the palace would light themselves, automatically. Once he sang Deepaka for too long, and he became overwhelmed with heat. For six months he was in agony; nothing relieved the heat until in a village he came across a pair of sisters, Tana and Riri, who were experts in Megha. When they sang Megha for him the heat finally abated. Even music can be dangerous!"

"And this had something to do with the Surya and Chandra Nadis."

"Naturally. The whole purpose of music is to help you stimulate your consciousness so that Kundalini can be triggered up. When Tansen overdid it his prana was affected."

"Maybe he should have been self-identifying with a deity instead of with a flame," I put in.

"Maybe so," said Vimalananda, laughing. "The great benefit of Indian music is that it helps you self-identify with your deity. Whenever Narsi Mehta (a famous poet-saint from Gujarat) played the Raga *Kedara* (the Field Melody), for example, Lord Krishna would come and dance before him."

"Can anyone learn to call Krishna with Kedara?"

"No, Kedara is not specific for Krishna; you would not necessarily see Krishna even if you learned to play Kedara perfectly. It is only because Narsi Mehta visualized Krishna dancing whenever he played Kedara that Krishna Himself would come to dance.

"You mean he used Kedara like you use 'La Paloma,' to remind him of Someone he loved."

"Yes, he made Kedara into his sadhana, and it got him into serious trouble one day. A sadhu asked Narsi for some money to go on a pilgrimage. Narsi wanted to help the sadhu but was broke, so he mortgaged Kedara to a grocer in order to get the money."

"He *mortgaged* Kedara? How could he mortgage a raga?"

"He promised never to sing it until the money was repaid. Back then people's words were their bond. If a man mortgaged his moustache to you, for instance, he would not fail to repay you because he would rather die than have his moustache shaved off. Think of what a tremendous penance this was for Narsi! He mortgaged the thing he loved best—the dance of Lord Krishna, which he could see whenever he played Kedara—to help someone else out.

"Unfortunately the sadhu never returned. That in itself would have been bad enough, but meanwhile those people who were jealous of Narsi Mehta's success had been busy poisoning the king's ears against him. Finally the king, Rao Mandlik, called for him and said, 'I hear that whenever you sing Kedara Lord Krishna appears. Do it now! Prove to me that you are not a false saint.'

"Narsi Mehta told him, 'Maharaj, I can't do it; I have mortgaged Kedara.'

"The king of course lost his temper at being refused, and said, 'Well, I see now that you are indeed a false saint. Tonight you shall be tied to a post in front of the Krishna temple so that you can reflect upon your crimes. If Krishna does not save you by tomorrow morning you will be executed.'

"Now Narsi Mehta was really in a fix. There was nothing for him to do but remember Krishna as he waited for sunrise. But Lord Krishna is never so cruel to His devotees. He loves His devotees more than anything else in the universe. That evening a mysterious person—it was Krishna in disguise—went to the grocer and paid Narsi's debt, and just as day was dawning the cancelled mortgage note wafted from out of nowhere into Narsi Mehta's hand. Narsi began to sing Kedara. Suddenly the locks on the door of the temple undid themselves, the doors flew wide open, and the necklace which was around the neck of the deity flew through the air and landed around Narsi's own neck. The cords binding him to the stake dropped away.

"This of course created a big commotion among the people who had gathered to watch Narsi's execution. They started to mob him, to get him to intercede with Krishna for themselves, and he started to run. They pursued him, close behind.

"Outside of town an Aghori was sitting, enjoying the excitement. As Narsi approached him, frantic, the Aghori said to him, 'Here, take the shelter of my back.' By the time the crowd arrived there was only the Aghori in sight, and Narsi Mehta was never again seen in the world of men."

Nada Yoga

"So any kind of music, Western, Indian, or anything else, can give you results if you are sincere about it and make it into a sadhana," I said.

"You can. I am sure that if Tukaram Maharaj, who lived here in Maharashtra almost four hundred years ago, were to come here to Bombay today and we were to play some nice Western song for him he would sit quietly and listen and enjoy it—or at least he would look as if he were enjoying it. All the time on the inside he would be hearing his mantra— 'Rama Krishna Hari, Jai Jai Rama Krishna Hari; Rama Krishna Hari, Jai Jai Rama Krishna Hari'—set to the rhythm and melody of the music.

"In my own case, whenever I ride a train pulled by a steam engine my own mantra starts to repeat itself in rhythm with the engine. The same was the case when I worked with textile machinery: the noise of the spindles would give me a rhythm. People who are serious about their mantras and put them into their hearts and souls will say them all the time. In fact, I personally find Western music better than Indian music for doing japa, because Western rhythms are simpler than Indian ones, which require more attention to avoid getting lost." Aha! No wonder he enjoyed the rock music I brought for him.

"Of course, there is more to using rhythm in sadhana than merely repeating your mantra to the rhythm of the driving wheels of steam locomotives or to the sound of the electric guitars of Barbados. I think you have heard me play the *Ganesh Paran* before."

"Yes, I have." It is a little-known rhythm designed to invoke Ganesha.

"Once, in a small Indian principality named Datia there was a *pakhawaj* (large two-headed drum) player named Khudav Singh. He was an expert at pakhawaj because he worshipped the Goddess Durga. In fact, before he would begin to play he would throw the pakhawaj into the air and Ma would strike it three times. Then he would catch it and start to play.

"The sister of the Maharaja, a young girl of sixteen or seventeen, loved Khudav Singh's music and used to listen to him play whenever she could. Eventually she fell in love with Khudav Singh himself. This enraged the Maharaja, who told her to give him up. When she refused, the Maharaja demanded that Khudav Singh reject the girl. But Khudav Singh said, 'She loves and appreciates my art. Why should I tell her to go away?' The Maharaja then said, 'All right, since you have disobeyed me you will be crushed under the foot of an elephant.' Kings dispense justice like that.

"The king invited all the people of the kingdom to the execution as a warning to them not to act foolishly like Khudav Singh had. The elephant was fed wine until its eyes became red, absolutely. The Maharaja asked Khudav Singh if he had any last request. He replied, 'My pakhawaj, which has been my life to me, should be crushed along with me.' He was given his pakhawaj. As the elephant advanced, Khudav Singh began to play the Ganesha Paran. When it is played properly Ganesha must come before you; He has no choice, He can't escape. This was a way for Khudav Singh to call his chosen deity: 'Mother Durga, please call Ganesha, help me!'

"Durga, who is after all Parvati in another form and as such is Ganesha's mother, requested Her son to aid Her devotee. Ganesha agreed, and entered the body of the elephant. The elephant then sat down in front of Khudav Singh and began to caress him with its trunk. For half an hour the soldiers prodded, poked, and goaded the elephant, but it refused to attack.

"Then the Maharaja realized his mistake and said, 'Let my sister be given to Khudav Singh, and let the elephant wander freely in my kingdom. Wherever it goes, those lands are to be given to Khudav Singh.' And until a short while ago Khudav Singh's family possessed those lands."

"Will the Ganesha Paran work for anyone?"

"It will if you know how to play it properly, and if you visualize Ganesha in the right way while you play it. It is a musical sadhana, created especially for the purpose of invoking Ganesha.

"All the various sadhanas which use music are part of *Nada Yoga*. In Nada Yoga you worship the *Nada Brahman*, the music of the spheres, the Absolute expressed as the sound Om, which emanates from Lord Shiva. If you follow this sadhana to its conclusion you will finally see that you and the universe are not different—One-in-All, All-in-One. This is what I mean when I say, 'Everywhere I see, everything is Me!'

"Anything that has sound has shakti, and all shakti has sound associated with it. The Absolute Itself is silent; It has no qualities whatsoever, which is why there is no Bija Mantra for Lord Shiva. Shiva has no melody to Him; He is pure rhythm, the father of music. This is why Shiva is always depicted carrying a *damaru* (small two-headed drum), the first musical instrument ever created. Since *laya* means both rhythm and dissolution, a Pralaya, the periodic dissolution of the universe, is merely the return of everything to the *Pra-thama* (first) *Laya*, the first rhythm: the Absolute. The sound 'Om' is the first sound to arise when creation begins, and it is the last sound to disappear at the time of the Pralaya. But even after the melody—the manifested universe—has totally disappeared, its rhythm lingers on, first as anusvara and then as bindu.

"You know that in Indian iconography Shiva wears a crescent moon on His forehead; do you have any idea of what that suggests?"

"None."

"In the Sanskrit alphabet the sign for anusvara is a crescent."

I slapped my forehead in disgust; I knew that!

He smiled. "Here the crescent moon is an external sign of Shiva's internal consciousness, a sign that His consciousness is full of Nada, and that if you worship Him your mind can be filled with Nada too, which will enable you to follow that sound back to anusvara and bindu, to the source of sound."

"Oh. Is the bull He rides on related to all this also?"

"Of course. One of the Sanskrit words for bull—*go*—also means both 'sound' and 'sense organ.' This indicates that Lord Shiva 'rides' His senses—He permits them to function but controls their movements perfectly—and that He moves with the help of Nada.

"I have told you that bindu is the source of all sound, which in the human begins with intention and culminates in vocal speech. Laya involves withdrawal of all our projections into bindu, the source. Speech begins with Para, progresses through Pashyanti and Madhyama, and then reaches Vaikhari, verbal speech. This is the path of *pravrtti*, creation. If you want to use sound to follow the path of *nivrtti*, the path back to the source, you have to begin where you are, in Vaikhari, and progressively refine your consciousness back through Madhyama and Pashyanti to Para, to bindu."

"Nada Brahman is central to Kundalini Yoga. You may recall that when Kundalini passes through the Anahata Chakra you hear the sound known as the Anahata Nada. It may sound to you like Krishna's flute or like Shiva's drum, depending on what sort of sadhana you are doing; it is the same sound, interpreted differently by different minds. At first you hear this sound in your right ear, because the left ear is meant for spirits. Remember this: when you hear someone talking only in your left ear it is sure to be a spirit.

"Each individual hears a slightly different nada. There are 108 *gatis* (gaits, or modes) of nada; $108 = 1 + 8 = 9$, the number of chakras in the body, according to Aghora. Which mode of nada you hear depends on your past karmas, present tendencies, ancestry, and other things as well. The gatis are many, but once Kundalini reaches the top of Her course you hear only one sound: the Nada Brahman, the Great Sound.

"All rivers go to the ocean and not vice versa. If the ocean were to go into all the rivers, what would happen to the rivers? They would be finished, and so would be the surrounding land. In sadhana of Nada that ocean is the ocean of *bhava*, intense emotion. The rivers are the nadis, and the land is the human body. First you follow your rivers into the sea, and then if you are meant to return to embodied existence the sea will flood the rivers, which will overflow their banks and fill you with an overwhelming divine intoxication, which is Bhava Samadhi. If you keep at it you will progress to Maha Bhava Samadhi, which can lead to Nirvikalpa Samadhi. Did you know that the story of Krishna and the gopis is actually a step-by-step description of this type of sadhana?"

"No."

"I'll describe it to you sometime," he said as we went into the kitchen for lunch.

Krishna and the Gopis

He described it one evening shortly thereafter, over Scotch.

"My family belongs to the *Pushti Marga*, the spiritual path (*marga*) whose greatest exponent was Vallabhacharya, who lived more than five hundred years ago. Some people translate 'Pushti Marga' as 'Path of Prosperity,' and others as 'Path of Grace.' But when I think of pushti I remember a phrase from the Maha Mrytunjaya Mantra." He looked at me expectantly.

"You mean, 'sugandhim pushti vardhanam'?" I asked.

"Yes. The Maha Mrytunjaya Mantra is addressed to Lord Shiva, the God of Death. When you repeat it you are requesting Him to preserve your life and enhance your welfare. Vallabhacharya's philosophy is called *Shuddha Advaita*, 'Pure Non-duality,' and follows the principle of 'One-in-All, All-in-One.' Vallabhacharya never taught people to run away from the world and become renunciates; he taught everyone to live a Vedic life, to live in the world without becoming part of the world."

"So this is also Advaita Vedanta?"

"Most certainly! Thus far you have been exposed only to the Advaita of Shankaracharya, and the proponents of that school want people to believe that theirs is the only Advaita Vedanta. They like to debate reality; it's only natural, since that is what Shankaracharya did his whole life long.

"Shankaracharya taught 'Brhamam sat, jagan mithya': while the Absolute Unmanifested is absolutely true, the cosmos, the Manifested, is *mithya*, false. But Vallabhacharya believed, as we Aghoris believe, that since God

[191]

created the universe, and pervades it, the universe is as true as God is, which means that everything is true, since everything is part and parcel of God. Vallabhacharya did not care too much for debate; he preferred to spend his time worshipping Krishna and enjoying the bliss of the nectar of His sweet name and form. I like to call the Pushti Marga 'the Path of Sweetness,' because of the many sweet songs Vallabhacharya wrote, in Sanskrit, about his Beloved. Probably the most famous of Vallabhacharya's songs is the *Madhura-ashtaka*, the 'Eight Verses in Praise of the Lord's Sweetness.' Of all deities only Krishna is Madhu: pure, unalloyed sweetness. In fact, one of His names is Madhava, the 'Sweet One.'"

"Why isn't this sect better known?"

"Well, there is a lot of esoteric meaning in their doctrine, which makes it too complicated to explain easily. The Gaudiya Math, from which the Hare Krishnas developed, teaches devotion to Krishna in His exoteric, external form, and rejects any kind of esoteric doctrine; this makes it easier to comprehend. The Pushti Marga believes both in the obvious and the hidden, and that is why I think it is superior, not just because I was born into it. If Westerners were to study Vallabhacharya's teachings they would really learn something about Advaita Vedanta, about the hidden meanings of Krishna's play, and about how to be sweet.

"Krishna was something else entirely," said Vimalananda appreciatively, shaking his head in amazement. "You know, the word Krishna has two and a half syllables, and so does the word *prema* (romantic love). So it is only natural for Krishna's play to be full of prema. But He is no ordinary lover. In fact, He is a true thug; that's why He is called Chaliya, 'the Inconstant One.' He will play about with you when you worship Him. Some days He will be very close; other days you won't be able to find Him at all.

"As He plays with you, you will be run through the wringer; you will ache with longing. When He finishes with His play you will be completely tired out. You will cry with all your being, 'When are You coming to me?' When He does come He will catch hold of your hand and will never let go, not even through millions of births—except that there can't be millions of births for you once He has hold of your hand. Finally you reach the state of tadrupata—'two hearts but one beat'—and then you are identical with Him, if that is what you want. But most devotees of Krishna never want to unite with Him; they always want to maintain their own identities so that they taste His sweetness over and over again, forever and ever.

"Although He is Perfection Personified, Krishna still has to come to our world to play about. Do you know why? Because of His beloved, Radha.

Why does the name Radha sound so sweet to the ear? Turn the word around and you get *dhara*, the power to hold or fix. In this case it is the power to hold Krishna in mind. Everyone who has perfect dharana of Krishna, whose mind is firmly fixed on Him, actually calls Krishna to them. He goes wherever He is called. The person who calls may not see or sense Him, but Krishna plays about with such a person, and causes him or her to do so many things.

"Krishna is called Perfection Personified because of a siddhi he had which was far beyond all ordinary siddhis. This siddhi is called 'Kartum, Akartum, Anyathakartum.' *Kartum*: that which is difficult to do, but is doable. This refers to the adhibhautika, the mundane world. *Akartum*: that which is impossible for ordinary beings, which refers to the adhyatmika, the spiritual world. *Anyathakartum*: that which is beyond both the spiritual and the mundane and is inconceivable to humans, referring to the adhidaivika or astral world. This suggests that Lord Krishna has unlimited power in all three realms, which means in the entire cosmos. Krishna had only one fault: He had a habit of promising to do the impossible. He would set up a situation, promise to change it, and then change it—and no one would know what He had done. All the time this was going on He would stand to one side, admiring His own play.

"But even Krishna was baffled by Radha; even He could not understand her. Do you know the depth of Radha's devotion to Krishna? Even Krishna Himself could not know it. Her bhakti was so intense that when she was away from Krishna she felt as if she were being stung by thousands of scorpions all at once. If you want to awaken your Kundalini completely by means of bhakti your devotion must be equally intense, otherwise there will never be enough pressure to force Kundalini to rise into your head."

Oh.

"Radha was a *gopi*, one of the milkmaids with whom Krishna carried on a secret romance. They would work all day long taking care of their homes and families, and when night fell they would sneak out and make love to Krishna. Esoterically, Krishna is the Soul, the Shaktiman; the gopis are the nadis, the nerves of the astral body. *Gopi* literally means 'secret'; naturally, because no one else but the sadhaka can know what is going on within his body. The gopis went about their daily work as usual, but their thoughts were only of Krishna. Likewise, a good sadhaka goes about his own daily life while his consciousness is fixed entirely on Krishna.

"They say that Krishna had sixteen thousand wives, and of those sixteen thousand He was fondest of one hundred. This means that of your seventy-two thousand nadis sixteen thousand are predominant, and of those sixteen thousand one hundred are most important in Kundalini Yoga. Of these, three are supremely important, and of these three Sushumna is most important. Radha, the most beloved of Krishna even though she was not even His wife, represents Sushumna.

"Do you remember when I demonstrated to you and your friend Sergei how through the manipulation of just one nadi in the second toe a woman can become aroused, and even have an orgasm?"

"I remember it well." And so does, I am sure, the woman he demonstrated it on.

"Can you imagine what would happen if all your seventy-two thousand nadis were stimulated at once?"

"I can imagine it with some difficulty."

"Well, that is what love of Krishna can do for you. If that ever happens to you then you will know something about Krishna's Lila. Do you know the two main Sanskrit words for 'play'?

"Yes, lila and krida."

"*Krida* is unconscious play, like *rati krida* (love play). Krida is play which is controlled by someone or something other than the being who is playing. In love play the glands and the genitals do the controlling, not the two people who romance each other. The Rishis play is *lila*, cosmic pastimes in which they are always in control. This is why we talk about Krishna's Lila and Rama's Lila, the divine play of Lord Krishna and Lord Rama.

"Everyone here in India knows when Krishna was born, but how many people know the real significance of Krishna's birth? Only when the causal body begins to burn to ash is Krishna really born. At that time the Kundalini Shakti merges with its Lord in the sadhaka's head, and then all the seventy-two thousand nadis begin to dance in the cosmic rhythm. Each nadi vibrates with bliss, thinking that she alone possesses Krishna, but in fact Krishna being the Soul is everywhere, and dances with them all. This is the way the Rishis celebrate Krishna's birthday: they enjoy the cosmic dance between Krishna and the gopis in their own bodies, utilizing the Kundalini Shakti. This is the real Rasa-Lila of Krishna."

"So it is at least theoretically possible to experience the *Rasa-Lila* (the divine dance of intense emotion), even now during Kali-Yuga."

"Let me put it this way. When Narsi Mehta was kicked out of the house by his sister-in-law he ran in desperation to a Shiva temple and threw himself across the Shiva Linga. He lay there for seven days and nights, forgetting to eat or drink, allowing snakes and insects to crawl over him as they pleased. Finally Lord Shiva was pleased with his penance, and appeared to him to offer a boon. Narsi Mehta told Him, 'Lord, just give me whatever you like best.' Shiva said, 'Well, I love best the Rasa—Lila of Krishna, so I will give that to you.' Some people say that Narsi Mehta is the only human in Kali Yuga who has ever seen the real Rasa-Lila of Lord Krishna."

"Of course that is too faraway for most of us," he added when he saw the far away look in my eyes. "But if you sing of Krishna's exploits with sincere devotion you can develop intense love for Krishna, which will give you immense bliss. And if you know the esoteric meaning behind the songs, they can send you into ecstasy.

"In one a gopi complains to her companion: 'On the banks of the river Yamuna, Nanda's son (Krishna) flung a stone and broke the water pot on my head, which caused all the water to flow out and lighten my load.' You know that Indians frequently carry their heavy loads on their heads. The gopis, like most Indian women, used to fetch water from the river in large pots which they would carefully balance on their heads as they carried them back to their homes. Krishna, to tease them, would throw rocks and break the pots. This is the surface meaning, easily understandable by every woman who has ever carried a pot of water on her head. Such a song thus helps even illiterate village women to increase their devotion to Krishna.

"When you sympathize with someone you self-identify with that person to some extent. If you can sympathize with the gopi in this song it will be easier for you to relate to Krishna, even if it is only to scold Him for breaking the pot. We in India do not believe that devotion has to be respectful and polite at all times. When you are in love with someone, is the course of your romance always smooth? No, it is not; it can't be, if you are really in love. Sometimes you will fight, sometimes you will weep, and so on, if you really love your partner. True devotion means falling in love with your deity.

"So, the gopi in the song seems to complain about Krishna's antics; this is the surface meaning. The esoteric meaning is something quite different. Never take anything here in India only at surface value. Our sacred writings are mostly esoteric and you should not take them at face value any more than you should take the books of Moses, which are also mostly esoteric, at face value.

"In this song the Yamuna River represents the Chandra Nadi, which flows in the left nostril. Bhakti requires the functioning of the Chandra Nadi. The gopis are the other nadis of the body. Krishna is the gopis' lover; He is the Soul, that which causes vitality and awareness in the nadis. The

Soul also causes blood to flow in the arteries, and so on. Doesn't your blood flow faster when you see your beloved?

"The water pot is the head, which is full of so many juices. 'Juice' is not limited to physical juices like hormones; it also includes 'mental' juices like tastes and emotions. Because an unenlightened person is selfish this water is poisonous, poisoned by the venom of selfishness."

"From the snake of the untamed ahamkara," I tossed in.

He nodded, pleased that I was following his meaning. "Krishna 'lightens' the gopi of her burden, making her 'enlightened.' After her head is lightened of the venom of the world the gopi becomes clairaudient and clairvoyant. Then all she wants to see is Krishna, all she wants to hear is the sweet music of His flute, and all she wants to do is dance with Him in the divine Rasa-Lila.

"Once Krishna hid in a tree near the Yamuna and waited for the gopis to come down to bathe. After they had undressed and entered the river Krishna stole their clothes, and when they realized what He had done they were too embarrassed to come out. But Krishna insisted, and they all had to emerge from the water and stand before Him naked."

"Naturally He wanted to see them naked; He was their lover."

"Yes. Before Krishna will dance with the gopis they must remove all their clothes: the three coverings which obscure Kundalini. The gopis are embarrassed in the beginning—their egos hesitate to leave familiar self-identifications—but Krishna is firm with them, and eventually they must become naked. Then the Kundalini Shakti becomes free to move through the various nadis in the body, and those nadis begin to dance."

Krishna and Shiva

He paused to sip his drink.

"When Kundalini enters the Anahata Chakra you begin to hear the Anahata Nada, which will sound either like Krishna's flute or Shiva's drum depending on which path you follow. Other Nadas are also described in the books, but these two are the most important.

"Let me try to explain to you the differences in Nada by describing how Krishna's hair differs from Shiva's hair. Krishna's hair has been compared to a swarm of bees. What does a bee do with its time? All day long it moves from flower to flower, enjoying the nectar at each one. The flower longs for the bee to come and take its nectar; many flowers in fact exist only because of bees. Likewise, Lord Krishna moves from girl to girl, from Shakti to Shakti, and enjoys with each one. They long for Him to come to them; they exist only for Him. By their longing they draw Him to themselves. Every sincere devotee of Krishna is female, no matter what sex the physical body might be.

"Bees are always buzzing, and the sound of Krishna's hair is likened by the Rishis to the murmuring drone that arises from innumerable intoxicated bees. That buzz is Nada. If you use this image to improve your concentration on Krishna you will begin to perceive this Nada when your concentration on Krishna becomes perfect.

"Lord Krishna has long, flowing, luxurious hair. Lord Shiva's hair is also long, but it is matted into thick locks; what do the West Indians call them?"

"Dreadlocks."

"Like dreadlocks. His hair, which is called a *jata*, is compared to a snake because it is long and ropelike, and because if you listen carefully you may hear a low hiss like a snake's coming from it. This is Shiva's Nada."

"And of course Shiva wears a snake around His neck."

"Yes he does. And yes, Kundalini is the Serpent Power. Think of this: Shiva wears a cobra around his neck, and Vishnu sleeps on Shesha, a thousand-headed snake. Just as Shiva allows Kali to dance on Him while He remains an inert corpse, a sadhaka who awakens Shiva in himself allows Kundalini to play about on him, but is never tempted to allow Kundalini to identify with any aspect of limited existence.

"Krishna has also subdued Kundalini, in a different way. Once He danced on the head of a venomous serpent named Kaliya in the middle of the Yamuna River, the Lunar Channel; Krishna used lunar energy to bring Kundalini under His complete control, and then He danced on Her! Normally Ma dances, but Krishna turned the tables on Her. This is why Shiva loves Krishna's play. But Krishna could do this only because His mind had been made totally firm by Shiva, which is why Krishna loves Shiva's play.

"How many people realize that sadhana of Shiva is sadhana of Krishna, and vice versa? Shiva cannot do without Vishnu and Vishnu cannot do without Shiva; it is a mutual bondage of love and necessity. It has to be; They are merely two aspects of the same Being. If you follow the path of jnana you must worship Shiva. In fact, only when you actually become Shiva will you really know how to worship Krishna. If you follow the path of bhakti you must worship Krishna, or some other aspect of Vishnu, and when you achieve Krishna, He will teach you about Shiva—that is, if you can still remember Shiva as you gaze at Krishna's beauty. One is the Absolute Unmanifested, the other is the Perfection of Manifestation."

"So on the path of jnana you actually become Shiva, while on the path of bhakti you worship but remain separate from Krishna."

"Yes; it is the difference between non-duality and duality. Shiva contains everything within Himself; He is the ultimate jnani. When the god of love came to Him to tempt Him, He incinerated that god with a single glance from His third eye, the eye of jnana. When there is no lust, no desire, there is no outward movement of energy, and the universe ceases to exist. The god of love was reborn as Krishna's son, because Krishna is *rasatmaka*, full of blissful emotion. This is why He dances the Rasa-Lila, and why He is called Ananda Ghana, the 'Mass of Bliss.' He loves all the fineries and luxuries of life; it is all His Maya. If you have become tired of Maya and want renunciation you must go to Lord Shiva. No other being in the universe has ever renounced as Shiva has. He has not renounced everything out of pride in His renunciation, but because He loves only Krishna, and always craves to see Him. He has renounced because He has given everything to Krishna.

"How few people understand Shiva! Shiva says, 'My Gopala loves beautiful clothes; let Him have them! To remind me of Him every moment, I will never wear clothes. Instead I will wear the ashes of burnt bodies. My Gopala loves jewels; I will wear a cobra, to remind me that I have offered all other garlands to Him. I will drink poison; all other food I offer to Him,' and so on. No one wants to come near Shiva in this state, so He plays with spirits; He doesn't even crave devotees. All He craves is Gopala. Once He went so far as to actually turn Himself into a gopi so that He could take part in the Rasa-Lila Himself.

"And if He craves Vishnu, don't you think that Vishnu will crave Him in return? It is only natural; Vishnu loves His devotees better than He loves anything else in the universe, and Shiva is His ultimate devotee. Do you know how strong Krishna's love for Shiva is? You have probably never thought about it. Even Krishna, Perfection Personified, died when He met Mahakala face to face; His love for Mahakala was so intense that He could not remain living separate from Him.

"It is this way for everyone. While they are alive people say, 'Rama, Rama,' or 'O Krishna' when they are in trouble; they invoke Vishnu and ask for His help. You rarely hear anyone saying, 'Hara, Hara,' because everyone is afraid of death. But really their love for Lord Shiva is much stronger than their love for Lord Vishnu. The moment they see Shiva they have to die, the emotion is so intense. This is how He performs His duty.

"Shiva is the Great Giver, and because He sees Krishna in every living being He gives people unlimited boons when He is properly propitiated. The problem is really not how to propitiate Him; the problem is how to get his attention. He is in perpetual samadhi, and it takes quite a lot of intensity to drag Him down into the consciousness of His surroundings.

"To give you an idea of what kind of giver Shiva is, let us take just one verse from the Shiva Mahimna Stotra, the 'Hymn to the Greatness of Shiva.' This verse describes how Vishnu was in the habit of daily offering one thousand lotuses to Shiva. One day Shiva stole one of the lotuses, as a test. When Vishnu found that one was missing and that His offering might be incomplete He thought to Himself: 'My eyes are described by my devotees as "lotus eyes." Therefore they are fit offerings to Lord Shiva.' He thereupon plucked out one of His two lotus eyes and offered it. Shiva was so pleased by this offering that He immediately appeared and converted the lotus eye into the *Sudarshana Chakra*, the discus which is Vishnu's favorite weapon."

"Does this story have anything to do with the Vishnu Sudarshana Mantra?" I wondered.

"It may." Though pleased that I remembered that reference of many months before, he was not so easily distracted from his point. "Here is a part of the esoteric meaning of this verse—not all, just a part. Vishnu's one thousand lotuses are in the Sahasrara; He offers them to Shiva daily by offering these internal shaktis to His internal Shiva. One day Shiva took one; what is that one? The ego, Vishnu's own personal Shakti. This naked Shakti then embraced Her Shiva. Remember the difference between Shakti and Ma: Ma is the maternal aspect and is very sweet—'Be prosperous my child,' and so on. Shakti, on the other hand, is immediate and impartial, like a knife: fast, sharp, cutting. This accounts for the 'plucking' of the 'lotus.'

"After the loss of His eye of duality (because it was Shakti) Vishnu had but one eye left: the eye of non-duality. Shiva took the Shakti and returned the Sudarshana Chakra. *Sudarshana* means 'good sight': clairvoyance. And why a chakra? Ask me that."

I tried to ask him that, but he continued to talk: "I'm not going to tell you the answer, though. What is the use of my telling you everything? There are some things you have to find out for yourself by experience.

"Shiva is pure consciousness. When you succeed in propitiating Shiva your own consciousness is transformed into a divine consciousness, so that forever after as long as you live you are in the world but out of it, like the lotus which grows from the mud but remains unsullied by it. The lotus is dear to Shiva because it is the very embodiment of discrimination.

"Ordinary people have minds filled with the heat of passion, caused by the friction generated by the mental turmoil due to *sankalpa* and *vikalpa* (certainty and uncertainty). Desire and heat are the same thing."

"Of course; *raga* means both 'passion' and 'melody,'" I said, "and in Ayurveda *raga* means 'inflammation.'" And, I thought to myself, it is cognate with the English word rage.

"Good. Coolness, on the other hand, means lack of mental turmoil. Lord Shiva is always doing penance, destroying the passions day in and day out, just as He destroyed the god of love with a single glance from His third eye. Shiva's terrific penances create heat, and so He needs to be continuously cooled off. This is one reason why he wears a crescent moon on His forehead, and a cobra around His neck. Snakes are cool to the touch, and are usually quiet and immobile unless disturbed; it is only when you disturb them that they will bite you. The image of Lord Shiva sitting immobile in samadhi in the extreme cold on top of Mount Kailash observing silence indicates the complete absence of sankalpa and vikalpa. Lord Shiva's mind is always as firm as a rock; this is why the linga is His symbol.

"Why does Shiva need to do penance when He has already achieved such a high state? Because He swallowed the terrible *Halahala* poison, the poison of samsara, which threatened to destroy the world. To protect creation, because He sees Gopala Krishna in all beings and cannot bear to see His Gopala troubled in any way, He drank this poison, and it stained His throat blue."

"Which is why He is called 'Nilakantha' ('The Blue-Throated One')."

"Exactly. Halahala manifested at the time of the Churning of the Ocean of Milk. We will discuss that event someday, but for right now consider that 'Ham' and 'Lam' are the Bija Mantras for the Vishuddha and the Muladhara Chakras respectively, so 'Halahala' represents the poison of everything which exists in the lower five chakras, meaning everything made up of the Five Elements. Because Shiva holds the poison of samsara above His Vishuddha Chakra and never allows it to affect him He is always above the samsara, in perennial samadhi.

"Ganga, the Ganges River, flows from the celestial regions down onto the earth, and Shiva catches her in His matted locks, breaking her fall so that Earth is not troubled by the force of her descent. It is well known that bathing in the Ganga can wash away one's evil karmas. The River Ganga was proud of this ability of hers until she learned that it was given to her by a Rishi who purified her each day, not for her glory but to provide coolness to Shiva. This Rishi loves Shiva so much that he is willing to take on millions of bad karmas daily just so Shiva will not be troubled. Only a Rishi could be so magnanimous."

"But there is probably an esoteric meaning to this story also."

"Of course there is, just as there is with bathing in the Yamuna. Evil karmas are definitely washed away when you take a bath in your internal Ganga, the right nostril. This is the bath of jnana."

"So finally it comes down to the two rivers, the Ganga and the Yamuna."

"Yes. Shiva and Krishna, jnana and bhakti; call them what you wish, they are the two paths to the Absolute."

Peaceful Offering of the Five Senses
**Mirror (sight); Lute (sound); Fruit (taste);
Perfumed Conch (smell); Cloth (touch).**

Wrathful Offering of the Five Senses

Eyes (sight); Ears (sound); Nose (smell); Tongue (taste);
Heart with Feather (touch).

IMMORTALS

Siddhas

"The universe is endless and beginningless." Vimalananda was in a mood to talk, and plenty of time lay before us. "If you are sincere and work hard you will eventually reach the state of continual awareness that you are the Universal Soul, the One, the Atman or Brahman. Then you can truthfully say to yourself, 'Aham Brahmasmi; I am Brahman.' Our mortal consciousness has three normal states: waking, dream, and deep sleep. Turiya is the state beyond these three. In Turiya you are continually aware of being Brahman, the Absolute Reality, and of Brahman being all. But it is only the beginning.

"In spite of knowing yourself to be the Brahman you cannot do everything the Brahman can. You cannot create, preserve, and destroy universes. It is all very well to know you are the Brahman, but there is an immense difference between imagining that you can create your own universe and actually being able to do so. While you and I are limited to the universe in which we live, a Rishi can create as many universes as there are stars in the sky. The difference between you and a Rishi lies in the power of will.

"To know that you are the Brahman is jnana, ordinary spiritual knowledge. When there is full knowledge of the Brahman no iota of ego remains; discrimination, doubt, and determination disappear. This is Nirvikalpa Samadhi. You can be satisfied that you have reached the Absolute once you have achieved Nirvikalpa Samadhi, but there is no joy in it; it is dry, it has no juice, no rasa. How can joy exist when everything—observed, observer, and observation—has ceased to exist? Jnana is good, but vijnana, special knowledge, is far better. When you reach the state of vijnana you realize, 'Oh, so there is someone behind the scene who is playing about and directing everyone else.' When this happens you become a Siddha. Only when you go beyond Turiya can you understand and know Siddhas.

"A Siddha is one who returns from Nirvikalpa Samadhi to perfect his vijnana. Here is how it works: You go from the state of ignorance in which you possess attributes to the attributeless state of jnana and then back to the qualified state again, with a difference. Just compare it to being in the belly of the Mother, from which you will have to be born over and over again, with being on Her lap, where you can play about as much as you like and She will keep an eye on you. You exist in relation with Maya either way, since you are manifested, but there is a big difference between being in the samsara and being on top of it. A Siddha does experience joy and sorrow, and the other pairs of dualities, but not in the same way as before.

"Both an ordinary man and a Siddha cry when they visit the smashan, which is the true temple of God, the place of Eternal Reality. An ordinary man cries tears of misery, because he suffers from separation; he thinks he has lost something he thought he possessed. A Siddha cries tears of joy, because he understands the play of Mahakala, the Lord of Time. Mahakala can have no effect on a Siddha, who has gone beyond time, space and causation. A Siddha can safely admire the play of Nature as an inviolate observer.

"Nowadays everyone who gets a little siddhi becomes a 'siddha.' Such people are only fooling the gullible and cheating themselves. Anything you strive to obtain is a siddhi, and you will find that in Kali Yuga many people are ready to strive for siddhis, for supernatural powers, but few are willing to strive for God. There are plenty of supernatural powers to be had, and many of them are very easy to obtain. One of the simplest is for the control of snakes. You can succeed at it in a single day. Our friend Chotu has done it. He doesn't show off any more, but in the beginning just for fun he would go up to a cobra or a krait, pick it up and hang it around his neck as if he were Lord Shiva, and the snake would not do a thing; it dare not. Even if he sticks his finger into its mouth nothing would happen.

"You Westerners have siddhis too, of course. You have made great technological advances in a very short time. You have learned how to see and hear across vast distances, how to fly through the air, how to harness the power of the atom. All these are supernatural powers. You have done your own researches and have demonstrated the results, and it is only right that you insist on seeing the results of our researches before you believe in what we say. The only thing is, all these achievements are outside the body. They are gadgets, external things which can always be lost or broken. Here in India we have turned our attention inward, and the results we get can never be mislaid or destroyed. This is the big difference between India and the West.

"Most gurus will tell you to shun siddhis like the plague, and this is correct, in the sense that it is so easy to get attached to them. Obtaining a siddhi is a great achievement, and when you obtain one it is natural to immediately think of showing off its power to others, but to do so is very foolish and dangerous. The real purpose of siddhis, which exist in the subtle body, is to remove one's karmas from the causal body, which is basically just a warehouse of karmas, and then to repay these karmic debts. The subtle body is the intermediary between the causal and physical bodies. It is less subject to gravitation than the physical body, so when it is released from the grasp of the physical body it can go higher and higher; there is no limit to the heights it can reach. But its main job is to go into the causal body and remove the karmas stored there.

"Being able to do this still does not make you a siddha. It is easy enough—relatively speaking—to learn how to take out your astral body. It is a greater achievement to be able to sit in one place and maintain consciousness of many different places and many different planes of existence all at once. But even that does not make you a Siddha.

"You must search long and hard before you find a real Siddha. You cannot become a Siddha over a weekend; nor can you follow a correspondence course and get a diploma by mail. No; you have to work your behind off, literally, sitting in meditation or sitting and performing rituals for lifetimes on end.

"And even after so much penance you must still be tested. Naturally the test for becoming a Siddha is very rough. I know the Mahapurusha in Girnar who is responsible for the testing of sadhus. He might come to a sadhu in any form, and his test would take only a minute or two. If the sadhu passed, wonderful. If not, his matted locks would be cut and he would have to leave Girnar. 99.5 percent failed. Five-hundred-year-old, one-thousand-year-old, even five-thousand-year-old sadhus couldn't pass. So it is no joke to become a Siddha."

Vimalananda used the term *Mahapurusha*, which literally means "Great Soul," to refer to any being who has become immortal as a result of sadhana.

Rishis, Munis, Naths and Siddhas are all Mahapurushas.

"But it is all worth it. To become a Siddha is a unique accomplishment, because you go beyond all the Elements and you can then play about with them as you please. A Siddha has no physical restrictions. You become immortal, which means that you are ethereal, but whenever you wish you can materialize a physical body for yourself and move about. Such a body is just like anyone else's body, as solid as can be. Once you've finished whatever it was you wanted to do, you just dematerialize; it's that simple. Each Element goes back to its source: Earth to Earth, Water to Water, etc.

"Once a Siddha was gracious enough to demonstrate this to me. He sat in front of me and within seconds, on the ground where he had been, there was a pile of some solid material, a little puddle of water and a warm breeze. Just to convince myself, I put out a finger and touched the water; it was real. After a few minutes of being discorporate he remanifested himself. But there was a flaw on his arm, as if some of the flesh had been dug out. When I asked him about it he replied, 'Didn't you remove a little of the water?' Then I understood. But even that is only the beginning. I know a Mahapurusha who has such perfect knowledge of the Earth Element that if he even shakes one of his matted locks with his hand the earth will quake, and giant waves will roll in the ocean.

"Mortals cannot understand how Siddhas play about. Sometimes, if he feels like it, a Siddha may remove his head from his body and walk around with it in his hands. People will be so amazed to see it that they will run after him just to find out what it might be. When they start to make too big a noise about it he will replace it on his shoulders as if nothing had happened. After staying in one place for some time he may become famous. Then, to prevent being trapped and made to do others' work he will discorporate and no one will be able to find him.

"Siddhas are too far away for most people. Unless a Siddha wants to meet you, you will never succeed at meeting him; it's just impossible. Besides, even if you could meet a Siddha would you know how to react? There are only two ways to react to something which is unknown to you. Either you do as most people do and define the thing according to all the old notions that you have been given by your relatives, friends, teachers, priests, and so on, or you look at it in a new, non-verbal way. If something is really new to you how will you be able to describe it verbally, since no word exists for it? For example, would you please describe for me the taste of sugar?"

"Ah, well, it's . . . sweet."

"Yes, but that doesn't describe anything. 'Sweet' can only be tasted, it cannot be described in words. You may hear about 'sweet' all your life, but until you taste sugar you will never really know what sweetness is.

"Likewise, you may get the general idea of a thing by talking about it, but words are no substitute for experience. The verbal way is second-hand, which is of no use to a jnani, who wants to experience Reality. How then can it be of any use to a Siddha, who is three steps higher than a jnani?

"Siddhas can experience things which most humans would never be able to imagine even after millions of lives. Just one example: the ancient bathing festival called the Kumbha Mela, the 'Pot Festival,' which is held every three years by turns in Hardwar, Prayaga (Allahabad), Nasik, and Ujjain when particular conjunctions are in the sky. They say that a bath in the appropriate holy river at these particular times gives you a drop of Amrita from the celestial pot of nectar.

"The most important of these festivals is held in Prayaga, at a place called the *Triveni Sangama* where three rivers come together: the Ganga, the Yamuna, and the unseen Sarasvati. The Sarasvati is hidden because here it represents Sushumna, the most important of the nadis, the nadi which carries Kundalini to the Unmanifest. Sushumna's course is hidden in the body, just as the River Sarasvati's course is hidden on Earth.

"Now, although a bath on the appropriate day in the Triveni Sangama provides some benefit, the Kumbha Mela is basically an esoteric festival. On Kumbha Day a Siddha need not bother to go to Prayaga for his bath. He has his own Triveni Sangama and his own pot of nectar right inside him. His Triveni Sangama is his Ajna Chakra, where the Surya and Chandra Nadis meet Sushumna. You know the two roads to the Ajna Chakra: the right and the left nostrils, jnana and bhakti. Whichever path you take, your own Triveni Sangama exists in the Ajna Chakra. A Siddha sits wherever he is and he—his ego, his Kundalini Shakti—takes a dip, by which he obtains a drop of Amrita from his own pot of nectar, his own head."

"So here," I interposed, "the 'pot' is like the pot of Ghata Sthapana and does not refer to the chest or to pranayama, even though the word *kumbha* is used."

"Oh, but it does refer to pranayama as well. On the specified day at the specified time the Siddha sits in a certain posture and concentrates his prana in the Vishuddha Chakra. His breathing slows down to two finger-breadths, then to only one. This is not forcible restraint, remember; this is the true 'kevala kumbhaka,' in which the breath slows and then stops automatically when the two flows become perfectly balanced. Once the Siddha has balanced his breaths he draws the prana from both into the Ajna Chakra. *Ajna* stands for what?"

"For *guru ajna*, instructions from the guru."

"Yes. Here the guru is the sun, the world's guru. Breathing slows almost to a stop when the Kundalini Shakti reaches the Ajna Chakra. It is not a question of holding the breath in; it is not inhalation, but rather continuous and complete exhalation. If you go for a swim and dive but inhale you will float. If you exhale you will sink right down to the bottom, which is neces-sary here. The ego must dive in and sink to the very bottom of the stream to be cleansed of all her blemishes. When she is totally cleansed she becomes the Kula Kundalini. At that point, when the Kundalini Shakti is in her purest form, she becomes eligible for holy nuptials with her Shiva. The result is Sadashiva, the eternal form of Shiva.

"Just as Krishna insists that the gopis show themselves to Him naked, Shiva will lie with Kundalini only when She becomes completely naked, completely stripped of all the three coverings, especially the Three Gunas. When I was a naked sadhu I would always ask any other naked sadhu I might meet, 'Just by taking off your clothes do you achieve anything? Do you become liberated? Only if you can remove Sattva, Rajas, and Tamas have you really taken something off; otherwise, no.'

"You probably were not very popular as a sadhu," I opined.

"No, but why should I be popular? I was not trying to win any popularity contests. A sadhu should be searching for truth, not approval, and to get to the truth you have to become truly naked. You have a phrase in English: 'the naked truth.' Translated into Sanskrit it becomes 'nagna satya,' which could also mean, 'Truth is naked,' or, 'Nakedness is Truth.' I like that last version: Nakedness is Truth. The true nakedness comes when you peel off the three coatings of the ego: the Three Gunas, the Six Tastes, and the Five Elements. Only then does She become true. They say Sanskrit is a dead language, but I think we've just created a new word.

"A water bath will not remove any of your real stains; it takes a mental bath to do the job. The stream of Amrita in which the ego bathes is a glandular substance, a secretion of the pineal gland. The conjunction of the constellations causes the pineal and pituitary to hypersecrete, releasing a stream of Amrita in which to bathe the ego. So, by bathing in one of the four holy cities on Kumbha Day you get your physical bath, and by this internal process you take a spiritual bath. Then you become eligible for your astral or adhidaivika bath, which unfortunately is indescribable. People come and go, enjoying the external Kumbha bath over and over again, but this spritual bath is something quite different. No one ever likes to return from this internal bath."

Rishis, Munis, Naths and Siddhas

After pausing to light a cigarette, Vimalananda continued.

"To become a Siddha is wonderful—marvelous—but it is not the ultimate. If your Kundalini should ever reach the Sahasrara you will see so many things that you will be amazed. You will see hundreds and hundreds of flowers of all colors. Each of those flowers is a shakti, and if you pluck one of them you will get that shakti, which will keep you on the periphery. You will form a little orbit for yourself, and you may remain there for ages. Siddhas usually stay in their own orbits because they are so fascinated by what they have achieved. Only if they are forcibly pulled further by some higher authority will they move ahead, and when they do they see that there are much better orbits to move into.

"To progress as a Siddha you must forget about everything else except going closer and closer to the center. It is almost impossible to reach the center, which is the preserve of the seniormost of the Rishis, but you can get closer and closer to it. If at any time you decide you've had enough of existence, you can completely efface your personality and merge into the center."

I strained to conceptualize it.

"Try to get some perspective on what I am talking about here. Even after you become a Siddha it takes time to progress further. Of course, a Mahapurusha, who has gone beyond time, space and causation has no value for time; but to you and me it seems impossibly long. After thousands of years of penance a Siddha may be permitted to meet a Nath and learn from him. If a Siddha works really hard he can even become a Nath.

"Naths are Aghoris. They make everything in their being self-identify with Lord Shiva even under the most trying and tempting circumstances. Their motto is 'Alak Niranjan'; *Alak* means 'a-laksha,' 'free from attribution or discrimination.' *Nir-anjana* means 'completely clean,' free of any fault, stain or blemish. What is that thing which is undefined and undefiled? The absolute imperishable Brahman.

"Most people would be terrified to see a Nath in his real form, with matted locks, big firetongs, bag full of ashes and fierce unblinking eyes."

"So all the Nath sadhus who dress this way are actually dressing in imitation of the real Naths, the immortals?"

"Yes, and each part of their costume has some meaning behind it; it's not just fanciful. Nath sadhus are known as 'Kan-Phatas' ('Pierced-Ears') because of the large earrings they are given by their gurus when they are initiated. The earrings stay in for as long as the sadhu lives, and the rule used to be that if an earring should break the sadhu should immediately commit suicide. I suspect that very few Nath sadhus follow this rule nowadays. Does the word 'earring' remind you of anything?"

"It reminds me of Kundalini, since *kundala* means 'earring.'"

"Correct. So there is a connection between the earring and Kundalini, or more precisely, between where the ear is pierced and Kundalini. The ear is full of important nadis, which is why the Chinese have gone in for ear acupuncture in such a big way. Nath sadhus are expected to be celibate, and one reason why they pierce their ears is because when you pierce the earlobe in just the right place you can prevent hydrocele, which may become a complication of celibacy. Of course if you are slightly off target you will become permanently impotent, so it is better to know before you pierce."

"If they are supposed to remain celibate what difference does it make if they become impotent; on the contrary, that should make them happy, shouldn't it?"

"Think about it; if they lose their sexual energy entirely, what will they have left to use to help awaken Kundalini?"

"Oh, right." You have to be virile to practice Tantra.

"The immortal Naths are passionately devoted to their guru *Dattatreya*, and they dress as they do in honor of *Adi Nath*, the first Nath: Lord Shiva. Thus Shiva is not the guru here; He is a fellow disciple of Dattatreya, the first of all Aghoris. Can you imagine what sort of being Dattatreya is if his original pupil was Shiva Himself?"

I tried to imagine Lord Dattatreya.

"Wah, wah," said Vimalananda admiringly, "Naths are really 'naths' (masters). They are masters of the ten senses. A special nerve is created, the eleventh sense, which permits them to receive their instructions telepathically.

Naths are higher than Siddhas because they get telepathic transmissions directly from their bosses, the Munis. This is why Naths are always waiting for adesha, for instructions: 'That which is heard without the ears, seen without the eyes, spoken without the tongue.'

"Because they are immortal and have complete control over their senses, Naths are masters of the physical world also. Just by pissing, or even spitting, on a rock a Nath can produce gold. In alchemy you have to use metal as your raw material, but a Nath only needs a rock. He has eaten and digested all types of poisons, which has changed his metabolism so much that he has become a touchstone himself. So naturally a Nath will have no value for gold, or for people like kings who do value it. They only have value for the gold of pure consciousness. A Nath is really a spiritual touchstone. Whoever comes in contact with a Nath must become spiritual, must become a real man or woman of God whether they want to or not. This is the power of a Nath.

"The Naths have a different way of teaching altogether. Once while Gorakh Nath was sitting at his dhuni he saw that the king's wife had died and that the king was crying as if his world had come to an end. Gorakh decided to go and meet the king. He brought along an earthen pot, and when he entered the king's presence he suddenly dropped it. It shattered into a hundred pieces, and Gorakh began to wail, 'I have lost my beautiful pot that I loved so dearly! Now it is gone forever!'

"The king looked at him in amazement and said, 'Have you gone mad? Are you crying over an old pot? You can buy hundreds of them at the market.'

"Gorakh said to the king, 'Maharaja, you are the ruler of the country, and in your harem there are many beautiful women. And besides, you can obtain any woman that you desire. Where is the need to cry over one lost woman?'

"The King replied, 'But she was so beautiful, so wonderful, and she had so many virtues that endeared her to me.'

"In answer, Gorakh took some ash from his shoulder-bag and threw it on the ground. Immediately two living women appeared, each a perfect copy of the king's dead wife. Gorakh asked the king, 'Can you tell me which of these is yours? If you knew her so well, you should be able to recognize her.'

"But the king couldn't distinguish which was his wife; both looked exactly alike. And then Gorakh said to him, 'King, you cannot even recognize your wife, and yet you are pining away for her. Now who is a fool, you or I?' And the king understood.

"The Naths are actually the creations of certain Munis, who in turn are merely the manifestations of a few Rishis. But each group in turn is kept in ignorance of their true nature so that the Lila, the cosmic play, can go on. They are limited in their new existences in order to perform certain tasks. If the Naths and Munis knew who they were, they wouldn't perform their duties properly.

"A Nath waits millions of years to meet a Muni, and after long austerities a Nath can finally become a Muni. Actually, a Muni should be called 'Mauni,' one who observes silence. He does not speak in Vaikhari at all; he communicates only with his eyes or telepathically. A Muni must wait Yugas or Manvantaras to catch even a glimpse of a Rishi, and then, if he is meant for it, after many billions of years of being a Muni he may get a chance to become a Rishi. The lower categories of Mahapurusha are all in orbit; each has his own orbit, but all are bound, however slightly. A Rishi, though, is totally free. He can travel to any star, any solar system he likes, in the twinkling of an eye."

"Does this apply to women too?"

"A woman who succeeds to the attributeless state comes back as a *Bhairavi* or *Yogini*; here also the hierarchy is very strict. After so many Yugas she moves up to become a Great Goddess, and finally she retires to the background, like the seniormost Rishis do, to let others enjoy the play. Actually those in the background control all the players, like a puppeteer pulling the puppets' strings. But no one is aware of it except the seniormost Shaktis and Shaktimans."

A flicker of confused emotion crossed my face, and Vimalananda increased his vehemence.

"Yes, I know what I am saying. The Rishis are the puppeteers, and all other beings in the universe, mortal and immortal, are their puppets. The Rishis go around creating rnas (karmic debts) for people to work off, to bind people down and help them progress. If you want to quit being a puppet, you must perform sadhana.

Notable Siddhas

"To meet a Nath, Muni or Rishi, or one of the Supreme Shaktis, is almost impossible. But you may be able to meet Siddhas. I was very fortunate to have met Telang Swami (see *Aghora*), who was a great Siddha. When I was in the Himalayas I met Babaji, the Siddha who Yogananda talks about. Babaji is a good Siddha, no doubt, but his sister is even better than he is!

"Let me tell you about another Siddha I met. He is a very unusual person, even among the many unusual people in this universe. Some years ago a policeman saw a man wandering around in the backwaters of Cochin, in what is now the state of Kerala. When the policeman stopped him and asked his name the man replied, 'My name is Prabhakaran, and I have come to look after the interests of my great-great-great-grandchildren.' The police-man thought he was trying to be funny and asked him his age. The man replied, 'More than seven hundred years.' The policeman ran him in.

"Prabhakaran told the policemen at the station house that he did not eat or drink anything, so the jailers informed him, 'We are going to keep you in solitary confinement without food and water, and no toilet either.' Prabhakaran said, 'O.K.' When five days, six days later Prabhakaran was still in perfect shape the jailers had to admit to his abilities.

"Then they asked him, 'Does anyone know you?' Prabhakaran replied, 'Ask C. P. Ramaswami Aiyar; I once saved his life.' As soon as they telephoned Sir C. P. Ramaswami Aiyar, who was then the Prime Minister of Travancore (also now part of Kerala) he immediately flew to Cochin to meet Prabhakaran, and insisted that Prabhakaran return with him to Travancore. But Prabhakaran said, 'No, I prefer to go back to the sea.' As soon as he had seen to the well-being of his descendants he walked out into the ocean. But that was nothing for him. He had already spent four hundred years in the Himalayas, and two hundred years in the sea. He is a Siddha, after all."

I recently learned that a man whom some had identified as Prabhakaran had been living on land for some years in an ashram, spending most of his time dancing in Bhava Samadhi. Eventually he announced to everyone that he had had enough of existence after seven hundred years, and that he had decided to leave his body in ten days. And so he did.

"And then there was Vishuddhananda. He was the pride of India, a real Siddha, not like these babas who produce ash from the air and so on. On the day I first met him in Benaras he was in such a fine mood that he began to press the area around his navel, and suddenly a lotus stalk came out, like the one at Vishnu's navel! As he continued to press, it became longer and a red lotus blossom appeared. Why red? Because red represents the Fire Ele-ment, which resides at the navel, the Manipura Chakra. There was a beauti-ful fragrance. After some time he pressed it, and it returned into his body, back through the navel. You may believe it or not, I don't care."

Nor did he pause to discover whether or not I believed it.

"The navel is really a very interesting structure. If you know the technique you can take in water through your navel and excrete it through your penis. Everyone in the world today performs creation, or rather procreation, with the penis, but Brahma, the Creator of the cosmos, does it with his navel, because He is Himself created from Vishnu's navel.

"After this performance Vishuddhananda's chief disciple, Pandit Gopinath Kaviraj, who was the greatest authority on Indian culture of his time, permitted a big smirk to escape onto his face. He was thinking, 'Yes, my Guru Maharaj can do this. What can you do, you bedraggled Aghori?' I looked at him and said, 'Have you ever heard of Vajroli?' He said that he had. 'Bring me some mercury,' I told him.

"Now, Vishuddhananda was doing research on mercury and there was plenty on hand. They brought a fifty-six-pound sealed tin and opened it in front of me. I sucked the mercury up with my penis. They were all gaping. Then I said, 'Aghora Nath is going to show you a little something about mercury. Wring my hair!' And all the mercury that had been taken inside was recovered from my matted locks. That put us on a more equal footing.

"Vishuddhananda was an expert at *Surya Vijnana*, the knowledge of how to make best use of the sun. Do you think this is simple? Never! Only when you understand the significance of the phrase 'Surya Putra, Agni Mitra' ('son of the Sun, friend of the Fire') can you even hope to know Surya Vijnana. It has something to do with purification of the Fire Element in the body, of course.

"Vishuddhananda would take an ordinary object, like a cookie, and put it on a large tray. Then he would direct sun rays onto it through certain yantras and the cookie would become a little puppy! Yes, it would come alive and move about. He would allow it to play for a bit, and then he would change the yantras slightly and the puppy would become a flower. Another change and a living human baby would appear. Finally he would change the thing into a sprig of *tulsi* (holy basil), and would give it to someone to be offered to the River Ganga.

"He would store the beads of his rosary in his arm. When he wanted to do japa he would remove them, string them, and use the completed rosary to count his japas. After finishing the number of japas he had decided to do he would unstring the rosary and replace the beads in his arm. And there was no hole, no scar, nothing to show where they had gone in or come out. He even used to keep a Shiva Linga made of solidified mercury in a hollow in his palate.

"I spent some time with him in Benaras. One day while he and I were together he became rather intoxicated with his powers, and suddenly a skull he was holding began to move its jaw, as if it were talking. I got the idea, and suddenly two rocks lying nearby began to knock into one another, over and over again, until they were pounded into rubble. And he also got my idea: when two people compete, the outcome can only be destructive, just as the rocks destroyed each other.

"Vishuddhananda was a true Siddha: he learned his vijnana at Lake Manasasarovar in Tibet. But even he had one fault: he showed himself off to too many people, and when he was ready to leave his body for good he had to suffer from diarrhea to purge all the samsara from him. Excess in all things is to be rejected."

Vishuddhananda lived for many years on the portal of the main post office in Benaras, so it was not easy for him to avoid people. The Law of Karma, however, makes no allowances.

"He did not need to die, of course; he was a Siddha. But he wanted to die so that he could continue to make further progress. To become a Siddha is a great accomplishment, but it is nothing compared to being a Rishi."

Rishis

Vimalananda lit yet another cigarette.

"Nothing is ever lost in the universe. Even things which happened millions of years ago can still be known, because their sound still exists. Sound, which is vibration, a series of waves, can be transmitted in many ways. Light can carry sound; even modern science has proved this. Humans usually perceive sound via molecules of air that vibrate; in light something else vibrates, but sound is there within light all the same. It may be in a form subtler than the ear can hear, but it is there nonetheless, and anyone who has access to subtle sounds can hear it.

"This is why the Veda is called shruti, 'that which is heard,' to distinguish it from later texts written by men, which are called smrti, 'that which is remembered.' Think of what happened to the first person to become aware of this subtle sound. One day, as he is sitting blankly, he starts to meditate on 'what is'; it's natural to do so. After prolonged meditation he remembers the first sound, the original word, the strongest mantra of shakti. This first sound that he hears is the Adi Natha, the most ancient: the sound Om, which is none other than Lord Shiva. As he continues with his meditation he progresses from stage to stage to become a Paramahamsa, then a Siddha, a Nath, and a Muni, and finally a Rishi.

"The word *rishi* means 'he who sees.' A Rishi is a Seer who sees with the divine eye of perception; who hears, with the divine ear, everything that has happened in the past. And when he speaks he speaks with the divine tongue; whatever he says must take place. The Vedas are made up of mantric hymns which were 'seen,' not composed, by certain Rishis. They 'heard' the subtle sounds which make up these hymns, and translated them into words, sounds that the human ear can hear. These mantric hymns can provide evolutionary leaps in the progress of those who know how to properly use them. The Rishis throw these hymns around, checking to see who can take their power.

"Some sadhus and yogis call themselves Rishis, but I'm afraid they are all talking out of their wits. The Rishis are very different from ordinary humans like you and me, in every way. A Rishi is an immortal being, a being who lives for spans of time which are almost inconceivable to us humans. A Rishi can create a body for himself whenever he pleases, and whenever he is through with that body he can dissolve it. In this way a Rishi can know every particle of every dimension, because he knows the characteristics of and has experienced every possible womb.

"The books say that there are eight million four hundred thousand wombs in which to be born. The numerological significance of this number is $8 + 4 = 12$ and $1 + 2 = 3$, the Three Gunas which make up the ocean of Maya in which we are all floundering. Actually, though, no one knows how many wombs there are in the universe, because wombs are innumerable. Any situation into which your consciousness is riveted when you die acts as your womb.

"Once Narada asked Lord Shiva this question of how many wombs there are in the universe. Shiva replied, 'I only take life, I do not create it. Please ask Vishnu.' But Vishnu told Narada, 'I only preserve life; I am not in the business of creating either. Please go to Brahma.' And Brahma said, 'Listen, I just create the wombs. I haven't been keeping count of how many I have created. You'll have to ask someone else.' But there was no one else to ask. Only certain Rishis have experienced all the existing wombs, so only they really know how to commiserate with all suffering beings. This is why a Rishi is a *Mahanubhavi*, a 'Great Experiencer.' This is also why a Rishi is the embodiment of motherliness, and why there is so much to learn from a Rishi—if you can ever locate one."

"That, of course, is the problem."

Time and Space

"It is a problem only because you lack patience. If you decide that locating a Rishi is the thing you want most to do you will set about doing it, no matter how many lifetimes it may take. It is only a matter of time, after all.

"Being immortal the Rishis are not subject to time as we know it. They have gone beyond the reach of Mahakala, the God of Death, whose name is Time. Mahakala is the center of all the universes, the boundary between form and formlessness. Death provides limitation to form with the help of time. All of us who are born are destined to die, and as long as we live all of us exist within the stream of time. Once we die we drop out of time until we are reborn.

"While we are alive time is real for us, but it is relative; you see this every day in your own life. At the office time seems to pass so slowly; it just drags by, especially if you have no love for your work. But when you are busy doing something that you enjoy, like sex, then you say, 'Oh, my goodness, how time flies!' Time actually passes at the same rate; the difference is only because of your point of view. But if such a small difference in viewpoint can have such a major effect on how you experience time, you can imagine what a difference there must be between the human viewpoint and the cosmic viewpoint.

"You can only know a particular time or space if its frame of reference is appropriate for you. A human would find it difficult to live for long on the moon or other planets because the human body is made to live in the time and space of Earth; Earth is our frame of reference. The Rishis, who are able to use the sun as their frame of reference, do not have this problem. While you and I count our years according to how long it takes the earth to move around the sun, the Rishis count their 'years' according to how long it takes the sun to revolve around—well, around something else. Obviously their perspective on time is very different from ours. They have gone beyond all limitations of time, so they can experience time in any frame of reference that they choose.

"Since all time cycles are relative, and depend on the observer's frame of reference, doesn't it seem at least possible that a Rishi, who has harnessed the power of the sun, should see things according to the sun's life cycle? Because of this different viewpoint a Rishi's senses of sight, hearing and memory extend to cosmic days the way the human memory extends to ordinary days. With this sort of perspective a Rishi can both plan well into the future and see far back into the past. Each Rishi likes to contribute what he can to the cosmic Lila, the play of existence. Just as countries create five-year plans to facilitate their development, the Rishis create developmental plans, for our world and for all the other worlds in the cosmos. And their plans are in an entirely different time frame from ours.

"Since Rishis are beyond all limitations of time, and since time and space form a continuum, as our modern scientists tell us, can the Rishis have any limitations as far as space is concerned either? No, they can move wherever they like in the universe in the twinkling of an eye. Einstein believed that nothing could ever go faster than light in a vacuum, but he was wrong. Thought is faster than light. A Rishi merely thinks that he wishes to go somewhere, and he arrives there immediately.

"The Rishis are beyond all limitations of time and space that we can conceive, but even they have some exceedingly subtle limitations which they must live with. They never quite transcend all attributes and distinctions; if they did, how could they continue to exist separate from the cosmos? So they continue doing their penances, getting closer and closer to absolute perfection without ever reaching it. They are totally perfect from our frame of reference, but from their frame of reference they still fall short of the Ultimate. How must they feel, if you and I feel bad that we haven't made much spiritual progress?

"But whatever their limitations, the Rishis are far, far beyond us humans. By now you should have some idea of how little you can understand the state of a Rishi, and about how fortunate we are that the Mahapurushas come here to play about. The Rishis are especially interested in our world of death and impermanence because it is here that beings can change their innate natures very quickly."

"But you are always pointing out to me people who in spite of all their efforts to improve remain as crooked as a pig's tail, and saying about them, 'Jati svabhava na munchyate' (inborn characteristics don't change)," I protested.

"And I've just got through telling you that time is relative. Most people will not be able to totally transform themselves within the space of a single human lifetime, although as you well know there are those who can and do; what about Jean Valjean? But from the cosmic viewpoint things happen here in the World of Death at breakneck speed. In just a few lifetimes you can achieve great things, whereas on other planes of existence it may take you millions or billions of years to get anywhere. Even the gods vie to be born here.

"The Rishis, in spite of being completely unlimited by any orbit, love to come down to Earth and play about, to help lighten Mother Earth of Her load. They visit all parts of the world, but they find the earth of India most to their liking."

"Does India have some sort of monopoly over them, then?"

"No, no; why they prefer India has something to do with the gravity here. There have of course been other civilizations, like that of Atlantis, which have made great spiritual progress. The Atlanteans, and the people of the civilizations which were related to them, like the ancient Egyptians, Assyrians and Babylonians, could take out the astral body and move about with it, but they could never progress as far as our Rishis did. They produced a few Siddhas, but they were really too conscious of the physical world to advance much spiritually. How can I say this? Well, look at the pyramids and the sphinx and what-have-you. How massive they are! The kings and their priests were more interested in this sort of worldly glory than in true spirituality.

"Incan culture was also based on that of Atlantis, but it never quite reached the same stage of advancement. You know, the Incas used to worship a form of *Bhairava* (Shiva as 'The Terrifier'), to whom they offered human sacrifices. The priestesses knew a crude form of Vajroli, enough so that they could regenerate themselves. They worshipped blonde people; most of the royalty was blonde, in fact. They were shorter and better built than the Red Indians, which suggests that they were of different stock.

"Atlantis sank under the ocean, and the ancient cultures of Egypt and Peru and the rest have vanished almost without a trace. But in spite of all the destruction that has happened here some part of India's ancient culture still remains, thanks to the blessings of the Mahapurushas who come here to enjoy their Lila.

"Even when the Rishis lived here openly, in physical bodies, they never wanted anyone to know them, since then they would have no peace, because even in Satya Yuga there are plenty of people around to trouble Rishis with requests for help. So, since they need peace and quiet for their researches, the Rishis would pretend to be ordinary people, and would live quiet lives with their wives in ashrams in out-of-the-way places. They always worship fire internally, but just to fool everyone they would make a show of worshipping the fire externally. If people knew that they did not need an external fire, everyone would rush to the Rishis and insist that all their work be done immediately.

"Of course, if you were clever you could recognize who was a Rishi; something would give them away, like their voices. Rishis would not talk much in words, of course; they usually communicated in Para Vani. But when they would talk their voices would be like thunder! I loved that picture *The Ten Commandments*, but one thing I have never been able to figure out is how Cecil B. DeMille was able to imitate God's voice so well. It sounded exactly like a Rishi's voice; maybe it could have been a little deeper, but that richness was there, just like a Rishi. Where did he get the idea, I wonder? Such touches are what make a film maker really great.

"Almost all our ancient Rishis were householders, which is another reason they could commiserate with the plight of embodied beings. No one is ever turned away from a Rishi's ashram, and everyone who comes there is automatically benefited. Tigers, rabbits, jackals, deer and other wild animals all live peacefully together inside the ashram's precincts. If a tiger should chase a deer into the ashram the tiger's personality will suddenly change as soon as it crosses the boundary, and it will forget to kill for as long as it remains there.

"The Rishi makes sure that all the ashram's inhabitants—plants, animals, humans, even rocks—feel confidence in themselves, so that they grow to become the best they can be, in their own ways. No one is told that he or she is bad, foolish, hopeless, or helpless. In return, all the inhabitants, even the trees and the flowers, always try to contribute their best to the ashram. Even a very dull boy who comes to the ashram, one who cannot understand even the simplest sadhana, is taken care of. The Rishi will assign him an ordinary task, like farming, or caring for the ashram's cows. When he sees that the boy is finally ready then the Rishi will initiate him, and then he too can progress.

"Actually, a Rishi is the embodiment of motherliness. In the old days, when a Rishi's wife would scold one of her husband's spiritual children for some foolishness, the Rishi himself would take the disciple aside and say, 'Don't worry about it. Do you want to do this? All right, go ahead and do it, I am here to look after you.' Don't ask me how I know all this."

He chuckled, and then spoke more softly.

"A Rishi and his wife also have a beautiful play together; far more beautiful than any of the modern relationships I see. Because the wife is half and the husband is half, it was a beautiful partnership back then; the wife would see to the details of running the ashram, the mundane aspects of life, and the Rishi would take care of the spiritual and astral aspects for both of them.

"Veda Vyasa was the Rishi who wrote the Mahabharata, and who divided the Veda into four parts. His wife was totally devoted to him and never questioned what he told her to do. She knew he was Shaktiman, the directing, controlling factor, and she knew from experience that whatever he would direct her to do would be the right thing. He in turn never had any reason to question what she did, because he knew she was the perfect executive. What a partnership!"

"Do you believe then that a woman should never question her husband?"

"What do you think?" he replied testily, to show his contempt for the foolishness of my question. "No woman should obey her husband blindly unless she is sure he never makes mistakes. Yes, if her husband is a Rishi that is one thing; but not every woman can marry a Rishi. Now may I continue with my story?"

I kept quiet.

"Because of her tremendous faith in her husband, which was her form of niyama, Vyasa's wife could carry water without a pot. Food should be filling, full of love and emotion; but the water you drink should be light, almost ethereal. Vyasa's wife simply carried a cloth whenever she went for water, and the force of her purity made the water so light that she could bind it in the cloth and carry it home with her. This is no ordinary capability, let me tell you; such power was involved that it was almost on a par with the ability to make solidified mercury impervious to the effects of fire, one of the most difficult of all transmutations.

"One day when she went down to the river to fetch some water she happened to see a pair of Gandharvas sporting in the water. She admired them, and thought, 'Ah, if only God had seen fit to permit us to have a child!' This was her only thought on the matter. She did not dream of returning to the hermitage and indulging in love-play with her husband; she did not envy the Gandharvas their romance. She just thought that one little thought—but that was enough to ruin her concentration. When she tried to pick up the water in the cloth as usual, it all spilled out.

"She tried again two or three times, with the same result. She began to get flustered, knowing that she had to bring some water for her husband. Finally she went and got an earthen pot and filled it, and returned to the hermitage.

"That evening Vyasa, who had been in samadhi all day long, came back to the ashram and asked his wife for a drink of water to soothe his parched throat. As soon as he drank the water he knew something was wrong: the water was heavy. Naturally it was heavy; it had been in that pot, and had absorbed some of the qualities of the earth of which the pot was made. One of the Earth Element's chief characteristics is heaviness.

"Very gently he brought this fact to the attention of his wife, who told him the whole story. Now it was his turn to make a mistake, because he accused her of being enamoured with the desire for romance, the base desires of the flesh. She showed him how wrong he was.

"Indignantly she replied, 'All I did was admire them, and you accuse me of falling into the trap of sensuality! Never would I do that!' To prove her point, she added, 'If my words are true, the cloth will again hold water!' And it did.

"Vyasa then had to retake his words. This is the play of Shakti and Shakti-man. She had previously been able to hold the water in the cloth on the strength of her husband's austerities, but when she made the cloth again hold water, it was her own power which did it. Jnana versus bhakti; isn't it beautiful?"

Anasuya

"It is very beautiful."

"A Rishi's wife is an amazing being in her own right. What about Anasuya, the wife of the Rishi Atri? Her very name means 'absence of envy.' What more could one want in a wife? And just as she was without envy, everyone was envious of her. Even Lakshmi, Sarasvati and Parvati, the wives of Vishnu, Brahma and Shiva, became envious of her, and one day they got together and decided to tell their husbands to go and disturb her penance so she would not stand out as the example of what a wife should be. Being henpecked, Brahma, Vishnu and Shiva gave in to their wives, and decided to disturb Anasuya's penance."

A theatrical pause, to emphasize how ill-advised this action was.

"First of all, what gave Brahma, Vishnu and Shiva the right to disturb her penance, even if Their fiat rules the whole world? Nothing; even though They are gods They had no right to interfere with a Rishi's Lila. Right from the start, then, Their mission was doomed to failure because They were try-ing to do something They had no right to do.

"They visited the hermitage of Atri and Anasuya in disguise, choosing a time when They knew Atri would be away. Anasuya invited Them in and, knowing that guests should be treated as gods, asked Them what They would like to eat. They replied, 'You may serve us whatever you like, but please feed us only after you have become naked; that is our desire.'

"This was the second mistake these three mischief-makers made. What right did They have to embarrass her modesty? None whatsoever. The time had come for Them to pay for Their evil karmas.

"Confronted by this most impertinent and unreasonable request, Anasuya decided to act. She went to her husband's *kamandalu* (water pot) and took some water from it. Sprinkling it over the three gods she said, 'Shishuvat bhava!' ('Become like babies!') And in that instant the three chief gods of the universe were changed into babies.

"Then Anasuya became naked. She took off her clothes, and she also took off the 'three coverings' from her ego; she became a perfect example of 'naked truth.' Since Brahma is the personification of Rajas, Vishnu the personification of Sattva, and Shiva the personification of Tamas, by removing all her 'coverings' she went beyond the provinces of all three of these cosmic forces.

"Once she was naked Anasuya took each baby by turn and fed Them from her own breasts. By doing this she complied with Their request—she fed Them while naked—but They could not embarrass her as They had planned to do. A baby has no idea what its mother's breast is; it knows the breast only as a source of milk. When in the Bible they talk about Amnon 'knowing' his sister Tamar they mean that he had sex with her. Only when you 'know' what the body is meant for can you be embarrassed by it. When you are too young to know, or too advanced to care, then your mind is no longer in your body; it is in your heart, where it knows other people's hearts and doesn't care for their bodies one way or another.

"The ego self-identifies with whatever catches its fancy. Ma in Her infinite compassion provides one with whatever one desires. It is only when the ego says to Ma, 'I have seen You in all of Your various costumes; now I want to see You naked, I want to see Your true self,' that She will make you like a child and let you sit on Her lap. Then you are a true child. This is why great saints are always childlike, when they are not acting like demons or madmen.

"Well, when Atri came back to the hermitage and saw what his wife had done he was so overwhelmed with joy that tears welled up in his eyes. On the other hand, the three wives of these miscreants were sitting at home, waiting for the moment when their husbands would return to dally with them and bring them the satisfying news that Anasuya had been humbled. They might have waited there forever had not the celestial troublemaker, Narada, happened onto the scene and told them where they could find their husbands, and that they would have to find them because the husbands could not find their way back home on their own, having been transformed into babies.

"Hastening to Atri's hermitage the three wives saw that Narada's words were indeed true. They went to Anasuya and said, 'Please give us back our husbands!' They knew they had to be polite.

"Anasuya said, 'Pick out your husbands and take them away if you like.' Unfortunately, they couldn't. How could they? As long as they saw their husbands as gods, as the embodiments of Sattva, Rajas, and Tamas, how could they identify them as children, in which the Three Gunas have not fully manifested? And because they were limited to the Three Gunas, how could they know the bliss of that which is beyond the Gunas? So naturally they were at a loss.

"Then Anasuya, who represents the purified ego, let herself descend into the Three Gunas again, and she delivered the appropriate babe to the appropriate wife. Then the three gods, restored by Anasuya to their normal forms and looking awfully sheepish, each blessed Anasuya that she would give birth to a great son. Soma, the moon, was born as a result of Brahma's blessing. From Shiva's blessing was born the great Rishi Durvasas. Vishnu's blessing was responsible for the birth of Dattatreya, the immortal guru of the Aghoris.

"It is said that Dattatreya received some of the blessing from Brahma and Shiva also, and that he is really an incarnation of all three gods, which means all Three Gunas. As guru of the Aghoris he went beyond all Three Gunas, beyond all those who blessed him. Hence the two meanings of his name: 'given to Atri,' which is certainly true, and 'having given up the Three,' meaning the Three Gunas. This makes sense, of course; since his mother was able to give up the Three Gunas and play about with them, doesn't it make sense that her son would be able to do so as well?"

"It does."

"This is why Dattatreya is called *Digambara* ('sky-clad'); by removing the clothing of the Three Gunas he has become truly naked, completely unaffected by anything in the manifested world. When he decided to test his students Dattatreya took to drinking wine, and created a beautiful Shakti to sit on his lap. Most of his disciples were orthodox, and they were disgusted with this sort of behavior; they could not see beneath their guru's outer 'clothes.' As Dattatreya held his Shakti's breast he watched all but one of his disciples disappear; this last remaining student was the one he taught."

Vimalananda sometimes used a similar method to rid himself of "excess baggage," as he sometimes called those people of less-than-sincere motives who tried to become his "children." He openly flouted his drinking and use of intoxicants, made no bones about his sexual activity, and was not above inventing details of his excesses if he thought it necessary. This sort of drama was usually sufficient to turn the average "spiritual groupie" away from his door.

Avataras

"Dattatreya is unique. But then, his father was a Rishi. Each Rishi offers his own experience to the world by sending down his essence to be born as a prophet or a saint, to guide and teach. When things on Earth come to such a pass that the continued existence of the Rishis' Lila seems threatened, a Rishi will send down an emanation of himself to guide the errant sheep back to the fold, as Jesus tried to do. As Lord Krishna says in the Gita, 'Whenever righteousness declines and unrighteousness increases I then take birth in the world, to protect the just, destroy the wicked, and re-establish righteousness.' Krishna, Rama and Jesus were all *amshas* (fragments, fractions) of Rishis. They were very different from you and me; they were avataras, embodiments of divinity.

"*Avatara* literally means 'downward-crossing'; an avatara crosses back from perfection into imperfection, solely because He loves us and wants to help us out. The Rishis are beyond our limitations of time and space until they choose to live on Earth, and then they make themselves subject to some of the rules which regulate us. They allow Mahakala to rule them while they remain with us, and permit the Law of Karma to direct their activities. This is why the saints and prophets always live lives of misery; they are trying, by taking on our limitations, to show us how to live. They make examples of themselves so that we can learn from their examples.

"When one day the Baby Krishna got tired of being treated as a child by His foster mother Yashoda Ma, who could only see His body and had no idea of who He was, He opened His mouth and showed her the entire universe within it. He could do this because His Kundalini was able to self-identify with the entire universe. She naturally became speechless in amazement.

"Then Krishna realized that the play would never be the same if she was allowed to remember His real nature. After all, she and everyone else who was close to Him were celestial beings who had taken birth for the express purpose of taking part in His Lila. Krishna decided it was more fun to play with His beloved devotee on a relatively equal footing rather than to have her remain awe-struck all the time, so He made her forget what she had seen, and she lapsed back into her normal role of being His mother.

"Jesus likewise could have enlightened His parents instantaneously, but then they would have been so fearful of offending Him that they could never have treated Him as their son any longer, and what fun would that have been? A play is really enjoyable only when the actors and actresses completely self-identify with their parts.

"Any emanation of any Rishi is an avatara. Because Jesus was the emanation of a Rishi we can also call Him an avatara. Each avatara is the projection of a particular Rishi, who appears as that avatara all during that kalpa. That role is his prerogative, his personal play, his birthright, you might say. No other Rishi will even attempt to take over his role. There are as many stars in space as there are grains of sand in the sea, so each Rishi can play as he likes on so many different planets. And they do play in many places, and in many different ways, according to the roles assigned to them.

"There have been many avataras of Vishnu, the Preserver, all of which were impelled by different Rishis, each of whom provided a different flavor to the emanation. Dattatreya is one of Vishnu's avataras. Ordinarily, though, when people talk about avataras they mean the Ten Avataras of Vishnu, a particular group of ten emanations Who came to support and protect the earth. In each cycle of four Yugas the same Ten Avataras of Vishnu appear. Do you know why there are Ten Avataras? $1 + 0 = 1$, the only One—Him, capital H, the Preserver of the cosmos. But there are eleven Rudras (Lords of Death): $1 + 1 = 2$, duality, since it is because of the Rudras, who end our limited human play, that the world exists.

"In Satya Yuga, when the first avataras appear, mankind is very much in tune with Nature. Everyone communicates telepathically, and they know things by intuition. In Satya Yuga people are spiritually very good, very advanced, but because they don't bother about material things they are technologically imperfect. And because they rely so much on Nature to take care of them they are more like animals than they are like the people of Kali Yuga. An animal has to rely on God; there is no other way for it to survive.

"Little by little, as the human intellect develops, people begin to think that they can improve on Nature. This is the origin of society and civilization. Still, though, they are very much in tune with Nature during Treta and Dvapara Yugas. It is only in our era, Kali Yuga, that we forget all about Nature and try to do everything on our own, and you can see the results all around us.

"Someone whose mind is subtle will see that the concept of the Ten Avataras has similarities with Darwin's theory of evolution. In fact these avataras represent stages in man's mental evolution during the cycle of the Four Yugas. Look at the Ten Avataras. The first is *Matsya*, the fish, who swims in the ocean—the ocean of jnana, which is perfect, undivided consciousness. Then comes *Kurma*, the tortoise, who is amphibious. The tortoise can live both in the ocean, the field of consciousness, and on land, the field of individual activity. Next comes *Varaha*, the boar, who lives only on land, but can swim when necessary. Do you remember the name of our current Kalpa?"

"The White Boar Kalpa."

"Boars are much more closely related to humans than are fish and tortoises. Why do you think cannibals call human flesh 'long pig'? And why do doctors use some of the pig's body tissues for organ grafting? But there is more to it than the merely physical; we'll come to that.

"After Varaha comes *Narasimha*, the Man-Lion, Who has the body of a man (nara) and the head of an animal, the lion (*simha*). He represents a transitional stage between the animal/primitive and human/rational natures. Narasimha is ferocity personified when He appears to save his beloved devotee Prahlada, who alone is able to pacify Him.

"Next we come to *Vamana*, who is a perfectly formed man, but is not of full stature; He is a dwarf. Vamana = va + mana, which indicates esoterically that the future evolutionary value (*va*) of the human race is mental prowess (*mana*); likewise the word *vanara* (monkey) indicates that after evolution (va) a monkey has the potential to become a human (nara). The Vamana Avatara is unique in that Vishnu in all His other Avataras gives something to the universe, while as Vamana He begs the cosmos back from the Asura King Bali who had conquered it. This begging was the foundation of the Krishna Avatara."

"How did that work?"

"That I will explain to you—eventually. *Parashurama*, who comes next, is a man of full stature, but He is very wild and primitive. His is a life of bloodshed; He kills all the warriors in the world many times over until He is vanquished by *Ramachandra*, the perfect man Who comes next in the line of avataras. Ramachandra, who is usually known simply as Rama, was the ideal king, a perfect example of equanimity whose life everyone can profitably imitate even though He lived a million or more years ago.

"Although perfect, Rama is still subject to certain limitations; some duality is still present. He represents endurance; His personal life was miserable, but He never lost control of Himself. His Shakti, His wife Sita, was external to Him; He even 'loses' Sita for some time, or rather, He fell under the delusion that He had lost her. Rama's limitations were primarily due to the absence of two of the Three Gunas: He existed in Sattva alone, and had no Rajas or Tamas at all.

"After Rama comes *Krishna*, the totally perfect man. Krishna was beyond all limitations except death. He embraced all the Three Gunas and then went beyond them. Krishna's Maya, His Shakti, is a part of Himself; the whole play is combined in one being. Both Nature and man reach their highest perfection in Krishna. There is no one else in any universe, past, present or future, who can be compared to Krishna. Even the Rishis marvel at His play.

"After Krishna leaves the earth Kali Yuga begins. Then comes *Buddha*. *Buddhi* means discrimination, and Lord Buddha represents the perfection of discrimination, though He is devoid of aesthetic experience. He is a man whose logical faculties are fully developed, but Who is trying to do without Maya altogether because of the many temptations of Maya, which increase in strength as Kali Yuga develops. He is not willing to live in the world and enjoy it; He wants out of the world. Lord Buddha is called the Compassionate One because even though He is no longer in the world He longs to help others who are trapped in the cycle of birth and death to escape also.

"The last Avatara is Kalki, who is yet to come. Kalki is actually the wrong word; it should be *Nishkalanka*, 'the One without any stain of any kind.' When Kali Yuga is at its worst He will appear and will destroy all but a handful of people. Then He will change the consciousnesses of those whom He allows to live so that they will remember something of their true selves, and Satya Yuga will begin all over again."

"So this whole business of yugas and avataras is basically one long loop of evolution from the extreme of intuitive consciousness to the extreme of intellectual consciousness, and then back again?"

"More or less."

"And it just keeps going on, over and over?"

"Yes, it does, but it is more like a spiral than a circle, since the events of one cycle act as a foundation for the events of the next. There is a continuous progression. Now, this idea of the Ten Avataras as reflections of the evolution of human consciousness is just the beginning; every concept should have many layers of meaning. The Ten Avataras also reflect individual spiritual evolution.

"You know, our ancient seers were not the simpletons that some modern historians make them out to be; they just didn't tell everything they knew. They believed in keeping the highest knowledge secret, because they knew that it would be dangerous in the hands of those who cannot digest it. If you drink a large glassful of ghee you will have a good nice purge unless you are used to it or are taking medicines which can digest it for you. Similarly, if you overimbibe knowledge you will not be able to retain it. It will all flow out of you unless you have had plenty of practice in digesting knowledge, or your guru predigests it for you.

"So I look at the ancient texts in a very different way than the historians do. For example, when the texts say that it is good to drink cow's milk, I read 'milk' to mean the 'milk' of sense perceptions, because 'go' means both 'sense organ' and 'cow.' To 'drink milk' then means to retain these perceptions inside, within the mind."

"But it also means actual cow's milk, doesn't it? You always say that if you can digest it cow's milk has a better effect on the mind than does the milk of other animals."

"It is better, no doubt; that is another layer of meaning of this saying. But I don't like to harp on the physical, because in Kali Yuga everyone is too attached to the physical anyway.

"When this milk of sense perceptions is mixed with the starter culture of discrimination and it is left for some time the yogurt of cultured intellect is prepared. But still it is not finished. This yogurt must be churned by constant discipline until the result is the butter of jnana, spiritual wisdom. This is still raw, however, because it is only theoretical knowledge. Only when this butter is boiled by the fires of intense longing will ghee be formed. This is the real ghee, the ghee mentioned in our tradition as 'ghrtam ayuh, ghrtam vishnor tejah' ('ghee is life, ghee is Vishnu's effulgence') because then you see Narayana everywhere. Like pure cow's ghee this knowledge is golden in color, the gold of truth. And yes, cow's ghee is the best fat to eat if you want to be healthy, but this is not an advertisement for cow's ghee!

"The doctrine of the Ten Avataras also has an internal meaning. Look again at the Avataras; the first is Matsya, the Fish. The Fish is born to save the Seven Rishis from a deluge, like the biblical flood. He also retrieves the Vedas from an asura who had stolen them and taken them to the bottom of the ocean. The ocean is the ocean of the body; the bottom of the ocean relates to the Muladhara Chakra. And do you remember Panchamakara?"

"So the Fish does his work via the breath somehow?"

"Correct. Next comes Kurma, the Tortoise. Have you studied pulse diagnosis in your Ayurvedic college?"

"A little bit." Vimalananda never bothered with taking anyone's pulse; he would always take his own pulse and then tell the person what was wrong with them. No one taught that sort of pulse diagnosis in my college.

"Have you heard of the 'tortoise' at the navel?"

Then I remembered; the plexus of nadis at the navel is sometimes called a "tortoise" because it is said to look like a turtle, with large nadis appended at roughly the positions where the turtle's legs, head and tail would be.

"Now think about this story: The devas and the asuras had agreed to cooperate to churn the ocean of milk in order to obtain the treasures hidden within. They used Mount Mandara as the churning rod and the serpent Vasuki as the churning rope. Forget for now the celestial events that this represents; think instead of the fact that this churning of the ocean happens inside every sadhaka. The devas and the asuras are your good thoughts and your bad thoughts, respectively. The mountain represents your spine and spinal cord. Ordinarily the spinal cord is a chain which binds you down to the world, just as the causal body is a chain of karmas which binds you down to rebirth. The spinal cord binds you down because it causes you to project your consciousness out into your body. I don't need to remind you of the significance of the serpent.

"At first attempt, nothing happens, because the mountain is too heavy and sinks to the bottom of the ocean. Then Vishnu incarnates as the Tortoise, and with the rod resting on His back the churning proceeds. What would you guess is the meaning of this event?"

"I think it suggests that you have to have a firm base when you try to use Kundalini to churn your being, because otherwise your attention will keep slipping down into the mundane again. The churning is done with prana, I take it, since the Tortoise is involved."

"Good guess. The process of enlightenment is chemical, with certain hormones and other glandular secretions being created when these processes occur. The 'churning of the ocean' is also a neurochemical process, during which so many internal treasures are produced, one of which is Amrita, the glandular secretion which is the nectar of immortality.

"The first thing which happens, however, when you churn your consciousness is that you separate it from the poison of the samsara, the ocean of manifested existence. This emerges as the Halahala poison, which Shiva consumes in order to keep it from descending any further than your throat. When you become a sadhaka you must keep the outside world outside, and cultivate interiority; otherwise you will be poisoned. You must stop identifying with the samsara; otherwise how will you be able to get any perspective on it? As long as the Serpent Power sleeps at the base of the spine She identifies Herself with the poison of the limited individual personality. When She awakens, She realizes She is by nature unlimited and free and She relinquishes the poison, which must then be dealt with. And there is no one in the universe like Shiva when it comes to dealing with poison.

"After the poison the treasures began to emerge: the wish-fulfilling cow, the celestial horse, the celestial elephant, the celestial tree, a celestial jewel, the apsarases—"

"Since the apsarases are really special nadis, could all these treasures be nadis?"

"They could be; but don't jump to conclusions. Then came the goddess Lakshmi, which Vishnu took for Himself, followed by the goddess of liquor, which the asuras took for themselves, since Vishnu had taken Lakshmi. Finally Dhanvantari, the god of physicians, emerged; in his hand was the pot of nectar.

"Now, the agreement had been that the devas and the asuras would evenly divide this nectar, but since Vishnu decided that the asuras could not be trusted with it He took the form of Mohini, the Enchantress, and it was agreed that She would distribute the Amrita. The asuras were so overwhelmed with lust when they looked at Mohini that they overlooked the fact that Vishnu was doling out the Amrita only to the devas. When the spell was broken they suddenly realized their mistake, but it was too late; all the nectar was gone. A great battle ensued, but because the devas had been invigorated by the Amrita the asuras were defeated.

"Internally the same sort of struggle occurs when Amrita is produced. All the selfish aspects of your personality want their share, but your spirit, your Indwelling Ruler, deludes them until they fight back and, weakened by your practices, are destroyed. Unfortunately, like the asuras, they eventually revive and return to fight another day. This is why sadhana is so important."

"The asuras come back to life?"

"Yes, but that is another story. Now we come to the Boar, Who emerged from one of the Creator's nostrils. His job was to dive deep into the ocean and retrieve the earth, who had been kidnaped by the asura Hiranyaksha. So the Boar is also tightly bound up with prana and with the earth. Earth Herself was created when she emerged from one of the nostrils of Brahma, the Creator, which suggests that Earth must also have some connection with prana. This is not surprising; the earth is Mother Nature, the ultimate root of all life which lives on Her. But how exactly is She connected with prana?

You may try to reason it out for years and years and yet you will never discover it. It is beyond the process of reason."

"Inside the body, though, the implications seem fairly obvious," I said. "After the body is revivified with Amrita and the prana is well controlled, the Indwelling Ruler can dive down to the Muladhara Chakra, the seat of the Earth Element, and bring Kundalini out from under the waters of the ocean of manifestation so that She can start Her return journey to Her Beloved. Is this close?"

"Very close. Next comes the Man-Lion. Narasimha saved Prahlada by killing his father Hiranyakashipu, who was king of the asuras. Hiranyakashipu, who had conquered the cosmos in a rage after the Boar had killed his brother Hiranyaksha, demanded that Prahlada should worship him alone. But right from his birth Prahlada, who was a spiritual type born into a family of materialists, was a dedicated devotee of Vishnu. Even when his father threatened to kill him several times, Prahlada's faith never wavered. His very name suggests this; *prahlada* means 'especially joyous.'

"Prahlada's devotion to Vishnu increased his power of discrimination tremendously, which helped him survive. For example, once his father ordered him to embrace a red-hot pillar. When Prahlada inspected it closely he saw ants walking on it, and realized that his father had only made it appear to be red-hot using the magical powers which all asuras possess innately. He then fearlessly embraced the pillar. But when his father really did lose his temper and was really ready to kill his son, Vishnu in the form of the Man-Lion stepped in and saved his devotee Prahlada."

A brief pause.

"You know, you can go on for years and years reading all the holy books, and unless someone tells you or you suddenly develop insight of your own, you will never understand any of their real meaning. Narasimha puts Hiranyakashipu on His lap, disembowels him with His claws, and garlands Himself triumphantly with his entrails. This is what the books say, and most people take this story at face value and leave it at that.

"But a person with subtle intelligence will wonder how many people have ever been so fortunate to have been taken on the Lord's lap. The answer is very, very few. So even though he died in the process, Hiranyakashipu must have been tremendously blessed by the Man-Lion. Hiranyakashipu had performed tremendous austerities, and in his arrogance tried to rival Vishnu Himself. His envy and hatred of Vishnu were so intense that he remembered Him almost constantly, and this drew Vishnu to him, to save him by slaying him. We call this *virodha bhakti* (perverse devotion).

"Why did Narasimha rip open Hiranyakashipu's belly? Because of the Manipura Chakra. Another name for Shiva is 'Hara,' 'The Snatcher.' When Mahakala snatches the Jathara Agni from the body life ceases, since your tissues lose their ability to feed themselves, and you die—or at least the mundane 'you' dies. If you have already converted Jathara Agni into Bhuta Agni, however, there is nothing for Hara to snatch, and you are immortal.

"So Narasimha split Hiranyakashipu's belly and awakened his Manipura Chakra, causing all the Jathara Agni, all the physical digestive fire, to be converted into Bhuta Agni, the spiritual fire, the fire of life. After such a conversion there is no need to eat at all; you can digest whatever prana comes your way. This is real freedom, or at least one aspect of it. It is freedom enough to make one into a Siddha, an immortal being, which is what Narasimha did to Hiranyakashipu.

"This is the meaning of the entrail necklace that the Man-Lion wears: He has removed all the Jathara Agni, which is contained in the guts, from the asura's body, and forcibly prevented Apana from moving downward any longer. Vishnu transmuted Hiranyakashipu's violent anger and hatred toward Him into an intense spiritual fire. The Man-Lion can do for you, too, if you are ready for it.

"Narasimha, Who is the embodiment of Fire, was not born; He emerged suddenly from a pillar in Hiranyakashipu's palace. This 'pillar' was of course the spinal cord. Sadhakas who are filled with false, demonic ego get disemboweled by the Fire Element as Kundalini awakens; the Man-Lion creates forcible purification, often at the expense of life itself. But to His devotees like Prahlada Narasimha offers His protection, and preserves their lives when they reach this stage."

Vimalananda fell silent here, and so I prodded him: "What about Vamana, and the other avataras?"

"A little at a time, Robby. There is so much to know, but you must digest what you learn if it is to be of any use to you. And we have only scratched the surface of these stories; there are so many things left to consider. Right now, though, we have something better to do: to sing the sweet name of God!"

Skulls & Skull Cups

The Esoteric Ramayana

Vimalananda used to organize a small function each year on *Guru Purnima* ("Guru's Full Moon"), the day on which one's guru is worshipped. He would arise well before dawn and worship his own gurus, and then all day long his spiritual "children" would drop by to offer their thanks for what he shared with them, and to request his blessings for further spiritual development during the coming year. Lunch would be prepared and served to everyone who came, and the afternoon and evening were reserved for the singing of devotional songs.

Because of the difficulty in fitting everyone into his flat, one year we decided to rent a marriage hall for the purpose, and hired a female *kirtankar*, a sort of spiritual bard, to recount stories of the Lord for us. While we were waiting for her to arrive, someone turned on a prerecorded cassette of a recitation of Tulsidas' Ramayana, performed by M., a very famous *kirtankar*.

The story of the Ramayana is the story of Prince Ramachandra. Just before He is to be crowned king of Ayodhya His father's third wife Kaikeyi reminds His father King Dasharatha of two boons the king had given her long before. For her two boons she asks that her son Bharata be made king, and that Rama be sent to the forest for fourteen years. Rama is joined in this penance by His wife Sita and His brother Lakshmana. After many adventures Sita is stolen by Ravana, the demon king of Lanka. Rama has to search long and hard to find her again, and once He finds her He has to invade Lanka with an army of monkeys and bears headed by Anjaneya, and kill Ravana in order to get her back. This is the mission for which He was born, because Ravana had oppressed the whole world.

The tape we were listening to covered only a small fragment of this epic, and when it ended Vimalananda asked, "Do you know M's story?" I did not, and if anyone else did they did not let on. "He was once a schoolteacher in Saurashtra (a region of Western India). When he was small his grandfather used to sit the boy on his knee and recite the Tulsidas Ramayana to him. Eventually M. memorized the entire book. While he had his teaching job he used to recite this Ramayana here and there for a few hundred rupees at a time.

"One vacation he went to Mount Girnar, and while wandering about came across a sadhu who was very fond of Anjaneya. The sadhu requested him to recite the Ramayana for him, and M. did it so well that the nearby statue of Anjaneya started to shed tears. The sadhu himself was so overwhelmed with joy that he blessed M.—really speaking, it was Anjaneya Himself who delivered the blessing, through the medium of the sadhu.

"And the result? M. now lectures before audiences of tens of thousands of people who sit in pindrop silence attending on his every word. People are ready to give him millions, but he doesn't accept any money, except on one day of the year: today, Guru Purnima. Which is a good thing, since Tulsidas did not write his version of the Ramayana in order to make money off it, and certainly not so that someone else could make money off it."

At this point our kirtankar suddenly arrived, and Vimalananda interrupted his story. A few days later when a convenient moment to resume it arose, I casually suggested to him that we listen to another of M.'s Ramayana cassettes. At the end of one side I switched off the tape player and looked expectantly at Vimalananda, who gestured to me to sit down and prepare to listen mindfully.

"The Rishis script everything before it ever happens," he began. "There is some room for improvisation, just as there is in any stage play, but the basic story does not change."

He motioned to me to light him a cigarette. "Thanks to the Rishis and their Lila India has been blessed with two great epic poems: the Ramayana, which as you know is the story of Ramachandra, the seventh Avatara of Vishnu; and the Mahabharata, which is basically the story of Krishna, Vishnu's eighth Avatara. For thousands of years these epics have been the foundation of India's culture. I have already told you a small part of the Krishna Lila, and how it relates to Kundalini Yoga.

"Most Indians know the outline of the story of the Ramayana, and there are so many people, like M., who make their living by reciting and interpreting the Ramayana. Many of them, like M., are good people; but how little most of them really know of the Ramayana and of Rama! The esoteric Ramayana, the true spiritual essence of the story, is something very few people know. But it is something you should know about, because it relates to the awakening of Kundalini.

The Script

"We would never have had the Ramayana at all had it not been for the Rishi Valmiki and his concern over how to spread out the karmas he had incurred through his chosen profession. Valmiki was not born a Rishi; in fact, he was a bandit. His job was waylaying people and robbing them. Sometimes he would hold them for ransom, or even kill them. Occasionally he would let them go. One day Valmiki caught the celestial troublemaker Narada, and told him that he would have to die because he had nothing of value to steal.

"Narada told him, 'All right, I am ready to die, but please tell me why you rob people.'

"Valmiki replied, 'Because I have to feed my family.'

"Narada then asked him, 'Do you think that they are all as willing to share in your karmas as they are to share in your income?'

"Valmiki said, 'Of course they are!' But deep inside his mind doubt suddenly took root. Narada told him, 'Before you kill me and add to the weight of your karmas, why don't you first make sure that your family is willing to share them with you?'

"Valmiki returned to his home to inquire and got the shock of his lifetime when one after another his family members refused to have anything to do with his bad karmas. His parents told him, 'We raised you and supported you while you were growing up; now you have to pay us back. We don't care where the money comes from; that is your problem.'

"His wife said, 'I have borne your children and run your household. You owe me a living, and I am not interested in how you provide it. All your karmas are your responsibility.' His children informed him, 'We never asked to be born here. You have created us, and now you have to look after us at your own expense. You will have to worry about your karmas yourself.'

"A shaken Valmiki returned to Narada, who had of course foreseen what would happen. Narada then taught Valmiki about how devotion to Vishnu can eliminate bad karmas. Because Valmiki could not pronounce Sanskrit correctly he could not repeat 'Rama, Rama,' so Narada ordered him to repeat 'mara, mara,' instead. *Mara* means 'killer,' which was something Valmiki could relate to.

"Both 'mara' and 'Rama' have the same letters, the same Bija Mantras, which means there must be a definite connection between them. There is also a definite difference in effect between them, due to the order in which the letters are pronounced, in the same way that there is both a connection and a difference between 'Hara' (Shiva) and 'raha' (secret).

"Valmiki sat down and began to recite. He sat in one position for sixty thousand years without moving. Ant hills grew over him . . ."

He paused, I interjected: "Naturally, since 'Valmiki' means 'he who lives in a *valmika* (an anthill or termite mound).'

"That's right. By repeating 'mara, mara' at top speed Valmiki actually started to repeat 'Rama, Rama.' When he finally emerged he was a Rishi.

"The Ramayana was composed long before it ever happened. First the Rishis got together and decided that they wanted a certain type of Lila. Then they commissioned Valmiki to write the script. It was just like writing the script of a drama or a movie for him. Actually it was even simpler; he simply opened himself up, and the senior Rishis wrote the Ramayana through him."

"So his sadhana made him a vessel fit to hold the shakti that the Rishis wanted to manifest in the world through him."

"Yes. This is what I mean when I say that the Rishis are the puppetmasters and we are merely the puppets. They decide what is to happen and then arrange for it to happen. The events that followed the writing of the Ramayana were entirely preordained. And people think there is such a thing as free will."

"So there is no such thing as free will?"

"There is really no such thing as free will for beings like us. Until you become a Rishi your options are to follow the script or not to follow it, and if you don't follow the script you will eventually regret it. You can however choose just how you will follow the script, if your will is strong enough."

"Will is the power to direct the mind, especially when there are contrary thoughts or tendencies within it. The mind governs the senses and the senses dominate the body through the nervous system. If the mind is untrained, as it is in most people, the will loses its authority and the body functions stupidly. You know that it is bad for your health to eat a thick juicy steak, and yet you do it. Your tongue overrides your willpower. You know that sleeping with a prostitute may give you a disease as a fringe benefit, but you go ahead and do it because your penis overrides your will. This is a type of mental impotence, an inability to control your actions, and it leads inevitably to unhappiness and frustration.

"All spiritual progress exists in the cultivation of a controlled mind. I am not talking about a closed mind, one which suppresses its desires. I am talking about a conditioned mind which maintains close watch over the senses by force of will. This is why I so love Anjaneya. He is immortal, he is a superman, and yet his mind is always focused on Rama, and his will is always subordinated to the will of Rama.

"Take a leaf from Anjaneya's book, and learn some humility," he said, focusing his gaze firmly on me. "Very few people know that Anjaneya actually introduced the story of the Ramayana to the world for the first time. He wrote his version with his fingernails on blocks of stone. After some time he realized that if his version became popular it would interfere with the fame of Valmiki's version, and he also understood that in Kali Yuga no one would be able to understand his Sanskrit properly, so he threw those blocks into the sea at Rameshwaram. They are still there somewhere, underwater. What did he care for name or fame? He cared only for Rama, so he could afford to be generous."

Mentally I bowed to the will of Rama.

"From one angle, episodes from the Ramayana take place every day in everyone's body. If people knew about this they would marvel at it. The Ramayana has seven divisions called Kandas which represent the Six Tastes in the body plus the one Parama Rasa, or Supreme Taste. Which Kanda you relive depends on which Taste you experience. If you are overwhelmed with lust, you relive the kidnapping of Sita by Ravana, and so on. But there is more.

"The story of the Ramayana is the story of the spiritual progress of an individual soul. All of us have the main characters of the drama present within us, and all of us who do sadhana live through the same sort of trials and tribulations that Rama and Sita had to endure. Rama, Sita and the rest had their own personalities, and therefore their own Kundalinis, but they also represent actors in the epic which is performed by everyone who does Kundalini Yoga. If you want to try to grasp the hidden meanings that exist within the story, and understand how it might affect you, first try to understand the characters.

The Players

"Rama, the Indwelling Spirit, is called *Raja* (King) Rama because He is king of the seventy-two thousand nadis. Krishna also rules the nadis, but His Lila is different; He has a love affair with them. Some people find it easier to relate to the Soul as King; others prefer to relate to It as Lover. You must find which way agrees best with your temperament, and relate in that way. As they say, 'the Truth is One; the learned describe It in many ways.'

"Rama's brother Lakshmana represents the power of concentration which helps the Soul to regain its Bride. His name, from the word *laksha*, suggests one-pointed concentration, and in fact Lakshmana did focus his concentration on a single goal: his brother Rama, the individual soul. Sita, Rama's wife, is the Kundalini Shakti, the power of Ma on an individual level. Sita was not born from a womb, as Rama was; she was found when her father King Janaka was plowing the ground to build a sacrificial altar. She comes therefore from *Bhu Garbha*, the 'womb of the earth.' *Janaka* means 'creator'; it is Janaka who by removing Sita from the Earth Element 'creates' her, or if you prefer, 'awakens' her."

"'Awakens' seems more appropriate, since the Earth Element is at the Muladhara Chakra."

"Exactly. Janaka, Sita's father, the king of Videha, was a truly amazing man. He had so purified the Fire Element within him that he used to sit on the throne with one foot resting in a blazing fire—not near it, *in* it—and with one of his queens sitting on his left thigh. He would cup her left breast in his hand, and go about the business of kingship without the least disturbance whatever. This is the real significance of the word *videha*, which means 'bodyless.' Even though Janaka had a body he behaved as if he had none.

"When Rama came to Janaka's court to attend the Swayamvara Ceremony at which Sita would decide who she would wed, He was given Lord Shiva's bow to bend, which no one had ever been able to bend before. When Rama first bent and then broke the bow, Janaka realized that Rama was meant to marry Sita. Esoterically—well, this is something which cannot be communicated in words, but I can tell you this: Shiva's bow relates to the medulla oblongata."

"The medulla oblongata?"

"Yes, the ancient Rishis were well aware of anatomy, as you have glimpsed somewhat from your study of Ayurveda. Now, Rama and Sita have to leave for the forest almost immediately after being married. Lakshmana refuses to be separated from them—how can the power of concentration be separated from the soul and the ego?—and accompanies them. When Kundalini unites with the soul the two withdraw from the senses, which wither and die from lack of shakti. And in fact King Dasharatha died very soon after Rama left Ayodhya. Dasharatha means 'Ten Chariots': the ten senses. The senses allow us to become aware of the soul; this is how Dasharatha is Rama's father.

"All would have been well with Rama and Sita in the jungle had not Sita fallen prey to curiosity and disobeyed the orders of her brother-in-law Lakshmana. Which is precisely what I keep telling you: just because your Kundalini starts to get awakened does not mean that the job is over. In fact, your job is only beginning. Because she strayed from perfect concentration on the soul, Sita was abducted by Ravana.

"Ravana, the demon king who abducted Sita, represents the limited personality which constantly contemplates its greatness: 'I am everything, I am lord of Lanka.' 'Lanka' is Lam Bija, the Earth Element. Ravana was a very powerful being; he had become lord of the manifested universe. His ten heads also stand for the ten sense organs. He propitiates Shiva by chopping off these heads, which means that he forcibly restrained his senses from perceiving anything except Shiva. His offering is selfish, however; he is a demon.

"Once he had realized Shiva, Ravana wanted to carry Him down to Lanka to live with him there. But Shiva is above the manifested universe—within the brain—and so when Ravana lifted Mount Kailasa, Shiva's home, in order to carry it and Shiva back with him to Lanka—the Muladhara Chakra—Shiva pressed Ravana down with His toe, and Ravana's hands were trapped under the mountain. Ravana had to bellow hymns to Shiva for thousands of years before Shiva took pity on him and allowed him to escape."

Ravana means 'howling.'

"Rama lost Sita to a formidable foe: the limited, demonic human personality which wants to use her for its own gratification. Rama had to wander far and wide before He could find any trace of Sita, just as you must search strenuously for Kundalini once She has self-identified with something other than the soul. Lakshmana, the one-pointed concentration which helped Rama regain His bride, was his brother's only companion for much of His search, until they met Anjaneya, who immediately enlisted in Rama's service. Anjaneya is prana, the son of the god of wind. Properly harnessed, prana clears Kundalini's path to return to her Lord, which is what Anjaneya did for Sita and Rama at every step."

Anjaneya's Role

Vimalananda paused for a moment and looked up to an image of Anjaneya, better known as Hanuman. His lip quivered almost imperceptibly with emotion as he spoke again.

"Anjaneya flew to Lanka, located Sita, and assured her that Rama was coming to rescue her. Before returning to Rama with the news of Sita's whereabouts Anjaneya allowed himself to be captured and taken before Ravana to make Ravana aware of the gravity of what he had done. Then Anjaneya burned the city of Lanka to the ground, destroying Ravana's lovely fantasy world.

"Actually Sita was responsible for the burning of Lanka. Ravana's minions wrapped Anjaneya's tail in oil-soaked rags to torment him. But when they lit the rags Sita prayed to the god of fire to refrain from burning his flesh, and Anjaneya felt no burning. In fact, he felt a wonderfully cool sensation; he felt cool enough to go calmly about his work of destroying the city. This prayer of Sita's is actually a mantra; if you know it you can sit in the fire for years on end and not even one of your hairs will be singed. After all, Sita is *shita*, cool. Wah, Ma, wah!

"Anjaneya was able to burn Lanka with the help of his tail. Think of the esoteric meaning here: Lanka stands for the Muladhara Chakra and the Earth Element. So that the Earth Element can no longer exert any effect on him whatsoever Anjaneya burned it, using his tail, which is attached to his body near the Muladhara Chakra. A sadhaka likewise totally 'burns' all connection between Kundalini and the Earth Element with the help of prana moving in the Muladhara.

"After burning Lanka, Anjaneya returned to Rama—he is totally devoted to Rama—and with the help of the other monkeys built a bridge so that

Rama could cross over to Lanka. This process is called *Setu Bandha*. Internally, this bridge connects the Muladhara Chakra to the Manipura Chakra, bridging the Svadhishthana Chakra. This particular bridge can only be built by a perfect celibate, someone like Anjaneya who is not in the least tempted by any enjoyment which the Svadhishthana, the sex chakra, can offer him.

"Anjaneya is strictly chaste, which is unusual for a monkey; most monkeys spend their days mating or masturbating. But then, Anjaneya is a monkey in form only. He is an incarnation of Lord Shiva, and he is sufficiently aware of his true nature that he is not affected, or is affected very little, by his simian nature.

"By bridging the ocean—the Water Element—Anjaneya was freed from being affected by Water. This is a permanent bridge; when Anjaneya does something it is impossible to change it. Even the external bridge that was built became permanent. Once Arjuna tried to be clever and destroy the real bridge, and he got nowhere. How could he possibly compete with the bravery and strength of Anjaneya, who is *Mahavira Balavant* (the 'Great and Powerful Hero')?

"You know the story of the Ramayana. Have you ever wondered why it was necessary to build a bridge over the sea from India to Lanka so that Rama and his armies could cross it?"

"No, I haven't."

"The bridge was necessary because the ocean refused to cooperate with Rama. When every other living thing in the world was cooperating with Rama because they loved him so much, why wouldn't the ocean cooperate?"

Good question; the story should be logical.

"Some people think it was because Anjaneya wanted to show off and become famous, but that is impossible; he is the epitome of devoted service, the single-minded servant of Rama. He has no other thought than for Rama. The answer lies in the Churning of the Ocean, at the time of the Kurma Avatara."

Of course! How elegant!

"The ocean was terribly tortured during the churning. How would you like to be churned? So although the ocean cooperated with Vishnu when Vishnu returned in the form of the Rama Avatara, it cooperated grudgingly, and partially. There was no alternative but to build a bridge."

"So after the ocean of the body is tortured by the churning of prana that is necessary to generate the Amrita, a new channel must be created—is this the idea?"

"You're getting there," he laughed. "Keep thinking about it. After the bridge was completed Rama, Lakshmana, Anjaneya and the monkeys invaded Lanka and the battles between the forces of Rama and Ravana began. At one point Lakshmana was seriously wounded. The chief physician reported that unless the *sanjivani* herb, which can restore the dead to life, was brought within a few hours, Lakshmana would die. That herb was available only on a certain mountain in the Himalayas. Rama was distraught at the possibility of losing Lakshmana, His right arm, so Anjaneya volunteered to bring back sanjivani. He flew to the mountain but could not find the herb, so in order to save time he uprooted the entire mountain and carried it back to Rama. Sanjivani was located, Lakshmana was saved, and Anjaneya returned the mountain to its proper place.

"You may have seen pictures of Anjaneya flying through the air with a mountain in his hand; they are illustrations of this story. Think about its meaning for a moment. I'm not going to spell it out for you; that would be too easy. But it involves Lakshmana, the one-pointed concentration of the mind; Anjaneya, who here is the body's prana; and the mountain from the Himalayas, the vertebral column which contains the spinal cord with its physical nerves and subtle nadis.

He let me think on these things for a few moments, and then said, "Now let me make this story even more complicated for you."

"Thanks," I replied sardonically.

"As Anjaneya flew over Ayodhya with the mountain, Rama's brother and regent Bharata saw him in the sky and, taking him for a demon, shot him down with an arrow. When he realized his mistake he was horrified, but Anjaneya reassured him and continued on his way. There was a sadhu I knew in Girnar who worshipped Anjaneya in the form of 'Langde Lal': Anjaneya who limps from the arrow in his thigh. In fact, the sadhu who blessed M. to be able to recite the Ramayana so well worshipped Langde Lal."

"Were they the same sadhu?"

"I don't know." He did know, clearly, and quickly proceeded with his point: "Think for just a moment: Anjaneya is immortal, a superman. How could an arrow shot by a mortal, even one so powerful as Bharata, even scratch his skin?"

Another conundrum.

He continued: "This is easy enough to understand: Bharata did everything in Rama's name. He even shot his arrow in Rama's name. Anjaneya is utterly devoted to Rama, and only when an arrow with Rama's name hits him does he fall. And only when Bharata, Rama's viceroy, gives him leave to go in the name of Rama can he depart."

"This is becoming difficult to follow."

"These things take time to digest. Keep trying! Anjaneya helped Rama conquer and kill Ravana. Now, Rama and Ravana both begin with 'R.' In India the first letter of a person's first name reflects where the moon is in that person's horoscope. Have you noticed how people whose names begin with the same letter, which means that they have the same moon sign, are often enemies? Astrologically it is not supposed to be this way; they should be friends. But often they are enemies: Krishna and Kamsa, Jesus and Judas, Gandhi and Godse."

"True enough. But of course Jesus and Judas were not from India."

"Ah, but remember the phonetic value of words. Names in India are given in this way to help balance out the mind; the moon controls the mind, especially the emotional side of the mind. Whatever your name, it is going to exert a strong effect on you, because everytime someone calls you by that name, and everytime you think of yourself by name, the phonetic value of that name will affect your consciousness, just like a mantra does."

Wow. "That means that there are billions of people out there in the world who have the wrong names! Which means their very names are probably unbalancing them even further!"

"Definitely. But after all, this is Kali Yuga, you know; you have to expect this sort of thing."

"What about my name?"

"As it turns out, your name should have started with 'r' anyway, so there is no problem."

"Quite a coincidence, or something."

"Or something. You share the same moon sign as both Rama and Ravana. 'R' represents Ram Bija, the Fire Element; anyone who worships Rama is actually worshipping fire. Ravana is Fire still polluted by the limited ahamkara; Rama is the Eternal Soul, pure Fire."

I understood: so long as my own innate selfishness remains I remain equivalent to Ravana, no matter how great and powerful I may become; but there is a chance, should I purify my own Fire Element sufficiently, that I might yet achieve Rama.

"After Anjaneya frees himself of all traces of egotism by helping Rama he is then free of all limitations associated with the Fire Element. A tiny trace of individual effort remained when he burned Lanka; this is why his tail was set alight. Even then Sita prevented him from being burned. Once he is free of every taint, though, Fire can no longer touch him at all.

"After Rama killed Ravana Sita was freed from the demon's clutches, and returned to her rightful husband. In the body of the sadhaka this suggests that the Fire Element becomes totally purified; the Kundalini Shakti is freed from the clutches of Jathara Agni and is returned to the influence of Bhuta Agni. When Sita is retrieved she must submit to an ordeal by fire to prove that she has maintained her purity, that she has not been tainted by Jathara Agni. You must submit to a similar, but internal, test at this stage; if you pass, you become free of the need to eat.

"From the Manipura Chakra the Kundalini goes to the Anahata Chakra. Rama, Sita, Lakshmana and a few others flew from Lanka back to Rama's capital Ayodhya in a sort of airplane, the Pushpaka Vimana. It is natural that they would fly, since the Anahata is the seat of the Air Element. Anjaneya is the son of the wind god. He is in his own element at the Anahata, and it is here that a sadhaka can meet him. The doors to his three lower chakras are irrevocably closed, so you will never chance upon him there; and when his consciousness is in the Vishuddha or higher, how will you be able to contact him? Beyond the Anahata he can see only Rama.

"Up to the Anahata you can still be aware of other individuals and have a desire to play about with them, though you see them all as forms of your Beloved. This is why fakirs (Muslim sadhus), once they reach 'chauthe asmaan,' the Fourth Heaven, are always doing work for people and helping out the helpless. The Fourth Heaven is the Fourth Chakra, the Anahata. Once you reach the Vishuddha, though, there is 'vishesha shuddhi' ('special purification') and there is no wish of any kind. And beyond the Vishuddha are the Ajna, where all that remains is the consciousness of individuality, and the Sahasrara, where nothing remains. No, if you want to meet Anjaneya you must do so at the heart.

"When you are endangered, why does your hand go to your chest? Because Vishnu is the presiding deity of the Anahata Chakra, and you are instinctively requesting him to save you, to preserve your life. Anjaneya, the servant of Vishnu in the form of Rama, is also a Rudra, an aspect of Shiva, the Destroyer. So it is no wonder that the Anahata Chakra is the place of both life and death.

"Have you seen pictures of Anjaneya ripping open his chest with his fingernails to show that nothing remains in his heart but the purest form of Rama?"

I thought for a moment before replying, "Those that I have seen usually show both Sita and Rama together in Anjaneya's heart."

"Yes, most do, but that is incorrect; Rama alone resides there. People sometimes speak of Anjaneya and Rama as different, but they are wrong. In fact, Anjaneya is Rama's heart."

"What?"

"Of course. Anjaneya is prana, the son of wind; he causes the heart to beat. How could Rama ever exist without His heart? Here is a story for you: Once Sita was complaining to Rama. 'O *Aryaputra* (Son of the Just),' she said, 'sometimes I want to have a private conversation with you, but we are never alone. Anjaneya is always with us. Please send him out now and let us talk alone.'

"Rama replied, 'O wife, what are you saying? What is there for you to tell me that Anjaneya cannot hear?'

"Sita answered, 'I have some private womanly work, and since Anjaneya is not married he cannot listen.'

"Rama said, 'All right, just to please you I will send Anjaneya away for a short time.'

"He turned and spoke to Anjaneya: 'I will inform you when the discussion is over; then come back in. Meanwhile, please go out and eat some fruit from the trees in the garden.'

"So Anjaneya went out to the garden. He looked at the fruit trees but couldn't bear to pluck any fruit from them; how could he hurt them? So he sat underneath a shady tree and began to sing a song in praise of His master Rama. Soon he was lost in samadhi.

"About this time Rama inexplicably began to yawn. But Anjaneya was so intent on his song—'Ram Ram Sitaram, Ram Ram Sitaram'—that he had completely forgotten his earthly existence, and he continued to sit and sing.

"Rama was in a fix. He was yawning incessantly and no one could cure Him. They called His personal physician, who checked His pulse and said that there was no underlying pathology. They called the astrologer, who said that all the planets were in good positions and there were no inauspicious signs. Finally, after calling a few more people, they called Rama's brother Lakshmana. He also did not know what to do, but he did remember to call Anjaneya.

"Anjaneya was out in the garden, deep in samadhi. By continuously chanting 'Sitaram Sitaram' into his ears for many minutes Lakshmana with difficulty brought Anjaneya back to earthly consciousness, and told him, 'Something is wrong with Lord Rama.'

"In one jump Anjaneya was in the palace, and the moment Rama saw Him the yawning stopped."

"The yawn was Rama's way of telling Anjaneya to return to the palace?"

"You are a student of Ayurveda; what can you tell me about yawning?"

"It is caused by an abnormal upward movement of prana—oh. I see."

"Correct. Anyway, Sita learned a good lesson: wherever Rama is Anjaneya must be there also, and vice versa. But it is also true that wherever Rama is Sita must be also. Once Sita asked Anjaneya, 'Do you like Rama's lotus feet better, or mine?' A tough question; how could Anjaneya insult either His beloved Rama or Rama's Shakti Sita? So He told her, 'Your lotus feet are the softest and most enjoyable, while Rama's are a little hard; but for liberation none can surpass Rama's.'

"Now, I have always loved Anjaneya; he is my most beloved deity. But here he was wrong. Without Sita Rama was nothing; there are so many instances that he had to come begging to Anjaneya for help. Only the Divine Mother can grant liberation; nothing is higher than Ma. Only a few, like Anjaneya, can go beyond Maya, the transitory, to Rama, the permanent, and they all do so by Ma's grace, nothing else."

Hmm. "So Rama requires Anjaneya, Sita and Lakshmana to be complete."

"Yes, which is why He is called Perfection Encompassed; He is the Perfect Man, but is subject to limits. This is why you always find all four images in a temple of Rama. They form a team; they cannot be separated from one another.

"After returning to Ayodhya Rama ruled as king, assisted by Lakshmana, Sita and Anjaneya. His rule, called *Rama Rajya*, was an ideal time in which to live; all was harmonious throughout His kingdom."

"And esoterically, I suppose, Rama Rajya happens whenever someone attains Rama-consciousness in this way."

"Of course. Regardless of when or where Rama lived and ruled on Earth, Rama Rajya happens whenever a sadhaka realizes the Rama within himself or herself and installs that Rama as the Inner Ruler.

"Rama ruled peacefully and happily for many years, but since all that is created must be destroyed, no matter how perfect it may be, one day Mahakala, Who is Time Personified, came to have a chat with Him. Mahakala stipulated that Rama must immediately disown anyone who might happen to disturb their conversation; He wanted no worldly influence whatsoever to interfere.

"As it happened Lakshmana did not know about this stipulation, and he inadvertently disturbed Rama and Mahakala. Rama, who always kept His word, had no alternative but to reject Lakshmana permanently. Lakshmana decided that life without Rama was not worth living, and so he jumped into the river which flows through Ayodhya, the Sarayu, and ended himself.

"Rama is the true, permanent, undying, indwelling Self. Lakshmana is *eka laksha*, concentration on a single point: the mind riveted on Rama. Even the last object or laksha in the consciousness must be dissolved before Nirvikalpa Samadhi becomes possible. In an individual sadhaka this final distinction jumps into the Sarayu in the forehead, a nadi which arises from Manasasarovara, the 'Lake of the Mind' within the brain. When concentration itself drowns and merges with the infinite only Rama remains, because Sita has meanwhile returned to her source, the womb of Mother Earth. The soul has now relinquished everything, even its own Shakti, its own personal Maya.

"After Rama loses Lakshmana He loses all desire to continue to exist, and after bidding farewell to Anjaneya He enters the river Himself. When Rama merges, there is Nirvikalpa Samadhi, and the play of the Ramayana is ended.

"Everyone dies or disappears in the end except Anjaneya. Rama tells Anjaneya, 'Although I am God incarnate I must also die. But you are the incarnation of Rudra, the God of Death Himself. You cannot die.' And it is true. Anjaneya can never die. He is immortal like Mahakala, the original Rudra."

"I know that Anjaneya is a matronymic, a name derived from his mother's name, Anjani," I said. "I also know how much you love Ma. But is there some specific reason you insist on calling Anjaneya Anjaneya, and almost never call him Hanuman or Maruti?"

"Well, being a worshipper of Ma I always like to remind myself of Her. And—Anjaneya may be a great hero, but even he has to listen to his mother.

"When Anjaneya went to meet his mother after Sita had been rescued he related the whole story of the Ramayana to her, and then told her, 'Ma, I have been true to your milk. I have dedicated my life entirely to Sri Ramachandra, so much so that I have even become a celibate. I will never even look on any woman except you and Sita Ji.'

"Anjani told him, 'How can you tell me that you have been true to my milk, when you could have taken Sita Ji back to Rama yourself directly without the need for any war? No, you have shamed my milk.'

"Anjaneya replied to her, 'No, Ma, I could not do that. I can only do what

Lord Rama orders me to do. If I had been so ordered I would have done everything myself and Ramachandra Ji would not have had to lift even his little finger. But by doing as I was told other good things happened. For example, all the *Rakshasas* (demonic beings) who saw me changed their inherent natures and started to worship Rama, thanks to the beautiful form you gave me.' And then his mother was mollified. Did you know that Anjaneya is described as 'koti kandarpa lavanya'?"

Let's see: 'the beauty of ten million kandarpas.' "But doesn't *kandarpa* mean 'onion' in Sanskrit?"

"Yes, it does, but is that its only meaning? Do you think anyone would refer to Anjaneya as having the beauty of ten million onions? Of course not!"

True enough. I stretched to think of other meanings of "kandarpa," and then told him, "Kandarpa is one of the names of Kamadeva, the god of love."

"Right. Now imagine how handsome the god of love must be, and then multiply by ten million. Then you will have an idea of Anjaneya's beauty. But that is not all. 'Kandarpa' also refers to a particular type of prana which is connected with Apana; the *kanda* is the nadi-plexus where Apana can be made to move upward instead of downward.

"Now here is another question for you: since Anjaneya always meditates on Rama, never forgetting Him for an instant, why hasn't he become Rama, according to the Law of Caterpillar and Butterfly?"

He was enjoying this. "I don't know."

"The answer is simple: He does not become Rama because he deliberately does not want to. He is Shiva, Who knows only how to give, not to take, even if it is only a question of form. This is why Shiva is called the Great Giver."

"Of course."

My concentration was evidently flagging. Vimalananda indulgently smiled at me like the Divine Mother Herself and ended our conversation by saying, "So now you know something of what I am thinking when I listen to the Ramayana."

Yantras of the Ten Mahavidya Goddesses

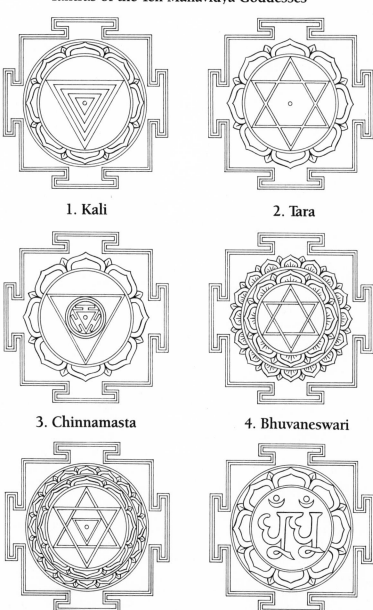

1. Kali

2. Tara

3. Chinnamasta

4. Bhuvaneswari

5. Bangala

6. Dhumavati

7. Kamala   8. Matangi

9. Sodasi   10. Bhairavi

The Ten Mahavidya Goddesses originate from the legend of Shiva and his first consort Sati. Incensed at the refusal of her father Daksa to invite her ascetic husband to the great sacrifice, Sati manifests the ten powerful forms of the Mahavidya Goddesses. Sati eventually destroys herself, and Shiva overcome with grief allows Vishnu to dissect her body and scatter it over the subcontinent of India. The places where the various parts of her body fell became the sacred sites (shaktipithas) of Devi worship, wherein the land itself embodies the sacred form of the dismembered goddess. From this legend derives the practice of Sati, where the faithful wife offers herself to her husband's funeral pyre. Some of the Mahavidyas, such as Kali and Tara, have several forms. Vimalananda self-identified with Tara, the second of the Mahavidyas, in her form as Smashan Tara. "Tara of the Cremation Grounds."

GURUS AND
DISCIPLES

A pleasing routine developed when Vimalananda visited Poona's Irani colony. I would come over early to help prepare lunch, and then would go off to college in the afternoon. In the evenings we would go to the stables to visit his "four-legged children," and on race days I would accompany him into the stands at the racecourse. After returning home we would sit together until late at night while he discoursed on spiritual subjects.

One night we were sitting with Chotu, one of Vimalananda's oldest friends, and with Sardar Dengle, the scion of a noble family of Poona. Vimalananda decided to have some drinks, and though he usually permitted his friends to drink with him this time he told everyone, "Please, I am in a different mood tonight, and I want to drink alone. You can give me company the next time."

"Ha!" said Chotu. "What do you think? Have I not lived with you day and night for eight years? Have we not always eaten and drunk together? If you are going to drink tonight, I am going to accompany you."

"Listen," said Vimalananda, "Don't insist. If you do drink I will not be responsible for what might happen to you."

"Leave off," said Chotu airily. "You are just saying that because you know I can drink you under the table without any difficulty. I am also going to drink," and he incited Sardar Dengle to drink as well.

"I warned you," was Vimalananda's reply, and I poured the Scotch. At his insistence I gave them only half a drink each. Although both these gentlemen measured their capacity in pints and quarts, after these particular drinks they were blind drunk. Chotu vomited all over himself and made a mess of the room before falling flat on his back in bed unconscious, leaving his grumbling wife to clean up behind him. I was assigned the task of dealing with Sardar Dengle. It took me half an hour to get him out the door, and another half-hour to steer him back to his home. Vimalananda enjoyed the whole spectacle immensely.

When Chotu came to he started to abuse Vimalananda roundly, and this caused Vimalananda to break into fresh peals of laughter. "Please abuse me some more," he told Chotu, "I expect it from you. I love to play with my 'children,'" he said, turning to me, "and they love to play with me; it is a mutual bondage of affection.

"I love to play with my children," he went on, "but they should do as they are told," looking pointedly at Chotu, who smiled broadly and foolishly. "Have you forgotten the story of the shakarpala?" We all leaned closer to listen to Vimalananda, while Chotu, who obviously knew the story, said nothing but continued to grin as if he had lost the ability to comprehend human speech.

"Once," Vimalananda began, "there was a wrestling club presided over by an old wrestler who was also a spiritual guru. His favorite among his many pupils was a shopkeeper, not because the shopkeeper was a good wrestler but because of a past karmic relationship. The shopkeeper, however, thought the guru loved him because he was the best pupil.

"The shopkeeper was always pestering his guru to let him fight a very eminent wrestler of the area. The guru knew his 'child' was no match for the bigger man, but he also wanted to fulfill his disciple's desires, so one day he called the boy to him and said, 'What makes you think you will be able to beat a professional wrestler?'

"The shopkeeper said, 'Well, I know that I am your best pupil, so that gives me confidence. I also know he will give me a lot of trouble, though, because he eats a whole goat every day.'

"The guru said, 'So what? Do one thing: Follow him out into the jungle in the morning and see how much he shits.'

"The shopkeeper started to object, but the guru told him forcibly, 'Now don't argue; if you want me to help you do as I say.'

"Unwillingly he did so, and came back the next day to report to his guru: 'About two pounds.'

"Then his guru said to him, 'You have nothing to worry about. He eats a whole goat, but he can't digest it. You have my permission to fight this big lug.'

"On the day of the match, just before the bout, the young shopkeeper did a full prostration to his guru, as is customary, and as the guru lifted him up from the floor he picked up a piece of *shakarpala* (a type of sweet), blew on it while repeating a mantra, and put it into the shopkeeper's mouth. The boy bounded out into the ring. The two wrestlers shook hands and began to fight.

"Within seconds the shopkeeper grabbed his opponent's leg, brought him down, and pinned him. He was so elated he began to dance, but his guru shouted at him, 'Hey, you rascal shopkeeper, sit down! Why are you dancing? It is the shakarpala which is really dancing.' Then the shopkeeper remembered himself and prostrated again to his guru, to thank him for the loan of shakti."

All of us listening realized that this story was aimed at Mr. Chotu and his prowess with the bottle, and we had another laugh at Chotu's expense. Vimalananda then decided to let Chotu off the hook, and changed the subject.

"Even my Junior Guru Maharaj, who is very strict, loves to play about. Back during the time I owned a dairy in Borivali he once came to visit Bombay, and my manager, Vasudev Pansekar, who we called Vasu, came to meet him. Vasu was a good singer of devotional songs, and after singing a few he invited Guru Maharaj out to visit the dairy. Chotu here, who lived with me out at Borivali then, is my witness. Do you remember, Chotu?"

Chotu, one of the most genial of men, smiled as he remembered Junior Guru Maharaj and nodded his assent.

"Guru Maharaj smiled at Vasu's invitation and told him, 'Of course I'll come, but you have to catch hold of me.'

"Vasu didn't think much of this, but late that night Guru Maharaj came to the dairy and strolled through. Vasu saw him and tried to catch him, but Guru Maharaj was moving too quickly, and disappeared. Or at least that is what Vasu told us the next day; I didn't believe him because Guru Maharaj had been sitting with us all during the time he was supposed to have been at the dairy. I told Vasu that without proof no one would believe him.

"Vasu said to Guru Maharaj, 'If you came to the stables and you were also here all the time, you must have come in your subtle body, and that is why you couldn't be caught.'

"Guru Maharaj said, 'All right, just to prove to you that I was there I will come again; this time be prepared.' Vasu replied, 'But none of this subtle body business; you must come in your physical body.' Guru Maharaj agreed.

"This time Vasu prepared a reception for Guru Maharaj. He marshalled together all the cowherds, armed them with sticks and ropes, and surrounded the corrals with thorns and barbed wire, so that once anyone got in, there would be no way for them to get out again. Late the next night while everyone was on guard Guru Maharaj appeared, and though all the cowherds strove their mightiest he eluded all of them. They drove him toward the barbed wire and thorns, but he walked right through the barrier; the barbed wire broke when he touched it.

"This was too much for Vasu. He and several cowherds immediately came to where I was staying. There was Guru Maharaj, chatting quietly with my friends. He had not left my sight all day long; I wanted to make sure he didn't try any funny tricks.

"Vasu said, 'All right, so we didn't catch you again this time; how can we catch you when you come in your subtle body, which is ethereal and gives us nothing to hold onto?'

"Guru Maharaj called him over and showed him the skin on his arm; there were thorns in it, the same kind of thorns that the barrier had been made of. 'I kept my side of the bargain, and here is my proof,' he said. 'I can't help it if you couldn't catch me.' How Guru Maharaj could have two physical bodies in two different places at once is something I cannot understand, but it happened."

We all knew that he understood how it could be. I asked: "What were the sticks and ropes for?"

Chotu answered, "To tie Guru Maharaj up and give him a good beating as a welcome."

I said, thinking of Guru Maharaj's august personage, "How could Vasu, or anybody else, dare to lay a finger on Guru Maharaj?"

Chotu smiled again, this time at my foolishness, and Vimalananda said, "Well, Guru Maharaj had challenged him; what was he supposed to do? Just lie down and let Guru Maharaj walk over him? Besides, did anyone catch Guru Maharaj? The old man knows how to take care of himself."

"It's just the idea," I replied.

"A disciple has every right to test a guru," said Vimalananda vehemently.

"Look how Chotu just tried to test me, and he isn't even my disciple. But then the disciple, or the 'child,' had best be ready to be tested in return. That is how it has always been: first you test the guru, to see if he or she is right for you; then the guru will test you, to find out what you are fit to learn, and what you deserve to learn."

Indeed; even in the Ayurvedic texts, a student is advised to first test a prospective guru thoroughly, and only when he is satisfied with the guru's capabilities should he submit his name as a candidate for discipleship. Then the guru gets his turn to test.

"A guru has to test his disciples, and if he is a good guru he will test the disciple until the disciple's resistance is completely broken. Your guru is trying to teach you to efface your ego, to disengage your consciousness from the limitations Kundalini has imposed on Herself by becoming embodied. Only when your ego is humbled can you learn. The guru is like a gardener, and the disciples like flowers. The flowers may be beautiful, but they shouldn't get a swelled head over their own so-called importance. When your guru ignores or insults you he is only testing to see how far your ego has been effaced. Never, never get angry in return. Just keep quiet, and see how you are benefited.

"I love my mentors, but they play hard, much too hard for most people today. I remember a good saint who once ran afoul of my Senior Guru Maharaj. This saint was called Joowala Sai (the 'Lice-Covered Saint') because his body was covered with thousands and thousands of lice and other tiny insects. Every day he would very carefully remove the insects from all over his body, talk to them, play with them, and then carefully replace them. One day Bapu, my Senior Guru Maharaj, happened to meet Joowala Sai, and Joowala Sai smiled at him. An instant later the smile left Joowala Sai's face, and there were tears in his eyes. He begged for forgiveness, and even stood on a hot road for hours, burning his feet, but nothing doing. Bapu said to me later, 'How could he afford to show me his teeth?'"

I obviously didn't understand, so Vimalananda explained: "It is traditionaly impolite to smile and show someone your teeth. When Joowala Sai smiled at Bapu it was a challenge to Bapu; it was tantamount to saying, 'See what a fine level of spirituality I have achieved!' Bapu had compassion for this fellow and so in a trice he stole all of his shakti. Joowala Sai immediately realized what had happened, and so he tried to placate Bapu, but to no avail."

"So then what happened?" I asked.

"What happened? Nothing happened. Joowala Sai had to start over again from the beginning. Eventually Bapu will have to do something nice for him—that's the Law of Karma—but Bapu is in no hurry."

"It hardly seems fair," I protested.

"Fair!" It was growing late and Vimalananda was tiring of my refusal to see his point. "What would you know about what is fair when it comes to people like Bapu? If Joowala Sai had been really advanced he should have been able to recognize that Bapu was infinitely more powerful than he. Then he would not have tried to show off, and he would still be happily playing with his lice today.

"You talk about fair because you still have a bee in your bonnet; you still haven't lost this filthy Western attitude that you deserve to be taught simply because you are fortunate enough to run across someone who can teach you. Unfortunately most Westerners have no patience. Your culture teaches that all desires should be immediately gratified. You see a girl you like and you go up to her and say, 'Hey, how about a nice screw?' No romance, no mystery, no excitement. 'Sex is a natural function,' say the scientists, and that is what you have made of it. In the West sex is now on the level of any other bodily function: whenever you feel the need to relieve yourselves you do. And you think the spiritual urge can be gratified in the same way. No wonder you people get only fake gurus.

"You cannot buy a real guru. If you try to purchase him or her you will get a nice kick on your behind; you'll be thrown out. If a real guru sees that his 'child' is becoming impatient for knowledge that guru will deliberately delay, to teach the 'child' a lesson. If the 'child' loses his patience and storms off, well, why should the guru care? One less burden for him.

"Of course Westerners are not entirely to blame," Vimalananda continued, calming somewhat. "Our friend from Germany who said that India is exporting 'godmen' is right, you know. We export them to the West where they steal money from people who come to them for knowledge. But the Westerners, and particularly the Americans, are partly to blame, because they think they can buy everything, including spirituality. When something cannot even be spoken how can it be bought? This is why Westerners are not being taught the true things. They only get false gurus; only a false guru will agree to teach someone in return for money.

"And they are not unique in this, of course. Rich people in every country, including India, think that because they feed, clothe, and house their guru that they are headed for heaven. It is not like that at all. A teacher can point the way, but he can't do your work for you. But if the disciple refuses to listen—and why should he if he has purchased and now possesses the guru?—what can the guru do about it? All he can practically do is refuse to teach—but it takes guts to turn down all that easy money.

"The knowledge I am trying to give you I gained after a lot of difficulty. Even if I could sell this knowledge to you, which I can't, the price would be so high that you would not be able to pay it. How can you put a price on the decades I have spent in smashans? Besides, a parent never expects money from a child, unless they are not true parents but merely procreators, like animals. I treat you as my son, Robby. After I have some drinks this feeling is magnified immensely, and I feel that there is so much I want to teach you. But you should be ready to learn it, and Ma should be ready to teach it. You know that the truth cannot be expressed in words; if it could be it wouldn't be true. I can only use words to point out the truth and other methods to transmit the knowledge directly without your even being aware of it. This is the way a gift should be given. But I need your cooperation in order to give it.

"Americans need to stop trying to possess saints and sadhus, and look for spiritual masters who will possess them instead. Only when you surrender everything to your guru, including especially your acquisitive nature, can you ever hope to progress. The Americans are the ones who can do it. They are interested in reality. I hate to say it, but most of today's Indians are cowards, the legacy of one thousand years of servitude to the Muslims and the Europeans. We Indians need to relearn this attitude of mind from the Americans, and they need to come to us, to some of us, for spirituality."

I began to feel a little distressed, not because he was upbraiding Americans, but because he still considered me so much of an American.

He saw this, and said to the others in the room, referring to me, "I know he may not like what I have to say, but I'm very blunt; I can't be sugarcoated quinine." With that he dismissed me for the night. I kept quiet.

The next time the subject came up was in Bombay, when one of Vimalananda's "boys" who had been studying astrology for a few months dropped by to ask some questions. The familiarity with which he asked made me remember the episode of Joowala Sai, and in fact Vimalananda told him, as he sat expecting to be patted on the back, "Please study for twelve years and then come back and discuss astrology with me. Astrology cannot be learned overnight. You know, I thought you were mature, since you are physically almost as old as I am. But I see now that you are still in your puppy stage. When a dog is small it bites its mother playfully; biting is an inborn trait in dogs. After it grows older it bites everyone else, but when it is a puppy it only has strength enough to bite its mother. The mother doesn't mind a bit; she knows it is her own puppy, and she allows it to do as it pleases."

It is no more polite to call someone a dog in India than it is elsewhere, so clearly Vimalananda was aiming to shock. Then, as his last sentence had promised, he showed his compassion.

"If you were to go to a sadhu he would say, 'First become my disciple and then I will teach you.' I don't want any disciples; I want to remain a disciple to my dying day. And I don't mind your trying to impress me with your knowledge, though I am not in the least impressed. But if you try to show off in front of someone else you may be humiliated, so please be careful; that is my advice to you."

The budding astrologer was ashamed of himself, and asked for forgiveness, but Vimalananda replied, "Forgiveness for what? The essence of motherliness is forgiveness, no matter what the child does." After the man left, Vimalananda went on.

"Like most people nowadays who study a little tiny bit of a subject and become experts, this fellow thought he knew quite a bit. I knew he was trying to show off his knowledge by the questions he asked and the way in which he asked them. If I were a sadhu I would have treated him roughly, shouting at him and upbraiding him for being cheeky, so that he would never do this sort of thing again. Because I treat him as my child I can't do that—but I can't let him get away with it either. So I had to be blunt. It hurt him, I know, but better he should be hurt a little bit now and learn his lesson than to have someone else burst his bloated balloon later, which might have hurt him a lot.

"Suppose a surgeon sees that he needs to operate in order to cure a certain disease. If the patient says to him, 'Oh, no, don't operate, it will hurt me a lot,' will the surgeon start to feel sorry for the patient and think, 'No, I mustn't operate; how can I cause him any pain?' Never! Not if he is a real surgeon. A real surgeon will cut, if he knows that is what the patient needs, because he knows that the end result for the patient, which is freedom from the pain of the disease, is worth the little bit of pain that it takes to achieve it."

I remembered his recent bluntness in Poona.

"I have never been and will never be a teacher. When you try to teach you usually end up cheating yourself. For one thing, most people are motivated by idle curiosity rather than a sincere thirst for knowledge. I have no time to waste my breath on people who want to know whether or not God exists.

For those who believe in God no explanation is necessary; for those who don't believe in God no explanation is possible.

"I will never claim to be God, or a prophet of God, or even a guru, as so many claim to be today. To be a guru you have to say, 'I know and I can teach you.' But if I say that, well, I'm finished. I can never learn anything else. I have shut myself off from anything new. If I remain a student all my life, though, I will always be ready to learn new things. I am nothing; the sort of nothing which has everything contained within it. That is the kind of nothing to become: the nothing which occurs when Kundalini leaves her dalliance with samsara and opens you to the universe of all possibilities.

"There are plenty of people around who think they are gurus and that they should try to enlighten the world. One of them is a famous swami from Bombay who has centers all over the place, in so many countries. I invited him to my house some years ago, just to see what he was about. When he arrived I offered him refreshment, as one does to any guest who comes, but he refused, saying, 'I never take any nourishment outside my ashram.' All right, I thought to myself, if you are being strict I will be strict in return.

"Then he asked me, 'Are you following some Yoga?'

"I pretended innocence and said, 'No, Maharaj, I am only an ordinary man. Yoga is too far away for me.'

"He said, 'You know, I am having my discourses on the Bhagavad Gita at the Oval. You should come and listen to them; you will be enlightened.'

"This was too much. I said to him, 'Maharaj, the Bhagavad Gita was spoken by Krishna, who was God incarnate, to Arjuna, who was a great yogi. Both of them were aspects of Rishis, in fact. You are not Krishna, and your listeners are not Arjuna. How can you expect that the kind of jnana which is in the Gita can be passed from you to them by discourse?

"'Not only that, you go day after day to the same place and speak the same things over and over again. The Gita was a spontaneous outpouring of joy from Krishna's heart. Arjuna was His beloved spiritual 'child,' and He had such a desire to make Arjuna understand that He couldn't control Himself. The Gita came from Krishna's lips spontaneously; even He was not aware of what was happening. That is why it is so great.

"'And when it was all over Arjuna said to Krishna, 'Lord, I have forgotten what you taught me. Can you tell me again?' Krishna replied, 'No, that time is passed, and it cannot be recovered.' Which means that the Gita could be only transmitted between its original author and hearer, who were both Rishis, at a certain time, because afterward that spontaneous outburst was gone. Now, Maharaj, how can you think that you are doing any good to anyone by babbling on about the Gita?

"Well, he got wild, of course, and told me, 'You are an atheist, I won't stay here any longer,' and stormed out. As he was leaving I said, 'Maharaj, the scriptures say you must control your anger.' That only made him wilder. Such are the sadhus we have nowadays. Only rarely will they recognize their mistakes.

"I don't mind meeting anyone who has a sincere desire to learn. I'm ready to teach anyone who is ready to learn, and as long as someone comes to me with humility I will do anything for them. But how many have real interest in spirituality, and how many have the patience necessary to wait for those spontaneous outbursts to happen when transmission can really take place? And besides, how many could endure learning with me? When I teach I am ruthless. No compassion; you must succeed or you'll die.

"If I were a sadhu, Robby, well, I love you but I would rip you to shreds before I taught you anything. That is the best way; then there is no fear of backsliding. As it is I am a householder, so you are receiving knowledge with much less effort on your part. I will never have disciples, only 'children,' because that is the way a real guru should treat a disciple: as a spiritual son or daughter. I can't afford to be as strict as a sadhu because I treat you as my son, and no parent ever wants to see his or her children suffer. I am willing to suffer on your behalf. In return I expect you to act in a certain way, and you do. I appreciate that.

"So," he concluded, "I'm afraid you have fallen in with a madman. Madmen can be dangerous; look out! Think twice before continuing to stay with me."

He laughed, and I grinned in reply, happy to be exposed to his sort of danger. I told him, "Hopefully my ego will come sufficiently under control so that I don't end up like Joowala Sai."

Vimalananda shook his head and said, "Poor fellow! He didn't realize who he was tangling with. Bapu is terribly strict about things like respect. One day he and I were sitting around here in Bombay when someone told us of a fakir who was very ill. My mentor immediately said, 'Take me to see him and I will cure him.' He is very loving that way. Now, I knew this fakir, and knew he was a good man, but I also knew that he was not yet ready for my Senior Guru Maharaj.

"I told my old man, 'Don't bother, he will not see you.'

"He became wild—as his disciple, I had no business contradicting him, after all—and said, 'I am ready to bet that he will see me.'

"I am a gambler, and I liked my odds, so I said, 'Be careful, Bapu! This is

Bombay; you don't know how people are here.' But he insisted, and we settled on a bet: one betel leaf.

"He went to the fakir's residence and asked to see the sick man. The people there refused to let him in. He told them, 'Look, I am a fakir myself, I want to cure him,' and all sorts of other things, but they steadfastly refused.

"Finally he lost his temper and said, 'Is he God, that he will refuse to see me? All right; he has a plaster on his chest right now, doesn't he? That plaster will remain on his chest until his dying day, just to remind him of the fakir he did not meet.' And it actually happened that way. You know it, Robby; you and Freddy have seen his photo with the plaster on his chest." Yes, we had.

"Of course then Bapu had to come back home and pay me my betel leaf, and he doesn't like losing any more than I do. I told him, 'Why do you become obstinate about such things? These are human beings; they can't pass the kinds of tests you dish out.'

"It always pays to give respect to spiritual people. Back in the time when the British ruled India there lived an Aghori in a small hut in a small forest on the outskirts of a small village. For some reason the government decided to build a road right through the sadhu's little hut. When the Englishman in charge of the road gang came to evict the old man he acted so highhandedly that the Aghori decided to teach him a lesson. He lengthened his penis, wrapped it around a nearby boulder which must have weighed tons, and towed it in front of the machinery in use on the roadway. Then he stood back and told the Englishman, 'Now please remove it.'

"The Englishman, of course, thought it was some kind of trick—wrapping your penis around a rock and dragging it along?—so he ordered his men to remove it. All of his men got behind it and tried to push it out of the way, but they couldn't budge it, not even an inch.

"Then the Englishman realized that something funny was going on, and he went to the sadhu and told him politely, 'Look, I have to build this road. It is my job; if I don't do it I'll be fired. Please help me out.'

"The sadhu looked at him closely and said, 'That's better; now you are talking properly.' Then he again·lengthened his penis, wrapped it around the boulder, and tugged it to one side, and the roadbuilding went on undisturbed."

By this time both of us were guffawing over the vision of the hapless Englishman and the Aghori who had lassoed the boulder with his penis. After the mirth died down Vimalananda continued:

"I accidentally got involved in one of these situations myself. It was in the

South, and it involved a Western couple who were touring India. One day while they were sightseeing a wild-looking man with unkempt hair started to stare at them. This made them uneasy and they asked him to stop. He ignored them, and continued to stare, wide-eyed. This went on for some minutes until the male tourist lost his temper and spat on the man.

"The man, who was a sadhu, picked up the wad of spittle with his fingers, looked at it carefully, looked at the couple carefully, and then walked away. The couple thought they were rid of him. How wrong they were!

"Next morning they began their day with bloody diarrhea. They tried all sorts of remedies, but nothing worked. Someone they knew knew me, and I was called onto the case. In the course of our talk about their health it came out that they had spat on that sadhu.

"'Oh,' I said, 'now I get the idea. You should never have insulted him like that. No wonder he has decided to teach you a lesson. Don't worry about a thing.' And I went to the smashan. The next day they were fine again, and I warned them strictly never ever to do anything like that again. India is a very strange and dangerous country.

"Two days later who do I see coming to visit me but the sadhu, who asked to be cured of his bloody diarrhea. I told him, 'Look, you are an old man and you are supposed to be matured and mellow. Why did you allow your mind to be disturbed by a couple of foreigners, who after all are so ignorant of our ways that they are no better than children?'

"He retorted, 'They come to India to stare at us, so I wanted to see how they liked it when someone stared at them.'

"I said, 'Yes, but you can't just use your power on everyone who irritates you, especially when those people don't know how to fight back. Besides, they are our guests while they are here, and we have to treat them as such. Anyway, they have learned a lesson, all right, and I hope you have too.' He agreed that he had learned a good lesson, and we parted as friends."

The unstated but clear message was of course directed at me: watch your step here in India, lest you land in quicksand!

"I have always tested my gurus, you know; only if they meet my criteria am I willing to learn from them. I have met and tested many sadhus, but most of them have been found wanting. One day one of my friends came raving about a certain saint: 'What heights this man has reached! He even talks to Lord Krishna!' I said to myself, 'Ah-hah, he talks to Lord Krishna!' I've always been willing to meet anyone who was willing to meet me.

"You were supposed to take a coconut and present it at his lotus feet, and then he would tell you what you wanted to know. I didn't take any coconut, and when my turn came he asked me where it was. I told him I had only come for his darshan and not to ask any questions. Then he started to say, 'Lord Krishna says this,' and, 'Lord Krishna says that,' and I got wild. Lord Krishna indeed!

"I told him, 'Whatever Lord Krishna may say, you had better watch out for yourself, Maharaj, because I think that within one month you will be trampled under the foot of an elephant.'

"Everyone there became very angry with me, of course, but I didn't care; I was so insolent then. And besides, I was just telling the truth. My friend tried to intervene: 'What are you saying? Ask Maharaj his forgiveness.' That only made me wilder, and I had to leave the room.

"Well, it happened as I had predicted. About a month later this sadhu was being taken out in a big procession on elephant back. Suddenly the elephant went berserk, picked the sadhu up with his trunk, threw him to the ground and trampled him. A horrible death.

"Like that I've met so many babas and holy men. I remember a fakir who used to sit on a big cushion of rich green velvet. When I met him I saw that he had a small spirit with him. The spirit was very unhappy because the fakir was taking a lot of work from him. I asked the spirit if he would like to be set free, and he said, 'Yes, I would like to repay this fakir for all the work he has taken from me.'

"As soon as the spirit was released he immediately grabbed that fakir's testicles and began to squeeze. My God, what a howl that guy put up! None of the disciples could see the spirit, of course, so they didn't know what was going on and didn't know what to do about it. As if there were anything they could do about it. His balls were squeezed mercilessly until the next morning, when he died and became a spirit himself."

My face must have hinted at disapproval, because Vimalananda continued by saying, "What should I have done? Left him as he was, to create more karma for himself and make the spirit more miserable so that when his end finally came his condition would be even worse?" Since I had no answer to this, the conversation ended there.

One day Vimalananda sat me down and outlined for me his criteria for testing saints:

"Some people follow what is called the Path of the Ant in their search for God: they scurry about hither and thither, moving backward as well as forward, taking many births to reach their goal. Those who are more determined follow the Path of the Fish, swimming strongly against the current. The Path of the Monkey, which involves leaping from limb to limb on the Tree of Knowledge, is more difficult still; but the most difficult is the Path of the Bird, the Path we Aghoris follow: you leap out into space, and your wings carry you to Him.

"Of course, if your wings fail, and you drop to the ground, you are finished, totally; you are dead. A monkey at least has branches to break its fall; a fish can rest behind a rock whenever it needs to. The Path of the Ant takes the longest time but it is the most secure, because an ant has nowhere to fall. The more difficult a sadhana is, the more necessary it is to have a guru. In Kundalini Yoga it is absolutely essential to have an expert guru. The guru is a spiritual aspirant's friend, philosopher, and guide; he guards the disciple against all dangers, and ignites the internal flames which eventually consume all the limitations of the disciple's personality. You can make spiritual progress without having a guru, it is true, but if you want to reach the highest states a guru is absolutely essential.

"No effort is ever lost. Even if you cannot succeed in this lifetime your effort is right there in your bank balance in an account that travels with you from birth to birth. It is such a wonderful account that you can never lose your passbook. The vibrations of your efforts exist indefinitely in a subtle form, so there is nothing to worry about. No matter where you end up you'll be dragged back into your spiritual practices. All the records of your past lives are available to anyone who knows how to locate them and who can perceive their subtle sound, so your guru never has any difficulty keeping track of where you are and what you are doing, no matter how far you may stray from him.

"But for you to have this sort of guarantee you have to have a real guru! Out of a thousand sadhus today perhaps one is genuine, because it is Kali Yuga. You will meet many sadhus, Robby, and you will need to know how to evaluate them. You should learn to smell saints out; yes, 'smell' them out. They say, 'Attar can be created only when flowers are crushed,' and it is the same way with a sadhu. Only after his ego has been thoroughly crushed so that his Kundalini can identify with God will he be able to give a sweet smell to all who come near him. So long as he retains traces of selfishness a stench will follow him wherever he goes.

"So long as your own mind and body are blocked up you'll never even be able to know what a saint is, or to sniff his scent; as you purify yourself, and your perception improves, you will learn more and more. This is like opening a bottle of attar in a room. After a moment or two everyone except someone whose nose is blocked up can tell that attar is present. The least-experienced person can say only, 'Attar is present.' Someone with more experience can identify it more accurately: 'It is rose.' Only an expert will recognize the fine nuances: 'It is Kabuli rose mixed with a little jasmine.' It is the same way with saints.

"If you want to find out whether or not a sadhu is genuine, first go to see him, but don't ask any questions. Sit quietly and don't say much; listen, and try to keep your mind blank. If when you sit near him you find yourself forgetting the things of the world and becoming more peaceful, then he is a good saint; his halo is quieting your mind. If not, run away!"

"Naturally if you yourself are purified it will be easier to know whether and how much your mind is being quieted," I observed.

"Naturally. Once your mind becomes purified there's no limit to what you can learn. You can know so many things about a person by simple observation. For example, check the saint's feces, like the shopkeeper who wanted to wrestle did. A real yogi excretes only an ounce, or at most a few ounces, a day; anything more indicates that he is bogus. If Jathara Agni has yielded most of its energy to Bhuta Agni, there will be very little physical digestive fire left. Yogis are disciplined by nature, and a good yogi will only eat as much as he is hungry for. If he eats more than he can digest he will have to excrete the excess, and you will be able to detect it. Or, if his bodily fire is generally weak, his assimilation will be poor and he will excrete more than he absorbs, which suggests that his mind will be as dull as his body.

"This principle makes Jain munis easy to test, because of their toilet habits. They never go outside the house to defecate; usually they do it on a outer balcony or somewhere like that. And they never use water to clean themselves afterwards, since water is life-giving and they regard it as sacred. So they clean themselves with a pebble or a stone and just leave the dung there for the rain to wash away. When someone told me one day that an excellent Jain muni had just arrived in town, I first went to see his droppings, and after I saw them I knew he would be no match for me. I went in confidently and defeated him easily at religious debate. He was actually rather dull. You can use this test for anyone.

"Whether or not you are able to observe a sadhu's droppings, look at his face. A good saint's face will begin to take on the form of the face of the deity he worships. You know how married couples start to look like one another after forty or fifty years? This is the same principle. There was a sadhu in Bombay named Kamu Baba who meditated on Sai Baba of Shirdi for so long that when you looked at him it was just like looking at Shirdi Sai Baba. At the end of his life my father looked almost identical to his own guru, on whom he had meditated for decades. This effect is magnified millions of times if your Kundalini has been awakened. Kundalini's power is self-identification, and she quickly takes on the form of whatever she identifies with.

"True saints rarely approve of having their photos taken. They don't like to be known by multitudes of people; they prefer to live alone and die alone so they can be nearer to God. Also, a photo gives a great boost to anyone who wants to self-identify with that person. Anyone who has a saint's picture can call that saint astrally and play about with him, which is all well and good. But suppose someone for some reason should hate that saint? Everytime they see his photo they will remember their hate, and send reinforced negative vibrations his way, which will have unpleasant implications for the health and well-being of the poor innocent saint. Only false sadhus who are anxious for publicity go out of their way to be photographed.

"While you are busy observing the sadhu don't forget to listen carefully to what he says. Do you remember that young woman who was born in India of Western parents? When she came of age she decided she wanted to marry a fellow-disciple of the same female guru. But when she went to ask her guru's permission the old woman said, 'No, how can it be? You are a foreigner and he is an Indian; such a marriage must never take place.' This shows the depth of that old woman's deficiency. If she really believed herself to be the Divine Mother incarnate, as she claimed, how could she discriminate between two of her children? Mustn't she treat them all equally? Her predjudice proves that she was not all that spiritually advanced. She could rightly have objected for other reasons, but not simply because of skin color.

"If the supposed saint you meet talks about collecting money to build ashrams and centers and so on, depart immediately. His disciples may talk about such things, I admit; disciples are always somewhat deluded. But a real sadhu says, 'Why should I bother about trying to establish something? If God wants me to have it I will have it.' This is the right attitude; it shows that the sadhu has full faith in his deity. Only if he has no faith will he try to collect money, or disciples, or whatever. We have a saying in Hindi: 'What is the use of a flower which has no fragrance? What is the use of a beautiful face which has no one to desire it? What is the use of a fakir or sadhu who is not a giver?' Fakirs and sadhus are always givers, because they have realized that everything belongs to God; how can they refuse to give to God in the form of a human being that which belongs to God?

"It is absolutely scandalous how many people are making money and fame for themselves off the Bhagavad Gita. I knew one Dada Maharaj, who had gathered a lot of disciples for himself by his discourses on the Jnaneshwari. You can be sure that a great Siddha like Jnaneshwar did not write the Jnaneshwari so that he could become famous; he did it so that common people who did not know Sanskrit could hear Krishna's story in Marathi, their own language, and keep it in their hearts, and bring themselves closer to Krishna in that way. When Jnaneshwar himself never commercialized his writing, why should anyone else do so?

"This Dada Maharaj was a barber who had promoted himself to religious lecturer. There is nothing inherently wrong in this, except that the Jnaneshwari is actually a wonderful treatise on spiritual subjects including Kundalini, and unless you have had personal experience in that department you have no right to open your mouth. You certainly have no right to develop a swelled head, as this man had done. He developed such a bloated ego that one day I decided to teach him a lesson. I went to see him, and I took a dog along.

"When I went in to him I performed a full prostration, as I always do in front of any saint, to gauge his or her qualities. This fellow, I could tell, had achieved absolutely nothing. He started to explain something when suddenly the dog burst in, as I had planned, and ran up to him. He shouted, 'Get that dog away from me!'

"Then I said to him, 'Maharaj, you claim that you are a great man, though by pedigree you are only a barber. Be that as it may, the book on which you give lectures states clearly that a sage looks with an equal eye on a realized soul, a cow, an elephant, a dog, and an eater of dogs. Are you better than Krishna, that you are offended by a dog?'"

"Then what did he say?"

"What will he say? He had no choice but to keep quiet. There's no use in jabbering on about all these things; you need to do the sadhana and have the experience. Then you will know, and there will be no need to talk. You don't realize the truth just by thinking about it; you have to go through the grind."

None of the saints, fakirs and babas that I met impressed me nearly so much as did Vimalananda, perhaps because none of them had gone through the grind as thoroughly as he had. Because he always preferred to have questions put to him mentally, so that he could answer them at the moment he felt most appropriate, I began to mentally inquire about becoming his disciple. One day he told me frankly that he was not a guru, but that I would meet my guru one day, if I had a strong enough desire to do so:

"People are always coming to me saying that they want to locate a guru, and I always tell them that if you have real bhakti, real spiritual love and devotion, then your guru will automatically come to you; you won't have to go out looking for him.

"You don't need to search, but you may well have to wait; remember Chang Dev." Chang Dev Maharaj, a sadhu who rode on a tiger and used a cobra for a lasso, had to wait fourteen hundred years for his guru. Every hundred years death would come for him, and he would go into samadhi to elude it. After fourteen hundred years he met his guru, Jnaneshwar Maharaj's fourteen-year-old sister Mukta Bai, and was released.

"Unfortunately," Vimalananda went on, "if you are not a superb yogi like Chang Dev you may not be able to know when you will meet your guru, or even recognize your guru when he or she comes to you."

"Meanwhile what am I supposed to do?" I retorted peevishly.

"Meanwhile do as I tell you to do, and you will continue to make progress. I didn't say I was not going to help you; I just said I am not fated to be your guru," he replied, warning me with a glance to behave. "Besides, first you need to be ready for your guru. Can you honestly tell me you are ready?" No, I couldn't.

"One of my friends asked my Junior Guru Maharaj in 1959 to make him his disciple. Guru Maharaj told him, 'I don't dare to do that, because once you become my disciple you will have to do everything I tell you. If you make any mistakes you will be guilty of *guru droha* (offense or treachery against the guru), and that could ruin you. You just be my devotee for twelve years, and at the end of that time if I feel you are ready I will accept you as my disciple.' But so far that has not happened, even though many more than twelve years have gone by." I got the hint. So did that friend, who has yet to become Guru Maharaj's disciple.

Just before Vimalananda's death he introduced a well-known Ayurvedic doctor from Bombay to Junior Guru Maharaj, who told him, "Get yourself a *shalagrama* (sacred river rock) of the variety known as Lakshmi Janardana and worship it."

The doctor replied, "Maharaj, you know much time it takes to worship a shalagrama properly," implying that he was a very busy man. "Give me a mantra to repeat instead, because otherwise I will have to carry that shalagrama around with me everywhere I go." As Vimalananda told me later, he forgot that you do not dictate terms to a sadhu, and especially not to someone like Guru Maharaj. There must have been some good reason Guru Maharaj wanted him to worship a shalagrama, but he was thinking only of his own convenience. Besides, on the one hand he asks Guru Maharaj for a way to advance spiritually, and on the other he says he has no time to do it properly. What does this tell us about his sincerity?

Guru Maharaj kept quiet, and the next day asked this doctor to prepare a medicine for a child with epileptic-type fits, a medicine whose recipe happened to call for equal parts of honey and ghee. The doctor objected again: "But Maharaj, Ayurveda forbids the mixing of equal parts of honey and ghee."

Guru Maharaj displayed great patience and replied, "This recipe also comes from the Rishis; please do as they have prescribed. Besides, there are other herbs in the medicine which will remove the poisonous effects of this combination and make it into nectar. What is poison and what is nectar anyway? Just do as you are told."

After this encounter was over Vimalananda took me aside and said, "You see how it is? Sometimes even when a guru wants to give some knowledge to a 'child' the 'child' refuses to learn it. You never get anywhere by arguing with a guru, and especially not with a guru who is a live wire like Guru Maharaj. What is a teacher to do with students like these? It is a great blessing to get a good guru, no doubt, but it is an even greater blessing to get a good disciple. Have I ever told you the story of Nagarjuna?"

"No, I don't think so."

"When Nagarjuna wanted to learn alchemy he located a guru and became his disciple. The guru assigned Nagarjuna to a room adjoining his, and for many days Nagarjuna worked on various preliminary sadhanas.

"One night just as he was going to bed Nagarjuna heard a strange noise from his guru's room. Wondering what it was he stared quizzically at the wall, and suddenly noticed a small hole in it. His native curiosity quickly overpowered any guilt about spying on Guruji, and he put his eye to the orifice.

Inside he saw his guru busily applying some sort of paste to his feet. After he had finished, he took hold of his staff—and flew out the window.

"Nagarjuna was momentarily stunned, but then his mind began to work again, wondering how he could learn that trick. He knew that asking his guru outright would prove fruitless, so he had to think of a workable plan if he was to gain the knowledge. Suddenly, it came to him.

"He waited up for several hours until his guru returned, and then, after waiting a respectful moment or two to let the old man catch his breath he rushed from his cell and knocked softly at the guru's door. When the door opened Nagarjuna explained, 'Guruji, I have been overcome with the desire to serve you. Please let me wash the dust from your feet.'

"The guru eyed Nagarjuna carefully, and then solemnly consented. He had expected this, of course; otherwise why would he have left a hole in the wall for Nagarjuna to peep through? He wanted to see how much initiative the boy had, and he was pleased with what he saw. But he didn't want to let Nagarjuna know how he felt, so he suppressed his praise.

"After washing his guru's feet Nagarjuna bowed low and returned to his room, where he exerted himself to the utmost to figure out the composition of the flying unguent. He tasted the wash water over and over again, and finally decided he could identify one of the ingredients. The next night he waited impatiently at the knothole, and finally, there went Guruji! Again he washed the old man's feet; again he tasted and tasted. Eventually, after many a night of this, he felt confident that he knew the recipe.

"And so one night Nagarjuna himself mixed up a paste, and smeared it on his soles. Then he walked to the window, and—off he flew! Unfortunately he did not have the formula down pat, so he didn't get very far. He fell out of the sky, and on his crash landing broke one of his legs. He spent the rest of the night outside, wondering what his guru would say when word of this excursion reached him.

"He need not have worried. He was found early the next morning, and his guru personally came to him to say, 'Of all my students you are the only one who has ever tried to discover the secret of that paste. You deserve to be taught.' And he was taught.

"A good guru always sets challenges for his disciples, to test them. Sometimes a guru will give a disciple a Shiva Linga made of crystal, or, if he is a really mighty guru, one made of solidified mercury, and make the disciple insert it into the mouth just above the hard palate. This is a type of penance; it limits you in many ways. For example, as long as it is in your mouth you dare not speak a lie; if you do, it will split into two pieces. If you can observe all the limitations you can achieve quickly, but if you fail, you fall. Never set out to attempt such things until you are absolutely certain that you can achieve them.

"The guru's order must be obeyed to the dot; then only can the disciple get results. Tukaram Maharaj once gave a rock to a man who was going on pilgrimage. This was no ordinary rock, of course; it was a philosopher's stone which could convert base metals into gold. The man had a fine pilgrimage, creating gold here and there whenever he needed more money to go on.

"At the end of the trip the man realized that he could not give the stone back to Tukaram Maharaj; he was too attached to it. What to do? He thought of a plan and hid the stone in his house. He then went to meet Tukaram Maharaj, who first asked for details of what he had seen and done, and then asked casually, 'Oh, yes, let me see that stone I lent you.'

"The man told him, 'Maharaj, while I was bathing in the Ganga the stone slipped into the water, and although I tried to catch it, it was lost. Obviously Mother Ganga has taken back Her own.'

"'So be it,' said Tukaram Maharaj evenly.

"As soon as the man got back to his own home he looked in his hiding place for the stone, but there was no stone to be found. He raced back to Tukaram Maharaj and shouted, 'Maharaj! The stone is gone!'

"Tukaram Maharaj told him, 'Stupid, of course it is gone. You just told me yourself that Mother Ganga had taken it back.' And that was that.

"So be patient, and prepare yourself," Vimalananda continued soberly. "So often a guru gives a disciple something like that philosopher's stone, and the disciple becomes so excited by it that he or she forgets altogether the guru who gave it to them in the first place. You can always lose objects, but you can't afford to lose your guru. If you hold tightly to the guru he can provide you with all the objects you'll ever need or want.

"One day a king decided to give away everything in his palace. Kings are like that; you can never know what they will do next. He told everyone in the kingdom that in between sunrise and sunset on a certain day they were all free to come and ask him for whatever they wanted from his palace, and it would be theirs.

"By late afternoon the palace was empty. There was absolutely nothing left in it, not even the throne. At five minutes to sunset a young girl entered the palace. The king told her, 'Oh, no, why didn't you come earlier? Now there is nothing left.'

"She said, 'You are wrong, Maharaj. Of course there is something left; you are left. I am taking you.' And they were married. After she became queen the girl told her husband, 'Now that I have you, I can use the money in the treasury to build and decorate fifty palaces if I like. I got the best bargain of all.'

Indeed she did, and Vimalananda paused briefly to let this sink in and to light another cigarette before proceeding.

"But why go so far away? Let us take an example that is close to home. I have taught you and several of my other 'children' to do homa. One of them, whom you know well, now spends all his free time wandering around the countryside performing homa. There is nothing wrong with this; it is a good thing. But he could learn even more if he spent more time with me, since I was the one who taught him to do homa in the first place. He has let his little bit of knowledge go to his head.

"Why should he spend more time with me?" I loved to spend all my time with Vimalananda, and needed no reason to do so, but I knew this question had a purpose. "Well, he is trying to convert himself from a caterpillar into a butterfly, from an ordinary human being into a worshipper of fire. He is still weak in visualizing his new role, still like a puppy; his Kundalini is not yet sufficiently awakened and freed from his normal, everyday personality. He is not yet able to disengage himself from his ego attachments. I could help him by visualizing for him, but he has to spend some time near me so that I can do it.

"The best example of this sort of practice that I can think of is that of Ramakrishna Paramahamsa. Whenever he saw his householder disciple Dr. Nag Mahashay, Ramakrishna would worship the Divine Mother Bhavatarini in him. He would visualize the Divine Mother in Dr. Nag's astral body, and eventually, by the force of Ramakrishna's will, the Divine Mother's form was actually created in Dr. Nag.

"When Ramakrishna saw Vivekananda he would visualize Shiva, and Vivekananda actually became the embodiment of Shiva as a result. When Gopaler Ma came to Ramakrishna she was already an advanced sadhaka; when she meditated on Gopala, Krishna in the form of a young boy, she could actually project a form of Krishna from her astral body. When she met Ramakrishna, that form of Krishna merged with Ramakrishna, and then she knew that he was indeed Krishna embodied. Ramakrishna began to work on her too, and eventually created the Divine Mother in her as well. This is the way a real guru works on his disciples.

"Do you think Swami Vivekananda, who was Ramakrishna's favorite disciple, could have done anything on his own? Never. When he went to Chicago and stood before the crowd at the Parliament of Religions, before he began to speak he mentally repeated this verse: 'I salute Lord Krishna, the embodiment of Supreme Bliss, by whose grace the mute speak and the lame cross mountains.' Then the Divine Mother Kali entered Vivekananda's body, and when he began, 'Brothers and sisters of America, I would like to talk to you today on "The Master as I Knew Him,"' all America went wild. *That* is the power of Ma, and of *guru bhakti* (devotion to the guru).

"Vivekananda had real guru bhakti. When Ramakrishna lay dying Vivekananda felt so much attachment to him that he actually ate the phlegm and pus that Ramakrishna coughed up. This was in fact a subtle test, and Vivekananda passed with flying colors."

"That was a test?" I asked.

"Yes, that was a subtle test. The same sort of thing happened with Samartha Ram Das, one of Maharashtra's greatest saints, who was actually an incarnation of Anjaneya. His favorite disciple was a boy named Kalyan, and of course all the other disciples were jealous of him. Samartha Ram Das decided that the jealous disciples needed to learn a good lesson, so one day he developed a big boil on his back. All the disciples showed plenty of sympathy, but didn't do much of anything of a practical nature to alleviate his misery.

"When Kalyan heard that his guruji was in pain, though, he was overcome with love. He ran to Samartha Ram Das, put his mouth over the boil and began to suck out the pus. But when he tasted it he found that it was not pus; it was nectar! His guru just smiled. This was a form of Shaktipat Diksha for Kalyan. The other disciples were ashamed of their jealousy when they saw that Kalyan did what they did not even dream of doing, and they never even suspected that he was getting anything in return for his devotion. Kalyan became the successor of Samartha Ram Das.

"Kabir says, 'You talk about lovers, but what do you know of them? Only the man who is ready to cut off his head at a moment's notice for his guru is a real lover.' Bhakti like Vivekananda's or Kalyan's is very rare, but I have seen an example of such bhakti. There was a nobleman named Jaisinghrao Ghatge, whose guru was a Muslim fakir named Mungshahji Maharaj. When anyone came to meet Mungshahji Maharaj he would throw feces at them, or if he knew they were vegetarian he would pick up a chicken bone and throw it at them, just to see how much they could take before they became angry.

"Mungshahji Maharaj lived with Jaisinghrao, and when the mood struck him he would throw his feces at the wall, set fire to the curtains, and break things. He would do anything he felt like doing, and Jaisinghrao never said a word. Jaisinghrao was so devoted to his guru that he used to perform full puja to Mungshahji Maharaj's feces.

"One day Jaisinghrao was in danger of losing all his land because his monetary position was very bad. He never spoke a word, but that day while he was paying his respects to his guru his mind strayed to his mundane difficulties and a single tear fell from his eye. When Mungshahji Maharaj saw it he said, 'Child, when you take such good care of me, never asking even the simplest favor, do you think I can bear to see a tear in your eye? What's the problem?'

"When he heard the problem, Mungshahji Maharaj said, 'Go! You not only will not lose your land, I am going to make you a billionaire.' Jaisinghrao kept his land, and when he sold it piece by piece he made in fact one billion rupees.

"At one point the entire population of a certain town petitioned the court that Mungshahji Maharaj be forced to stay with them. Jaisinghrao filed a countersuit, asking to retain custody of his guru. The learned judge was quite perplexed, and finally decided that since a fakir is free of all encumbrances he has the right to decide where he will stay. Mungshahji Maharaj then said, 'I will never desert Jaisinghrao, because he doesn't ask me for anything.'"

I interrupted: "Mungshahji Maharaj was called 'Maharaj' even though he was a Muslim?"

"Yes, because he had so many Hindu disciples. Jaisinghrao was a Hindu, after all."

"He must have been quite a saint."

"He was good. I met him because he had been trying to dig up a buried treasure. He had got partway and a cobra had appeared to block the path. Also, spirits could be heard howling around the area. He had heard that I knew how to get around such obstacles—I have dug up hundreds of things from the ground—so I came and grabbed the cobra and said, 'Dig!' Just before they were about to strike pay dirt I told them, 'You must donate this much to charity, this much to a particular trust fund, and then you can keep the rest for yourself.'

"Poor Jaisinghrao said nothing, but Mungshahji Maharaj's ego was hurt, and he said, 'No, it will be divided as I decide.'

"I let go of the cobra and said, 'Do it yourself then.' They couldn't, and the treasure remained buried. It is so difficult to keep the ego under complete control, even for great saints like Mungshahji Maharaj. But in spite of his guru's imperfections Jaisinghrao did well, because of devotion. It was the bhakti that did most of the work. Have I ever told you the story of Pyaredas?" He had, but I wanted to hear it again, so I kept quiet.

"Pyaredas was a drunkard debauchee who was very fond of women. One day this wastrel met a sadhu who told him, 'Pyare, you are completely devoted to flesh, skin and bone; if you were to love God as much as you love the physical body, what do you think you might become?' These words had such an effect on Pyaredas that he left everything and took that sadhu as his guru. He loved his guru very, very dearly, and was so terrifically devoted to him that he never left him for a moment.

'When it came time for the guru to leave his body he became worried that the shock of the separation might be too much for Pyaredas, so he told him, 'Pyare, you go to such-and-such a city, and I will follow you later.' After Pyaredas departed, his guru left his body.

"Pyaredas waited several days in that city, and when his guru did not come he returned to the guru's town and asked news of him. When he learned that his guru had left his body, and that a memorial stone had already been erected for him, Pyaredas went directly to the memorial stone and began to cry. He cried and cried and cried, so much so that he went blind.

"Finally he decided to end himself, and started to bang his head against the stone. After his head had become quite bloody and his skull was about to crack, his guru appeared to him in an ethereal form. He made Pyaredas to see again, healed the wounds on his head, and then entered his body. Then the two were always together, and they lived together in that body for a hundred years. Bhakti like this is very rare."

We were interrupted at this point, and some days later he continued this lesson.

"You can be dead sure that your guru will come to you when the time is ripe. The question is, will you be ready for him? Will you be ready to love him without any limits or preconceptions or conditions? The mother is high, but the guru is even higher. It is because of your mother that you have any physical existence at all, which is why you must worship your mother until the end of your life; but it is because of the guru that you are born again. A real guru will first destroy you and then recreate you, give you a new birth. When Jesus said, 'You must be born again,' this is what He meant.

"If you want to love God, or your guru, or whoever, you must have a waxen heart. That was Shakespeare's phrase, but I'm not sure he under-

AGHORA II: Kundalini

stood the full implications of what he wrote. You must have a heart which is ready to melt when the emotion becomes too great. And that is only the beginning. Once your heart melts, you must melt your bones so that there is no resistance left at all. You must surrender totally to your guru, making his will yours, so that your guru can have his way and perfect you. Unfortunately, only one in a million can surrender totally; everyone else must first learn how to surrender.

"The relationship which exists between guru and disciple is the deepest possible human relationship. They relate like parent and child, like chums. Nowhere in the universe will a 'child' ever find a pal like his guru. And they are like lovers. The guru will tempt the child in all sorts of ways, like Matsyendra Nath tested Gorakh Nath (see *Aghora*, pp. 156–7), but a good disciple will never be tempted. A good disciple loves only the guru, and wants only the guru.

"You well know that Guru Purnima is the day on which the guru is to be worshipped. Have you asked yourself yet, 'Why a full moon, and not some other lunar day?'"

"No."

"Well, it has to do with emotion. If two lovers find themselves alone on a full moon night they are likely to be overcome with the desire to unite sexually. They cannot endure the separation from each other; they must embrace. Full moon nights cause an overflow of emotion in the human psyche. On Guru Purnima the guru and disciple, whose relationship is much more intimate than that of mere lovers, experience a natural outpouring of emotion for each other. The guru, because of his tremendous love for his disciple, takes the disciple's karmic debts onto himself. The disciple responds with *guru dakshina*, an offering to the guru.

"Someone with subtle understanding will now ask, 'Why is the disciple supposed to give an offering to the Guru, if the guru has already taken all the karmic debts from the disciple? Then the disciple has nothing of his own left to give.' And that is very right. The disciple has nothing he can give the guru except love, and so he can do nothing in return except worship the guru as God incarnate; not to pamper the guru's ego, but to become more and more selfless so that the guru can work on him without interference.

"They say in Hindi, "Light comes from the moon, not the stars; love comes from one, not many." That one is the guru, and only when you have learned how to love your guru will you ever learn how to love God. The relationship between guru and disciple can begin only when the disciple forgets everyone else except that one; once that happens then everything follows.

[278]

"A guru always wants to make his disciple into his own guru. The Self, the Absolute Reality, is the true guru, because the gu-ru is that which is *gunatita* and *ru-patita* (beyond attribution and form). A true guru makes the disciple go beyond attribute and form. First he makes the 'child' go beyond manubandhana, the bondage of karmic debt. Then he makes the disciple realize the nature of the Self, and the two become guru-brothers (or guru-sisters). Then the guru worships the disciple's Self as the Supreme Guru, the First Deity, and the disciple is made.

"If this is what it takes to make a disciple," Vimalananda continued rhetorically, "how many real disciples can a guru have? One or two; a handful at the most. Jesus had only twelve, and not all of them had the same capacity or achieved the same things. Four of them, like John, had Sattva predominating in their natures; they were the ones who best followed Jesus' teachings. Four of them who became pillars of the church, like Peter, were dominated by Rajas; because the pillars were Rajasic, the Catholics and their church exist mainly in Rajas. And four disciples, like Judas, were full of Tamas. Poor Jesus did the best He could with the material He had available.

"A few gurus teach a handful of disciples each; some teach no one. A guru may have many devotees, but there is no use in creating hundreds of disciples who are all half-baked. Every guru should have one special disciple to whom to transfer his most precious knowledge. Make one, but make that one so thoroughly that the whole world will gape at his or her greatness. *That* is the real value in being a guru.

"The pride of seeing your 'child' succeed cannot be measured in words. But a guru can't just select a disciple arbitrarily; he must know the innate capabilities and aptitudes of each of his 'children' so that he can select one to whom to transmit the bulk of his knowledge. This is why a guru always loves to play with his 'children,' to test them.

"After he has been satisfied, and he wants to give Shaktipat Diksha to a disciple, he usually transfers that shakti through a vehicle, which might be a drink of water, the smell of incense, an intense gaze, or a tap to the spine or head. Perhaps he will transfer the shakti in the form of a mantra. When the disciple with closed eyes sees the mantra written in tongues of flame, in Devanagari script, a voice will tell the 'child' how to repeat the mantra and what restrictions to observe. It is better to do it this way, because mantras are never meant to be spoken.

"This is what happened to Tukaram Maharaj. He met his guru once only, in a dream. The guru showed him the mantra, repeated it to him, and told him to repeat it. That was it; no lengthy discourses, physical initiations or complicated rituals. He got his mantra and began to recite it. And it was not some sort of complicated mantra, either; it was the simple, beautiful mantra 'Rama Krishna Hari.' Because he had supreme faith in his guru, Tukaram Maharaj achieved wonders even without any personal guidance from a living guru. He was so advanced that he did not die in the usual way; like Elijah, a chariot from heaven came down and collected him. Not everyone who claims to have been initiated in a dream ends up like Tukaram Maharaj!

"And what about Kabir? He was initiated when he lay in front of Ramananda Swami early in the morning as Ramananda Swami was returning from bathing in the Ganga in Benaras. Ramananda Swami inadvertently kicked Kabir, whom he could not see in the darkness, and said, 'Ram, Ram,' which Kabir took as his mantra. He could achieve in this way, with a mantra which had been given to him offhandedly, because he was Kabir, and because he had full faith in Rama and in his guru.

"Kabir was a great saint who had a great son: Kamal. Kamal, which means 'amazing,' really was amazing, which meant of course that all of Kabir's other disciples were insanely jealous of him.

"Kabir loved horses, and one day he sent Kamal out to cut grass for the horses. Kamal found the grass, but when he went to cut it he started to think about how much that would hurt the grass. To make a test, he took the sickle and cut his own finger. When he felt the pain he decided that he definitely couldn't go through with cutting the grass.

"Horses have to eat frequently, and when these weren't fed they became uneasy. When some of the other disciples discovered that Kamal had not brought any grass they rushed out to cut some, and then ran to tell Kabir, hoping to see Kamal get a good scolding from the master.

"When Kabir heard the story he called for Kamal and asked him why he had not cut the grass. Kamal explained to Kabir that the grass was living just as much as he was and that he couldn't cut it; in fact, he would rather cut himself than cut the grass. Then Kabir understood, and composed a verse on the spot: 'Kabir told Kamal, 'You are really *kamal* (amazing). I have only been half-baked, but you are completely done.' This is the beautiful play of guru and disciple."

Perhaps because he knew he would be dying soon, Vimalananda sat me down one day late in 1983 for what would be a final admonition.

"Sooner or later, Robby, I am going to die."

"Yes, but you are not going to die any time soon."

"Can you guarantee that? Can you guarantee that you or I will be alive even one minute from now?"

"I can't guarantee anything about me, but I can guarantee that if you decide you want to stay alive you can do it."

He continued without comment. "Everyone is going to die. Maybe now, maybe later; but someday I will be gone, and you will be left here. You have learned quite a lot, and you have a lot left to learn. Never pass up an opportunity to learn.

"Because it is Kali Yuga there are no longer any Rishi ashrams here on the physical plane. But the Rishis are immortal, and they can travel anywhere they like in the universe. This means that a Rishi might be moving amongst us, in Bombay or anywhere else. Of course no one would be able to recognize him; he would be in disguise. You would only be able to recognize him if you knew the special signs on his body which distinguish him from ordinary human beings. Very few humans know these signs.

"If you do know these characteristics and are able to spot a Mahapurusha, even a Siddha, he will give you a wonderful blessing. Because this is Kali Yuga everyone's sadhana is imperfect, so you are not likely to be able to attract a Mahapurusha to you by force. But if you sincerely do the sadhana that you have been taught, and if you have an aching desire, one day a Mahapurusha will come to you, in disguise, and will let you try to catch him. See how they love to play about? Even though sadhana is very serious business, you must always keep an attitude of playfulness about you, like a small child. Everyone, and this especially includes celestial beings, loves children; but no one likes an adult who thinks he or she is too clever. The quickest way to be shot down in the spiritual field is to become too big for your breeches.

"This is the reason you must always see Narayana in the heart of each and every creature you meet. You can never know when, or in what form, your deity or a Mahapurusha will come to test you. If you pass you are made; your sadhanas have been crowned with success. If you fail—well, you will have to start all over again from the beginning, and no one knows how many lifetimes that might take. So don't make any mistakes.

"And remember, this is not the sort of test you can mug up for. You will never know it is taking place until it is over. Actually, of course, there is no such thing as a test. You think it is a test because 'you' are there—the false personality. Once the e-y-e 'eye' has been converted into capital 'I' there is no question of a test; who will you test? Yourself? But so long as duality is present—so long as Kundalini is not completely free of Her bonds—there is always the danger that you may not make the right choice, because of the play of karma and manubandhana.

"Whatever you are destined to have you will get, beyond the shadow of a doubt. How and when you get it depend on how well you can cultivate your mind. The function of Tantra and Aghora is to put the government of mind, senses, and body into the proper order to avoid misery. Life minus misery for a prolonged period produces satisfaction, which yields happiness; and when happiness is increased beyond all conceivable limits and is sustained it becomes bliss, what the Vedas call *ananda*. Sadhana is a means to this end. When Kundalini awakens, if body, mind and spirit are in good working order bliss is certain.

"Bliss is not something you have to create, or accumulate; it arises spontaneously. Just let God decide what is best for you, and God will provide it accordingly. So even at those times when your will power is weak and your mental control is poor, there is still nothing to worry about. Always, always remember that the supreme method of mind control, the supreme intoxication, is the perpetual repetition of the sweet name of God. Never forget God, and God will never forget you. And one day you will succeed."

Appendix

by Robert Beer

Yantras: A General Description

Yantra, meaning "device" or "instrument," is usually a geometric representation designed to identify the mind of a worshipper with his or her chosen deity. The *Yogini Tantra* says that the goddess may either be worshipped as image, mandala or yantra. A yantra is the outward form of a deity, while a mantra is the deities' subtle form. In essence the mantra is the deity, and when a yantra is inscribed with its bija mantras and empowered by consecration the deity is installed within the yantra. Empowerment is the entry of the deities' prana into the yantra, and without this the yantra is but an empty construction. When a yantra is consecrated by auspicious rites it brings prosperity and peace and removes all malevolent influences from the worshippers family. Yantras can be used for magical purposes and when employed in destructive rituals the yantra becomes more a prison than a palace for the deity.

A yantra is usually constructed with a circular point or bindu at the center embodying the seed or bija of the deity. Encompassing the bindu are usually triangles which may form a hexagram or geometric design, the upward pointing fire triangles represent the god, and the downward pointing wind triangles represent the goddess (yoni). Intersecting squares may house the center which usually rest on the circular bed of a lotus. Outside this in concentric circles are the petals of the lotus which normally number eight or sixteen. The whole diagram is contained within a square bhupura or ground plan with four gateways in the cardinal directions.

Yantras are inscribed on various materials according to their use and the function they perform. For peaceful and magnetizing rites: rock crystal and birch bark are often used; for enriching: gold, silver or copper plate; for destructive rituals: iron, skin or bone is employed. The metal plate is often smeared with a paste such as sandalwood, saffron or aloe, and inscribed with a stylus of gold, wood, iron, or thorn taken from shrubs such as acacia, bael or datura, depending again on the ritual for which it is used. Three dimensional yantras are sometimes commissioned for their enduring influences of peace and prosperity, skilfully carved from such precious materials as rock crystal, coral or lapis lazuli.

The Nine Nath Siddhas

The tradition of the Nine Nath Siddhas stems from the flowering of Shaivite Tantra around the tenth century. The word Nath is derived from the name of Shiva and its literal meaning is "Lord." The Naths brought to light various systems of tantric practices aimed at the transubtantation of the human body into a divine immortal body. Central to their methods were the practices of Hatha, Kundalini and Alchemical yogas. The North Indian tradition lists nine Naths and eighty-four Siddhas in its lineage, the most prominent of which were Matsyendranath and Gorakhnath. Many of these eighty-four Siddhas appear in the Buddhist tantric tradition, where it is sometimes said that they practiced Hindu tantra by day and Buddhist tantra at night. The various lists of the Nine Naths include: Matsyendranath, Gorakhnath, Jalandhara, Kanipa, Gopichand, Caurangi, Charpati, Dharamnath and Gaininath.

NATH SIDDHA ILLUSTRATIONS

The Nath Siddhas and Siddhas are illustrated in their Tibetan styles.
Page numbers refer to references or examples in the text.

The Nath Siddha Matsyendranath

Matsyendranath—the "Fish Lord," is the first Guru of the nine Naths. Along with Gorakhnath he is regarded as the founder of the Nath, Kaula and Kanphata traditions, and with instigating the practices of Hatha, Laya and Raja yogas. According to legend he was a fisherman from Kamarupa in Assam who hooked a giant fish and was swallowed alive by it, like Jonah. The fish came to rest on the ocean floor near a hidden palace in which Shiva had chosen to transmit his most secret teaching to his consort Uma. From within the belly of the fish Matsyendranath overheard these secret teachings and received his mantra directly from Shiva, who had no option but to make Matsyendranath his disciple. Matsyendranath spent twelve years perfecting his sadhana in the belly of the fish until he was eventually disgorged onto dry land. He had many disciples, the most prominent of which was Gorakhnath.

In Nepal, Matsyendranath is identified with the Buddhist bodhisattva of compassion, Avalokitesvara, who is himself identified with Shiva as Lokanath—"Lord of the World." Matsyendranath is the patron deity of Nepal, and is believed to have brought the first grains of rice to this Himalayan Kingdom.

The Nath Siddha Matsyendranath
(page 278)

The Nath Siddha Gorakhnath

The Indian subcontinent is rich with stories and miraculous anecdotes about the life of Gorakhnath. He was probably born in the Punjab around the tenth century, although legend often dates him to a far more remote past. He travelled extensively across India, from Sindh to Bengal and from Nepal to Sri Lanka. In Nepal he is said to have caused a twelve year drought by the power of his meditation, which was only ended by the intercession of Matsyendranath. The city of Gorka in Nepal is named after Gorakhnath and its decendants now form the tribe of the Gurkas. He is believed by his followers to be immortal and living to this day in the Himalayas; but at the vast temple complex in Gorakhpur in Uttar Pradesh is a tomb said to contain his body absorbed in Samadhi. His Hindu name Goraksha probably derived from "Protector of the Cows (Go)," or from a legend in which a barren woman, wishing to bear a son, received some ashes from Shiva's fire. Instead of swallowing the ashes she threw them on a pile of dung (ghor), and twelve years later Matsyendranath recovered a boy from this dung pile whom Shiva named after Gorakhnath—"The Lord of Dung."

Gorakhnath is said to have inspired such great luminaries as Kabir, Gopichand, Guga, Puran Bhagat and Guru Nanak—the founder of the Sikh religion; in one record he is even reputed to have been the foster father and teacher of the Prophet Muhammed. His followers, known as Gorakhnaths, Naths and Kanphatas form the largest Indian tantric tradition. The Kanphatas are named after the practice of splitting the center of the ear to accomodate large ear-rings, usually made from rhinoceros horn, ivory, conch, copper or gold. Great importance is attached to these ear-rings; if they are pulled out or the ear mutilated the Kanphata yogin becomes an outcaste. In certain parts of India such an occurance would result in the yogin being buried alive with no tomb erected over his body.

The Nath Siddha Gorakhnath
(pages 38 & 211)

The Nath Siddha Caurangi

Cauranginath was a disciple and contemporary of Gorakhnath. Legend relates that he was the son of King Devapala of Bengal. Devapala's first wife died while Caurangi was still a child, and his father took a new wife who resorted to deception in order to place her own son on the throne. Caurangi was taken to a forest clearing where his arms and legs were cut off. Here he was found by Matsyendranath who instructed Gorakhnath to care for the limbless youth. Gorakhnath taught him the yoga of pot-like breath retention (kumbhaka), and after twelve years of this practice his limbs were miraculously restored by the power of his own realization.

His name Caurangi probably derives from "Four Limbs (anga)," and the shape of his torso as a bulb (kanda) possibly refers to his practice of Kanda Manda yoga. Caurangi is said to have founded the great Kali temple of Kalighat in Calcutta. The main north-south thoroughfare across the city of Calcutta is now known as Chowringhi.

The Nath Siddha Caurangi
(page 114)

The Nath Siddha Jalandhara

Jalandhara, whose name means "Bearer of the Net," is also known in Bengal as Hadipa—"born from a bone (hada) of Shiva." He is named after one of the four most sacred sites (pithas) of tantric practice, Jalandhara, located in the Kangra valley of northwest India and close to the modern city of Jullunder.

In the Nath legends, Hadipa was a sweeper of Bengal who became guru to the young king Gopichand. Gopichand doubted his guru's integrity and caused Hadipa to be buried alive in a pit. After twelve years, Hadipa's disciple Kanipa was informed of this occurance by Gorakhnath, and Kanipa travelled to Bengal to release his teacher. When Hadipa emerged alive from his ordeal, Gopichand repented of his actions and abdicated his throne to follow the Nath path of his teacher Hadipa.

Jalandhara was a great exponent of Hatha and Kundalini yogas. Gorakhnath comments that the term Hatha meaning "forceful" is made up of the two syllables ha and tha representing the solar and lunar channels which are forced into union (yoga) in the central channel of Sushumna.

The Nath Siddha Jalandhara

The Nath Siddha Kanipa

Kanipa was said to have been born as a Brahmin in the Kingdom of Gaura near Bengal. His father is reputed to have been the fisherman who caught the fish from which Matsyendranath appeared. Kanipa's guru was Jalandhara and his legends are rich in anecdotes of the Bamarg or Left Hand Path. He was instrumental in the rise of the Kapalika and Carya traditions, composing a famous cycle of Bengali Carya songs known as the Caryagiti. He is also held to be one of the founders of the Aghori sect, and many snake charmers claim Kanipa as their root guru. In one anecdote a tantric feast was hosted by Matsyendranath and Goraknath and each participant was free to choose his own food. Kanipa's chosen dish was cooked snakes and scorpions, and he was promptly banished from the feast. In the Buddhist legend of Kanipa his untimely death was due to being cursed by a dakini. On his deathbed he taught the headless Vajra Varahi sadhana—a deity assimilated with the headless Mahavidya goddess Chinnamastra.

He is represented in a smashan wearing bone ornaments, holding a skull cup, double-sided drum and tantric staff. Above his head float seven drums and canopies, which often spontaneously manifested as signs of his accomplishment. He is seated upon the resurrected corpse of a vetala (vampire or ghoul).

The Nath Siddha Kanipa
(page 125)

The Nath Siddha Charpati

Charpati was one of the first great teachers of Hatha yoga, and composed several texts on this subject. He was one of the early disciples of the Kapalika lineage and his guru was Jalandhara. One of his legends relates the practice of Khecari Mudra, whereby the tongue is turned upwards into the soft upper palate of the throat. He lived around the tenth century and amongst his pupils was King Sahila Varma of Chamba state in Himachal Pradesh.

The Nath Siddha Charpati
(page 71)

SIDDHA ILLUSTRATIONS

The Siddha Nalinapa
(page 213)

The Siddha Chang Dev Maharaj
(page 270)

The Siddha Bhadrapa
(Chapter 7)

The Alchemist Siddha Nagarjuna
(page 271-272)

The Musician Siddha Vinapa
who attained realization through Nada Yoga
(page 188)

The Siddha Dengipa – The Rice Thresher
(page 218)

GLOSSARY

Abhisheka - Ritual bath of a deity or individual; if the latter it is initiatory.

Adesha - Instruction, command (by the guru).

Adhibhautika - The mundane or terrestrial sphere of action. The lower three Chakras, Muladhara, Svadhishthana, Manipura, are for adhibhautika accomplishments.

Adhidaivika - The celestial or astral sphere, the world of gods and goddesses beyond both the physical and the spiritual. The three Chakras in the head called Golata, Lalata, and Lalana are for the adhidaivika.

Adhyatmika - The spiritual world, the realm of the Self. The upper three Chakras, Anahata, Vishuddha, and Ajna, are for the adhyatmika.

Advaita - "Non-dual"; the designation of a system of philosophy characterized by the notion of the ultimate non-distinction between the individual self and the absolute Brahman or God.

Adya - Lit. "first, original." Used as a synonym for the Adishakti, the first or original Shakti which manifests from the absolute and is the Mother of all the worlds.

Aghora - Lit. "non-terrifying." Aghora is the most extreme of all Indian sects, concentrating on forcible conversion of a limited human personality into a divine personality.

Aghori - A practitioner of Aghora.

Agni - "Fire"; the God Fire.

Agnihotri - One who performs the Vedic fire sacrifice called Agnihotra, the offering of milk or rice into a sacred fire in the morning and evening.

Ahamkara - "I-maker"; the ego.

Ajagara - "Python."

Ajagara Sadhana - A meditation in which one becomes like a python.

Ajna - "Command"; name of the Chakra located at the center of the forehead, between the eyes.

Akartum - "Not to perform"; that which is impossible for ordinary beings, referring to the adhyatmika, the spiritual world.

Akula-Shiva - the Absolute Unmanifested; opposite of both Kula and Shakti.

Alaksha - "Unmarked; without characteristic."

Amrita - "Immortal", nectar.

Amsha - "Part, fraction."

Anahata - "Unstruck"; the name of the heart chakra.

Anahata Nada - "The sound which does not arise by striking"; the sound of the Anahata Chakra.

Ananda - "Bliss."

Anjaneya - "Descendant of Anjani"; a name of Hanuman, the monkey king, because his mother was named Anjani.

Anubhavi - "Experiencer."

Anusthana - An extended series of ritual or meditational sessions.

Anusvara - The nasal sound "m" that comes at the end of many Sanskrit words; its shape is a horizontal upward-pointing half moon (see bindu).

Anyathakartum - "To alter, act otherwise"; that which is beyond both the spiritual and the mundane and is inconceivable to humans, referring to the adhidaivika or astral world.

Apsaras - A class of semi-divine females who can change their shape at will; they move between water (ap) and clouds (saras).

Aryaputra - "Son of a nobleman."

Asana - "Seat, yogic posture."

Ashta - "Eight."

Ashta Pasha - The Eight Snares which bind us to the world: lust, anger, greed, delusion, envy, shame, fear and disgust.

Asura - "Demon, anti-god."

Atharvan - Name of an ancient Vedic sage.

Atma/Atman - The soul, the indwelling spirit which animates a living being.

The Jivatma is the individual spirit which imagines itself trapped in a physical form, subject to the limitations of embodied existence. The Paramatma is the Universal Soul, the totality of spirit in the cosmos. All Jivas or Jivatmas belong to the Paramatma.

Avatara - "Descent, incarnation;" usually denoting one of the ten incarnations of Vishnu: Matsya (the fish), Kurma (the tortoise), Varaha (the boar), Narasimha (the man-lion), Vamana (the dwarf), Parashurama, Rama, Krishna, Buddha, and Kalki (the future incarnation).

Baccha - "Child" (Hindi, masculine).

Balavant - "Strong, powerful."

Bandha - "Binding; a bond or fetter"; a sealing of a part of the subtle nervous system through yogic manipulation.

Bandha Koshtha - Constipation.

Bhairava - "The Terrifier"; a ferocious form of Shiva who often serves as a guardian deity. [also cf. Aghora glossary]

Bhairavi - A ferocious form of the Goddess;. A woman who gains an attributeless state in sadhana comes back as a celestial Bhairavi or Yogini.

Bhajan - Religious song or singing.

Bhakti - Religious or spiritual devotion.

Bhava - Any emotional or spiritual state.

Bhedana - "Dividing, breaking."

Bhogi - "Enjoyer"; usually characterized as the opposite of "yogi."

Bhojana - A meal.

Bhu - "Existence", name of the Earth Goddess.

Bhu Garbha - "Womb of the earth."

Bhuta - "A being"; usually, however, it refers to a disembodied spirit.

Bhuta Agni - "The fire of life."

Bhuta Shuddhi - Ritual purification (shuddhi) of unwelcome spirits from the body.

Bija - "Seed."

Bija Mantra - Any monosyllabic mantra, which is a "seed" representation of a God or Goddess.

Bindu - The dot appearing over the anusvara in superscript position in Indian scripts. The half moon and dot above the line are the anusvara and bindu. More esoterically bindu refers to a point or position without dimension; thus, the source of all sound.

Brahmana - A member of the priestly class of society.

Brahmarshi - A high level sage or rishi.

Buddhi - "Intellect."

Chaitanya - "Consciousnes."

Chillum - A pipe used to smoke marijuana or hashish mixed with tobacco. It is three or four inches long and is straight, tapering from a wide bowl to a thin mouth.

Chakra - "Wheel"; a sensitive subtle nervous plexus. The six Chakras usually described are the Muladhara, in the perineum; the Svadhishthana, in the pubic region; the Manipura, at the navel; the Anahata, near the heart; the Vishuddha, in the throat; and the Ajna, in the center of the forehead. From the Ajna one moves into the Sahasrara, which is not actually a Chakra. However, Aghora adds three more Chakras, all located in the head: Golata, Lalata, and Lalana.

Chakra Puja - A ritual in which one or more male tantric practitioners surrounds himself or themselves with female tantrics (8, 16, or 64 are recommended numbers). Sexual relations are the culmination of the long ritual which includes many offerings during which both males and females self-identify with deities.

Chit - "Consciousness, subjectivity."

Chit Shakti - The power of consciousness or subjectivity which identifies with the Unmanifested Absolute.

Dakshina - Payment or offering of gratitude after the completion by a guru or priest of a teaching or ritual.

Dama - Physical self-control.

Damaru - Shiva's small drum.

Dasharatha - Name of a great king, father of Rama.

Dattatreya - Name of a sage, son of Atri and Anasuya who was worshipped as a deity in the form of the triad Brahma, Vishnu, and Shiva.

Daya - "Compassion."

Deepaka - Name of a Raga or musical melody: the Kindling or Igniting Melody.

Deva - "Deity, celestial being."

Dhabawala - One who carries a vessel (dhaba); refers to men who bring hot home-cooked lunches to hundreds of thousands of workers in Bombay every day.

Dhara - The power to hold or fix, the syllables of the word Radha reversed.

Dharana - "Concentration."

Dhuni - The fire tended by a sadhu. A sadhu is said to sit "on" his dhuni, meaning close to it, concentrating on it.

Dhyana - "Meditation."

Digambara - "One whose raiment is the sky;" a naked mendicant, usually of the Jain religion.

Diksha - An initiation.

Droha - "Treachery."

Dvapara Yuga - "Eon of one-half"; name of the third Yuga in the series of four, in which one-half of the dharma or righteousness of Satya Yuga remains. In Dvapara Yuga the primary sadhana and means of achieving desires is austerities (tapas).

Five Great Elements - The elemental constituents of the physical universe: earth, water, fire, air, space.

Gana - "Attendents."

Gandharva - A celestial musician.

Ganesha - The elephant-headed god, son of Shiva and Uma (gana + isha, lord of attendents).

Ganesh(a) Paran - A raga for Ganesha during which Ganesha must come if sung correctly.

Garbha - "Womb."

Gati - "Gait, mode;" there are 108 gatis of sound (nada, q.v.). Numerologically 108 adds up to 9, the number of chakras in the body, according to

Aghora. Which gati of nada you hear depends on your past karmas, present tendencies, ancestry, etc.

Ghata - "Pot."

Ghata Sthapana - "Establishing of a pot;" name of a rite performed at the commencement of the Nava Ratri festival during which a clay pot is decorated and consecrated or established, then worshipped as the Goddess.

Ghee - Clarified butter.

Go - "Cow" (secondarily "sense organ" and "sacred word"); name of the supreme ideal world (loka) of Krishna.

Gopi - "Female cowherd;" the gopis were devotees of Krishna.

Gotra - 1) System of Vedic lineage ancestry, deriving from "protection of cows"; 2) "Protection for the senses."

Granthi - "Knot."

Granthi Bhedana - The piercing of the knots which obstruct the free movement of Kundalini in the nadis (q.v.).

Guna - Lit. "qualities" or "attributes." The Three Gunas are the three fundamental attributes of conditional or limited existence: Sattva (equilibrium), Rajas (activity), and Tamas (inertia). In its purest state the mind is pure Sattva, and the two chief mental disturbances are Rajas (overactivity) and Tamas (inactivity).

Gunatita - "Beyond the gunas."

Guru Bhakti - Devotion to the guru.

Guru Droha - An offense or act of treachery against the guru.

Guru Purnima - The full moon of the Indian month of Ashadh (usually in mid-July), during which the guru is worshipped.

Halahala - The world-threatening poison drunk by Shiva that turned his throat blue.

Hanuman - The monkey king of the Ramayana who is the archetypical devotee.

Hara - "The snatcher"; name of Shiva as the Lord of Death.

Hiranyakashipu - A great demon king, father of Prahlada (q.v.), was eviscer-ated by Narasimha, the man-lion avatara of Vishnu.

Hiranyaksha - A demon king, elder brother of Hiranyakashipu (q.v.), was killed by Varaha, the boar avatara of Vishnu.

Homa - General term for any ritual in which offering into a consecrated fire is the primary action.

Indriya - "Sense"; five senses are enumerated: touch, smell, taste, sight, hearing.

Isha - "Lord."

Jahnavi - A name of the Ganges River, also a word for the sacred thread worn by Brahmanas and others.

Janaka - A king of great spiritual prowess; father of Rama's wife Sita.

Jathara - "Belly."

Jathara Agni - "Fire of the belly"; the digestive fire.

Japa - Systematic repetition of a mantra or sacred name.

Japamala - A rosary on which japa is performed.

Jata - "Matted locks", worn by many sadhus (q.v.).

Jeevan Samadhi - "Living trance;" the act of deliberately entering into a state of permanent samadhi, tantamount to death. This act is only possible for the greatest saints, such as Jnaneshwar, and often will happen in a cave, after which the saint's disciples will seal off the entrance.

Jiva - The individual personality which undergoes rebirth, because the karmas stored in the causal body need a physical body to permit their expression. (see Atma)

Jnana - Transcendent wisdom. Knowledge (Vidya) is an outward projection or objectivization of this innate, living wisdom.

Jnani - One who has attained ordinary spiritual knowledge.

Kala - "Time."

Kala Ratri - The Black Night, the night just before Dipavali, the new moon of the month of Ashvin.

Kali - The lowest throw of the dice.

Kali Yuga - The fourth of the four ages through which the cosmos passes in cycles of 4,320,000 years. Kali Yuga is supposed to last 432,000 years, and is characterized by lack of interest in spirituality among the populace, which leads to materialism, atheism, and the perpetuation of various cruelties by stronger beings onto weaker ones.

Kalpa - A time period or epoch consisting of the four eons or yugas (q.v.)

Kanda - "Division, chapter;" also "bulb," or something bulbous, such as the nadi plexus where the breath or prana called Apana can be made to move upward instead of downward.

Kandarpa - "Onion; beauty;" name of Kamadeva, the god of love.

Kanya - "Maiden."

Kartana - "Cutting."

Kartum - "To do;" that which is difficult to do, but is doable. This refers to the adhibhautika, the mundane world.

Kaula - Followers of Tantra who perform the practice of Rasa Vidya in order to turn Kundalini into Kula Kundalini (q.v.).

Kavi - "Inspired poet."

Kevala - "Isolated, exclusive, alone."

Kevala Kumbhaka - Cessation of breathing for a lengthy period. Only when there is kevala kumbhaka can one's mind become completely firm, after which worship will become steady.

Kedara - Name of a Raga (q.v.), the "Field Melody", sung to attract Krishna.

Khanda - "Broken; a part or limb."

Khanda Manda Yoga - A sadhana during which the practitioner cuts off his own arms and legs with a sharp cleaver, and throws them into a roaring fire. After twelve hours these limbs reemerge from the fire and rejoin his body.

Khandana - "Breaking, dividing, destroying."

Khara - "Donkey."

Kilana - "Nailing"; particularly ritually nailing an ethereal being or deity to a specific location with mantra.

Kirtan - "Devotional song", often accompanied by discourse.

Kirtankar - "One who leads devotional singing and discourse."

Krida - "Play"; particularly unconscious play, such as rati krida ("love play"). Krida is controlled by someone or something other than the being who is playing. In love play, the glands and the genitals do the controlling, not the two people who romance each other.

Krura - "Cruel."

Krura Ratri - "Cruel Night"; the night before the spring festival called Holi, on the full moon of the month of Phalguna (in March).

Kshatriya - "Warrior"; a member of the warrior castes.

Kula - "Family"; "Supreme Consciousness of the Universe"; "form"; see Kula Kundalini.

Kula Kundalini - "Freed Kundalini." After the Kundalini is uncoiled and straightened out along the Six Chakras, She takes the form of the Goddess who is meant to be worshipped by the family (kula) into which you have been born.

Kumbha - "Pot."

Kumbhaka - Holding of the breath, rendering the abdomen and chest like a pot.

Kundalini - Cosmic energy that manifests along the spine and within the chakras (q.v.); the source and force of all experience.

Kurma - "Tortoise"; name of an avatara of Vishnu.

Laya - "Rhythm, dissolution;" see Pralaya.

Lila - "Cosmic play"; distinct from Krida (q.v.). The divine play of Rishis and deities, especially Krishna and Rama, is called Lila, cosmic pastimes in which They are always in control.

Linga - The phallic shaped symbol of Shiva.

Ma - Vimalananda's generic term for the Mother Goddess, the cosmic potentiality for creation. All females were to him embodiments of this universal principle of motherhood and motherliness.

Madhu - "Honey." Only honey can offer sweetness to the body without being digested first.

Madhura - This word has the suffix 'ra' following "madhu". The 'ra' refers to the Fire Element. Anything that is madhura must first be digested before its sweetness can be released into the system. Of the four levels of speech only Para is truly madhu. All other levels are madhura to various degrees because they must first be digested by the listener before their effect can be felt.

Madhyama - "Middle, in between"; the second level of speech, midway between the mundane and the spiritual; mental speech or intention.

Madira - "Wine", one of the Five M's. Esoterically, Fire, of the five elements.

Maha - "Great, immense, cosmic."

Maha Atharvan - Designation of a Maha Kaula whose Kundalini is completely awakened; As such he has gone beyond the limitations of the Atharva Veda, which is the source of Tantra.

Maha Bhava Samadhi - Emotional highlights, a state of madness with uncontrollable love and joy.

Maha Maya - "Great or cosmic illusion"; the covering on the individual self.

Mahakala - The God of Death.

Maha Kaula - Designation of a Kaula after a ritual initiatory bath (abhisheka) has been performed on him.

Mahanubhavi - "Great Experiencer", said of Rishis (q.v.).

Mahapurusha - "Great Soul"; refers to any being who has become immortal as a result of sadhana (q.v.). Rishis (q.v.), Munis (q.v.), Naths and Siddhas are all Mahapurushas.

Maharaj - "Great King"; also a common designation of a saint, who has achieved dominion over the spiritual world.

Maha Rasa - Transcendental flavor.

Maha Ratri - "Great Night", otherwise called Maha Shiva Ratri, occurring on the night before the new moon during the lunar month of Magha (February or early March).

Mahavira Balavant - "Great and Powerful Hero", description of Hanuman.

Maithuna - "Sexual intercourse," one of the Five M's. Esoterically, Ether, of the five elements.

Mamsa - "Meat," one of the Five M's. Esoterically, Air, of the five elements.

Manda - "Embellishment; creation."

Mandana - "Decorating, adorning; creating."

Mantra Siddhi - "Perfection of mantra"; the result of successful sadhana such as purushcharana (q.v.); the manifestation of the deity inherent in the mantra.

Mantra Chaitanya - A stage of sadhana (q.v.), beyond tadrupata (q.v.), when there is total union of consciousness and mantra.

Manu - A being who is the progenitor of the races who live on the earth during a Manvantara (q.v.).

Manvantara - A period of time comprising seventy cycles of the Four Yugas (q.v.).

Marga - "Path."

Marjana - Part of a purushcharana during which one's mantra is recited while water is sprinkled about the body (marjana).

Maryada - "Bounded, encompassed."

Maryada Purushottama - Perfection Encompassed; said of Rama.

Matsya - "Fish;" the name of the fish incarnation of Vishnu. One of the Five M's; esoterically, Water, of the five elements.

Maya - "Illusion"; usually indicates cosmic illusion.

Maya Shakti - The power of unconsciousness or objectivity which identifies with the world, the manifestation of the Absolute.

Megha - "Cloud"; name of a raga (q.v.). If you want rain you play Megha in a certain way and rain will come.

Mleccha - "Barbarian"; one of the common Sanskrit words for any foreigner.

Moha - "Delusion."

Moha Ratri - "Night of Delusion", which is Krishna's birth night, occurring in the month of Shravana (August or early September).

Mudra - "Parched grain", one of the Five M's. Esoterically, Earth, of the five elements.

Muladhara - The first chakra, located at the perineum.

Munda - "Skull."

Munda Sadhana - A spiritual practice that employs skulls.

Muni - An advanced being (yet lower than a Rishi [q.v.]), who communicates telepathically or through the eyes.

Nada - "Sound."

Nada Brahman - The music of the spheres, the Absolute expressed as the sound Om.

Nada Yoga - Sadhanas which employ music. In Nada Yoga the Nada Brahman is worshipped.

Nadi - Ethereal nerves; the body has 72,000, which are conduits of prana (q.v.).

Naga - "Serpent, naked"; a naked Sadhu who gives up everything except his fire.

Naga Kanya - "Serpent princess."

Nara - "Man."

Narasimha - "Man-lion", the name of this avatara of Vishnu.

Narayana - A name of God, esp. of Vishnu.

Nath - "Lord"; a highly advanced being, an Aghori.

Niranjana - "Stainless."

Nirvikalpa - "Without option."

Nirvikalpa Samadhi - A state of consciousness in which all dualities are finally transcended and only aware-

ness of the Paramatma (Ultimate Reality) remains. No consciousness of body or individuality is left.

Nishkalanka - "Stainless"; name of Kalki, the final Avatara of vishnu.

Nivrtti - Inward movement of consciousness toward its source.

Niyama - The second limb of yoga, internal disciplilne.

Nyasa - Ritual placement of a deity in a part of the body.

Ojas - That essence of physical energy which produces the aura as well as immunity (Ayurveda).

Paan - A common digestive consisting of the highly astringent areca nut and other ingredients wrapped in the pungent betel leaf.

Pakhawaj - A large two-headed drum.

Para - "Beyond"; the fourth and highest level of speech, purely telepathic. Only Rishis can access Para.

Parashurama - "Rama with the axe"; the sixth avatara of Vishnu.

Pasha - "Noose."

Pashu - "Animal"; Vimalananda's etymology: "he who is snared (like an animal for sacrifice) by a pasha", referring to any of the Eight Snares (Ashta Pasha.)

Pashyanti - "Seeing"; the third level of speech, seeing with the divine eye, clairvoyant perception. Certain immortals, including Naths and Munis use pashyanti.

Pitri - "Father; deceased ancestor."

Pitri Tarpana - A ritual performed for a deceased human, usually a father or mother or other progenitor, to satisfy any lingering cravings that individual might have had. Properly performed, this assures the individual an auspicious rebirth and enables him or her to maintain their spiritual progression.

Prahlada - Son of the demon king Hiranyakashipu (q.v.); a devotee of Vishnu.

Pralaya - The periodic dissolution of the universe in which everything is returned to to the first (pra-thama) rhythm (laya): the Absolute. This occurs at the end of each Kali Yuga, usually caused by natural calamities.

Prana - "Breath, life force." The five major breaths are prana (the forward-moving breath that regulates the process of breathing), apana (the downward-moving breath that regulates evacuation), samana (the evenly-distributing breath that regulates digestion), vyana (the all-pervasive breath that provides movements of the limbs and joints), and udana (the upward-moving breath that pervades the head).

Prana Pratishtha - "Establishing prana"; a rite in which prana is infused into an image of a deity.

Pranayama - "Control of the Breath"; any practice of breath-control.

Prasad - Any substance, usually food, which has been offered to a deity or saint, or to the image of a deity or saint, and which is then partaken of by a disciple or devotee. Prasad is supposed to contain a tiny amount of the deity's or saint's Shakti, which can exert a spiritualizing effect on the partaker.

Prasadika vani - "Words gifted from God."

Pratyahara - "Withdrawal" of the senses; the fourth limb of classical yoga.

Pravrtti - External movement of consciousness toward manifestation.

Prayoga - "Procedure"; any ritual or meditational procedure

Prema - "Love, esp. romantic love."

Puja - "Ritual adoration", especially of a deity or guru, with objects symbolic of purity, divinity, or grace such as flowers, incense, sweet fruit, coconut, etc. However, puja can also be performed mentally, and Aghoris can perform external puja with impure objects such as menstrual blood and feces.

Purnatmaka - "One whose nature is fullness."

Purnatmaka Purushottama - Perfection Personified, said of Krishna.

Purnima - "Full-moon."

Purushcharana - A lengthy and highly

controlled sadhana designed to achieve Mantra Siddhi.

Mantra Siddhi - For that you need to follow a specific process called purush-charana. First determine how many repetitions of japa you can do in a year. You must then do the same number every day. After completing that, ten percent of the total number must be offered as oblations into a homa fire. Then ten percent of that number must be offered into water (tarpana). Ten percent of that number must be then recited as you sprinkle water about your body (marjana). Finally, ten percent of that number is offered as bhojana, gifts of food, usually to children.

Purushottama - "Supreme person, highest being."

Pushti - "Grace, prosperity."

Pushti Marga - A path (marga) of Krishna devotion founded by Vallabhacharya (1479–1531).

Raga - "Melody"; any Indian musical scale.

Rajya - "Kingdom."

Rakshasa - "Demon."

Rama Rajya - "Rama's kingdom", symbolic of the ideal state wherein peace, harmony and dharma prevail.

Rasatmaka - "Full of blissful emotion", said of Krishna.

Rasa - "Flavor, emotion."

Rasa Vidya - "Knowledge of flavor"; Tantric alchemy.

Ratri - "Night."

Ravana - Name of the demon king who abducted Rama's wife Sita, later killed by Rama.

Ravi - "Sun."

Rishi - Lit. "Seer." Anything a Rishi sees or perceives becomes reality, because a Rishi is an ethereal being of the highest class, one who is almost totally unlimited, who can travel anywhere in the cosmos and do anything at all. The Rishis "saw" the hymns of the Vedas, from which all the knowledge of ancient India was derived.

Rnanubandhana - The bondage of karmic debt.

Roti - Generic name for Indian bread, usually indicating a chappati.

Rudra - Lit. "the Crier," or "He Who makes others cry." Rudra is the ancient name for Shiva, the god of death, and is so called because He makes everyone cry who comes into contact with Him, because He separates them from their limited existence, to which they are tightly attached.

Rupatita - "Beyond form."

Sadashiva - "Eternal Shiva", the state in which Shiva and Shakti are united. Sadashiva's left side is female and right side male, united through the operation of Kundalini.

Sadhaka - One who practices a sadhana.

Sadhana - Any spiritual practice. Aghora Sadhana is designed to replace the Aghori's personality by creation of the deity's form in the Aghori's subtle body.

Sadhu - "A good person"; a wandering religious mendicant.

Saguna - "With attribute, with form"; The Absolute can be expressed as Saguna or manifested, such as the form of a deity, or Nirguna, formless and unmanifest.

Samadhi - A state of profound or one-pointed consciousness, trance.

Samagri - "Collection, assemblage, especially of materials used for worship."

Samaya - "Time, occasion"; especially for regular functions such as worship or eating.

Sampradaha - "Complete incineration."

Sampradaya - "Sect, tradition."

Samsara - The cycle of birth and death, ensnarement in the web of worldly existence.

Samskara - Personality characteristic.

Samyama - "Complete control."

Sangama - "Confluence", as of rivers meeting.

Sanjivani - An herb that can restore the dead to life, brought from the Himalayas by Hanuman to save Lakshmana, the brother of Rama.

Sankalpa - "Intention; certainty."

Sankhya - "Number", e.g. the number of repetitions of japa that must be preformed.

Sarangi - A mid-sized string instrument played with a bow.

Sarvavidya - The totality of manifested knowledge. This is a Siddhi which involves control of all Shakti in the cosmos.

Satya Yuga - "The eon of truth"; the first and longest of the four yugas. In Satya Yuga, in which dharma or righteousness operates at maximum capacity, there is no disease or discord, and people obtain everything they need by power of will.

Setu - "Bridge."

Setu Bandha - The building of the bridge by Hanuman's army of monkeys from India to Lanka in order for Rama's army to cross the waters and rescue Sita. Esoterically, the internal Setu Bandha connects the Muladhara Chakra to the Manipura Chakra, bridging the Svadhishthana Chakra.

Shaivism - Sectarian worship of Shiva or his aspects.

Shakarpala - A type of sweet.

Shakti - Energy; the ability to perform some action. Shakti is always female in Indian philosophy.

Shaktipat - "Descent of Shakti."

Shaktipat Diksha - "Initiation by transference of Shakti."

Shalagrama - Fossil ammonite representative of Vishnu.

Shat - "Six."

Shat Prayoga - "Six Rituals or Procedures"; rituals of black magic which cause death, delusion, discord, hatred, obstruction, and enchantment.

Shava - A corpse.

Shavasana - A yoga pose (asana) in which the pratitioner lies down like a corpse (shava) in order to release and relax completely.

Shita - "Cool."

Shruti - "That which is heard", indicating the Veda because it has been transmitted orally.

Shuddha - "Pure, purified."

Shuddha Advaita - "Pure non-dualism"; name of the philosophy of the Pushti Marga founded by Vallabhacharya.

Shuddhi - "Purification."

Shudra - "Laborer"; member of the hereditary castes of laborers.

Shunya - "Emptiness, nothingness"; in the Shunya state all names and forms become extinct, and one is only aware of one's own individuality. The entire universe is contained in the Shunya state, in unmanifested form.

Siddha - An "accomplished one." Anyone who has obtained a Siddhi, or supernatural accomplishment, is a Siddha. Vimalananda restricted his use of the word Siddha to indicate those beings who have achieved immortality.

Siddhi - "Perfection, accomplishment"; especially success at sadhana.

Simha - "Lion."

Six Tastes - An Ayurvedic category: sweet, sour, salty, bitter, pungent or spicy, and astringent.

Smarahara - Name of Shiva. After the God of Love (Smara) disturbed his meditation, Shiva destroyed (hara) him with a single glance.

Smashan - A charnel ground; an area in which dead bodies are burned or buried. This word is derived from "ash-mashana," or "place where rocks lie," which suggests that burial was once more common in India than it now is.

Smrti - "Memory, that which is remembered"; recorded tradition, distinct from Shruti, the Veda, revealed tradition.

Sthana - "Location."

Sthapana - "Establishing."

Sudarshana - "Well-seeing."

Sudarshana Chakra - Vishnu's discus.

Sura - A god (identical to deva).

Surya - "Sun."

Sushumna - The central nadi through which the Kundalini Shakti travels.

Svapneshvari - "Goddess of Dreams."

Svatantra - "Independent, self-functioning", a primary goal of Tantra.

Tadrupata - "A state of being similarly formed"; a stage of sadhana, beyond tanmayata (q.v.), in which the practitioner becomes identical with the deity.

Tanmayata - "Togetherness"; a stage of success at sadhana in which the practitioner is with the chosen deity at all times.

Tapas - "Heat, austerities, penance"; karmas are burned away by tapas.

Tara - The Goddess Tara, She Who Causes One to Cross Over; from the Sanskrit, "to cross, swim."

Tarpana - Offerings into water .

Tattva - Lit. "thatness." A category of existence. For example, the Three Gunas are Tattvas because they are attributes, and the category of attribution is a Tattva. The Atma is also a Tattva.

Tirthankara - "Ford-Maker"; name for any of the 24 founders of the Jain religion. Esoterically, a Tirthankara is one whose Kundalini has successfully passed through all Six Chakras.

Trataka - A form of meditation in which one stares fixedly at an object such as a candle flame. If done properly it can open the third eye. In Treta Yuga people used trataka to obtain prana from the sun.

Treta Yuga - "The eon of three-quarters"; in which one-fourth of the dharma or righteousness of Satya Yuga is lost and three-quarters remains. In Treta Yuga, sacrifice (yajna) is the main sadhana.

Triveni Sangama - The confluence, at Allahabad or Prayaga, of the three rivers Ganga, Yamuna, and the unseen Sarasvati. Esoterically, it is located at the Ajna Chakra in the forehead, where the Surya and Chandra Nadis, the energy channels of the right and left sides, respectively, which generate

heat and coolness, meet the Sushumna (q.v.).

Tulsi - Holy basil.

Turiya - "The fourth"; the state of consciousness beyond the three ordinary
states of waking, dreaming, and deep
sleep, in which one realizes identity
with the Absolute Brahman.

Upanayana - The Vedic ceremony of
investiture of the sacred thread (Jahnavi [q.v.], Yajnopavita), the Gayatri
mantra, and eligibility to study the
Veda.

Vaikhari - The first and lowest level of
speech; vocal or physical speech, it
can only be used for mundane communication with external objects.

Vaishya - "Merchant"; a member of the
merchant class.

Vajroli - A yogic practice in which fluid is
sucked into the penis or vagina by
muscular force. During the sex act
Vajroli can be used to suck up the
partner's secretions for both physical
and spiritual benefit.

Valmika - "Anthill or termite mound."

Vamana - The dwarf incarnation of
Vishnu, he rescued the world from
the designs of the demon king Bali.

Vanara - "Monkey"; Vimalananda's etymology: after evolution (va) a monkey
has the potential to become a human
(nara).

Vani - "Speech"

Varaha - The boar Avatara of Vishnu.

Vasana - A tendency of the individual
personality which produces habitual
modes of action. often inherited from
one's ancestors. Vasanas make people
do what they do in spite of themselves
because of the power of the inherent
tendency.

Videha - "Bodiless"; name of the kingdom of Janaka (q.v.).

Vidya - "Knowledge."

Vidyut - "Lightning."

Vidyut Lata - "Lightning creeper"; said
of Kundalini.

Vijnana - Practical spiritual knowledge,
higher than jnana. In vijnana one

becomes a Siddha (q.v.), an immortal,
because the ego has become absolutely purified.

Vijnani - One who possesses Vijnana.

Vikalpa - "Option; uncertainty."

Vimala - "Stainless."

Vimalananda - "Stainless bliss"; a proper
name.

Virodha Bhakti - "Perverse devotion";
said, for example, of Hiranyakashipu,
whose hatred of Vishnu was so powerful that he remembered Him constantly.

Visha - "Poison."

Vishesha - "Special, extraordinary."

Vishuddha - The Fourth Chakra, taken
from the words vishesha shuddhi
("special purification")

Wah - An exclamation of amazement,
surprise or revelation.

Yajna - Vedic fire ritual. In yajna, deities
in ethereal worlds are invoked, then
fed with the fragrance of smoke from
the various burnt offerings.

Yajnopavita - The sacred thread worn by
Brahmans and others (also jahnavi)

Yakshini - A Hindu angel; an etherial
being who was once human and
because of his ability in sadhana
attained to this status after death.

Yama - Also called Dharmaraja, or King of
Righteousness. He is the judge of the
dead, evaluating their activities while
on Earth and determining which paradise or hell they go to while awaiting
rebirth. Also, the first limb of yoga,
external discipline.

Yantra - A diagram which acts as a receptacle for the power of a mantra. Tantra
is the ritual by which the Yantra is
empowered by the mantra. Any substance can be used for a Yantra, but
Vimalananda averred that the best of
all possible Yantras is the human
body.

Yogini - See Bhairavi.

Yuga - The Four Yugas or eras are Satya
Yuga, Treta Yuga, Dvapara Yuga and
our era, Kali Yuga.

Shri Yantra

(continued from page 12)

The Mahavidya goddess Tripurasundari is also known as Sodasi—'the divine sixteen year old goddess.' She is of a beautiful red complexion with four arms holding a bow, noose, arrow and trident hook. She sits astride the prone body of her white Shiva in sexual union, supported by a throne whose four pedestals are the gods Brahma, Vishnu, Rudra and Indra. This form of the Shri Yantra was worshipped for many decades by Telang Swami in the Anapurna temple of Benares.

BIBLIOGRAPHY

Avalon, Arthur (Sir John Woodruff), *The Serpent Power*, Madras: Ganesh & Co., 1913.

——. *Shakti and Shakta*, Madras: Ganesh & Co., 1929.

Campbell, Joseph, *The Inner Reaches of Outer Space*, New York: Harper & Row, 1986.

Jung, Carl, "Psychological Commentaries on Kundalini Yoga, Lectures One and Two—1932", Spring 1975, Spring Publications, New York.

Krishni, Gopi, *Kundalini: The Evolutionary Energy in Man*, Boulder: Shambhalla Publications, 1971.

Svoboda, Robert E., *Aghora: At the Left Hand of God*, Albuquerque: Brotherhood of Life, 1986.

Yantra of Smashan Kali

Yantra of Smashan Tarạ

Other Titles of Interest

Yoga Sutras of Patanjali
Translation & Commentary by Charles Johnston

Fulcanelli: Master Alchemist
Fulcanelli, translation Mary Sworder

Prodigal Genius, The Life of Nikola Tesla
John J. O'Neill

The Spirits' Book
Allan Kardec

Rhythm & Touch, An Introduction to Craniosacral Therapy
Anthony P. Arnold

The MU series (complete in five volumes) including
The Lost Continent of Mu
by Col. James Churchward
and other fine titles

COMPLETE BOOK LIST UPON REQUEST

BROTHERHOOD OF LIFE PUBLISHING
110 Dartmouth SE
Albuquerque, NM 87106-2218